NEW ESSAYS ON CANADIAN THEATRE
VOLUME EIGHT

Q2Q

ALSO IN THIS SERIES

ASIAN CANADIAN THEATRE
EDITED BY NINA LEE AQUINO AND RIC KNOWLES

NEW CANADIAN REALISMS
EDITED BY ROBERTA BARKER AND KIM SOLGA

LATINA/O CANADIAN THEATRE AND PERFORMANCE
EDITED BY NATALIE ALVAREZ

THEATRES OF AFFECT
EDITED BY ERIN HURLEY

DANIEL MacIVOR
EDITED BY RICHIE WILCOX

PERFORMING INDIGENEITY
EDITED BY YVETTE NOLAN AND RIC KNOWLES

CANADIAN PERFORMANCE HISTORIES AND HISTORIOGRAPHIES
EDITED BY HEATHER DAVIS-FISCH

ALSO BY PETER DICKINSON, C.E. GATCHALIAN, KATHLEEN OLIVER, AND DALBIR SINGH
Q2Q: QUEER CANADIAN PERFORMANCE TEXTS

NEW ESSAYS ON CANADIAN THEATRE
VOLUME EIGHT

Q2Q: QUEER CANADIAN THEATRE AND PERFORMANCE

EDITED BY PETER DICKINSON, C.E. GATCHALIAN, KATHLEEN OLIVER, AND DALBIR SINGH

PLAYWRIGHTS CANADA PRESS
TORONTO

Sky Gilbert's "Performing Your Fictional Identity: The True Imaginary" was originally published in *alt.theatre* 13.1, and is published here with permission.

Library and Archives Canada Cataloguing in Publication
Q2Q : queer Canadian theatre and performance / edited by Peter Dickinson, C.E. Gatchalian, Kathleen Oliver, and Dalbir Singh. -- First edition.

(New essays on Canadian theatre ; 8)
Based on papers presented at Q2Q: A Symposium on Queer Theatre and Performance in Canada held in Vancouver from July 20-24, 2016.
Includes bibliographical references and index.
ISBN 978-1-77091-913-6 (softcover)

1. Gay theater--Canada--Congresses. 2. Homosexuality in the theater--Canada--Congresses. 3. Canadian drama (English)--History and criticism--Congresses. I. Dickinson, Peter, 1968-, editor II. Gatchalian, C. E., 1974-, editor III. Oliver, Kathleen, 1964-, editor IV. Singh, Dalbir, 1979-, editor V. Q2Q, a Symposium on Queer Theatre and Performance in Canada (2016 : Vancouver, B.C.) VI. Title: Queer Canadian theatre and performance. VII. Series: New essays on Canadian theatre ; v. 8.

PS8169.H6Q82 2018 C812.009'35266 C2018-902034-2

Playwrights Canada Press acknowledges that we operate on land, which, for thousands of years, has been the traditional territories of the Mississaugas of the New Credit, the Huron-Wendat, the Anishinaabe, Métis, and the Haudenosaunee peoples. Today, this meeting place is still home to many Indigenous people from across Turtle Island and we are grateful to have the opportunity to work and play here.

We acknowledge the financial support of the Canada Council for the Arts—which last year invested $153 million to bring the arts to Canadians throughout the country—the Ontario Arts Council (OAC), the Ontario Media Development Corporation, and the Government of Canada for our publishing activities.

Canada Council for the Arts Conseil des arts du Canada

ONTARIO ARTS COUNCIL
CONSEIL DES ARTS DE L'ONTARIO
an Ontario government agency
un organisme du gouvernement de l'Ontario

Canada

Ontario
Ontario Media Development Corporation

CONTENTS

GENERAL EDITOR'S PREFACE

ROBERTA BARKER

When Ric Knowles founded New Essays on Canadian Theatre (NECT) in 2011, he set out to complement his previous book series for Playwrights Canada Press, Critical Perspectives on Canadian Theatre in English (CPCTE). Each volume of the CPCTE series offered a critical history of a key topic in Canadian theatre studies; most of the essays featured in these volumes were reprints of important articles in the field, though they were supplemented by newly commissioned works that brought novel perspectives to the questions at hand. With NECT, Knowles chose to foreground new work, under-explored subjects, and fresh viewpoints. As he wrote in his General Editor's Preface for *Performing Indigeneity* (2016), these volumes

> are designed to fill what I perceive to be gaps in the critical record, often . . . taking new approaches, often . . . from minoritized and under-represented perspectives, and in almost every case introducing topics that have not received book-length coverage . . . [T]hey are designed at once to follow, lead, and instantiate new and emerging developments in the field. (v)

Paired with play anthologies, many of them specially created as companions for the NECT volumes, these books strive to open exciting new avenues of exploration for artists, students, and scholars of Canadian theatre.

The six volumes published under Knowles's editorship richly fulfill this mandate, covering in the process a wide range of topics and approaches. Some, like *Asian Canadian Theatre* (edited by Nina Lee Aquino and Knowles) and *Latina/o Canadian Theatre and Performance* (edited by Natalie Alvarez), illuminate the vibrant and important work of key communities within the Canadian theatrical ecosystem. Others, like *New Canadian Realisms* (which I co-edited with Kim Solga) and *Theatres of Affect* (edited by Erin Hurley), strive to reconsider established genres and forms of theatre through new theoretical lenses. The 2015 volume, *Daniel MacIvor* (edited by Richie Wilcox), brings long overdue scholarly attention to the work of one of Canada's most beloved and innovative theatre artists. Finally, 2016's volume makes a particularly mighty contribution: *Performing Indigeneity*, edited by Yvette Nolan (Algonquin) and Knowles, is the first Canadian collection of essays on the topic to offer an all-Indigenous list of contributors. Many of these volumes, or the articles they feature, have been garlanded with scholarly prizes and awards: a fitting tribute to their impact on the field.

When I took over from Knowles as General Editor in 2017, I was both honoured and daunted by the task. Above all, however, I was inspired by the work of Knowles, his collaborators, and the many other brilliant scholars and artists who continue to transform our understanding of the field of Canadian theatre and performance. In the 2017 volume of NECT, *Canadian Performance Histories and Historiographies* (edited by Heather Davis-Fisch), a number of these writers set out to rethink the subject we have been used to calling "Canadian theatre history." They investigated the ways in which the influence of performance studies methodologies, the re-evaluation of diverse and underexplored forms of historical performance, and, above all, the insights offered by scholars and artists who speak from under-represented and minoritized perspectives have fundamentally challenged familiar ways of approaching the Canadian past. Seen from these angles, a field we thought we knew looks unfamiliar, unpredictable, challenging, and very exciting.

This latest volume of NECT, the eighth in the series, engages in a similar process of rethinking. *Q2Q: Canadian Queer Theatre and Performance*, edited by Peter Dickinson, C.E. Gatchalian, Kathleen Oliver, and Dalbir Singh, is inspired by a major conference held in Vancouver in July 2016. Bringing together the voices of many of this country's leading makers and scholars of queer theatre and performance, it showcases the vibrancy, diversity, and radically innovative spirit of today's LGBT2Q+ communities. Above all, this collection foregrounds the vivid, challenging, often discomfiting, and always passionate nature of the dialogues happening within and across those communities. The subject of queer performance in Canada is endlessly new, because the word "queer"—like the words "Canada" and "performance"—is one whose meanings are continually transformed as new folks take them up to articulate their own lived experiences. The vehement debates recorded in this volume offer us a range of fresh ways to imagine the complex histories—and the multivalent futures—of LGBT2Q+ performance in Canada.

Later in 2018, another new volume of NECT, edited by Jacqueline Petropoulos, will be the first ever edited collection to focus solely upon the work of the late, great Canadian playwright Linda Griffiths. Upcoming volumes will explore such timely topics as theatre and immigration, dance theatre, and digital theatre, among others. In each of them, the editors hope to follow the series's original vision of opening new vistas in Canadian theatre and performance studies. At the same time, they aim to reveal that fields we thought we knew are also full of something rich and strange—or rather, as this volume exemplifies, of something rich and queer.

ACKNOWLEDGEMENTS

We would like to thank Annie Gibson, Blake Sproule, Jessica Lewis, and everyone at Playwrights Canada Press for their belief in this volume, and for their patience as we have worked to put it together. Special thanks to Roberta Barker, General Editor of the New Essays on Canadian Theatre series, for her diligent care and oversight in shepherding this book through the editorial process. We additionally thank Blake for his expert copy-editing.

Many people have contributed to the making of this book, but we would especially like to single out the following individuals: Jan Derbyshire, Maura Doherty, Robert Leveroos, and Jonathan Seinen. All were members of the organizing committee of Q2Q: A Symposium on Queer Theatre and Performance in Canada, held in Vancouver in 2016, and from whence many of the essays in this collection derive. Jan deserves additional credit for coming up with the name Q2Q, which we simply could not leave behind.

Finally, we thank the Canada Council for the Arts, the Social Sciences and Humanities Research Council of Canada, and Simon Fraser University for providing the financial support that helped to seed many of the ideas in this book.

PUTTING THE QS IN Q2Q

PETER DICKINSON, C.E. GATCHALIAN,
KATHLEEN OLIVER, AND DALBIR SINGH

As Jill Dolan observes in her introduction to *Theatre & Sexuality*, attention to the role of sexuality in theatre and performance studies began in the mid-1980s and early-1990s as a two-pronged critical project (2). On the one hand, scholarship in this area was focused on historical recovery, shining a light on lesbian/gay/bisexual/trans/Two-Spirit/queer (LGBT2Q) plays, writers, and performers excluded from canonical surveys of Western drama. At the same time, queer theatre studies served as an interpretive rubric; drawing from post-structuralist theories of the performativity of gender and sexual identity, especially as advanced by Judith Butler in *Gender Trouble* and Eve Kosofsky Sedgwick in *Epistemology of the Closet*, scholars began to "queer" performances, characters, and plots by viewing them from a non-normative spectatorial perspective, or within a minoritarian discursive framework (such as camp). While these twinned scholarly endeavours have yielded a wealth of important book-length publications related to American and UK theatre and performance contexts (see Clum, *Acting Gay*; Román, *Performance*; Sinfield; S. Warner; and Wyllie), there has not been a similar research output focused on queer Canadian theatrical production and reception.

This is surprising for at least two reasons. First, as can be seen via the examples of John Herbert's *Fortune and Men's Eyes* (first produced in 1967) and Michel Tremblay's *Les Belles-soeurs* cycle (especially *Hosanna*, first produced in 1973), queer plays and playwrights are arguably at the heart of the modern theatrical canon in both English and French Canada. Second, the institutional longevity and the dramaturgical legacy of the pioneering queer and feminist companies Buddies in Bad Times Theatre and Nightwood

Theatre, both founded in 1979 in Canada's largest theatre-producing city, Toronto, point to the ongoing—and increasingly intersectional—exploration of sexuality and gender on Canadian stages, as well as to the development of diverse and alternative voices in key artistic, curatorial, and managerial leadership roles. Related to questions of institutional genealogy, while also troubling an exclusively bicultural model of theatrical canons in this country, is the fact that Native Earth Performing Arts was founded in Toronto just three years after Buddies and Nightwood, and has always shown a commitment to developing and staging Two-Spirit work, from early devised creations overseen by Muriel Miguel, to acclaimed plays by Tomson Highway, Daniel David Moses, and Cliff Cardinal.

As J. Paul Halferty notes in a 2014 reflection on queer theatre, performance, and scholarship in Canada, important articles and special journal issues focusing on queer theatrical topics have been published more or less continuously in this country since the 1970s, including three themed issues of *Canadian Theatre Review* (see Watmough; Wilson; and King, *Canadian Theatre Review*). However, to date there remains only one (out-of-print) "book-length investigation of queer Canadian literature and drama, addressing both work by gay men and lesbians in English and French" (Halferty 257), and only one stand-alone edited collection of essays focused on queer theatre in Canada published in the last decade.[1] As Halferty goes on to note, "The relative dearth of LGBT2Q theatre scholarship [in Canada] is not commensurate with the vitality of the work in the country today nor does it reflect the history of LGBT2Q theatre and performance in the contemporary period" (256). Citing the foundational example of Toronto's Buddies before listing the different professional queer theatre companies, performance spaces, and festivals producing and presenting new and acclaimed work, and noting as well the current generation of artist-scholars contributing to queer Canadian theatrical writing (see King, *Queer/Play*; O'Hara; and Wilcox), Halferty suggests that the scholarly narrative in this country has to expand radically to account for this diverse activity and its still "largely uncharted" historical lineages (256).

1 See, respectively, Dickinson, *Here is Queer*; and Kerr.

This volume sets out to address this challenge by bringing scholars of queer Canadian theatre and performance into direct dialogue with the artists, producers, curators, and administrators contributing to the vibrancy and diversity of LGBT2Q live arts scenes and cultures across the country. Most of the contributions emerge out of Q2Q: A Symposium on Queer Theatre and Performance in Canada, held in Vancouver in July 2016, and co-sponsored by Simon Fraser University and **the frank theatre company**; taken together, the essays and commentaries that follow provide a snapshot of contemporary queer performance practices (from playwriting to drag to performance art to musical theatre to digital performance) in Halifax, Montréal, Toronto, Lethbridge, Vancouver, and beyond, as well as what such practices can tell us about current audience appetites and potential future programming. At the same time, we understand that we cannot begin to map such futures without accounting for and documenting Canada's queer theatrical past. Anchoring this collection, then, is a two-part question: Why is it important not just to continue to tell queer stories on stage, but also to piece together the larger historical narrative of Canadian queer theatrical production and reception through our academic research? In scholarly articles, artist reflections and provocations, and curatorial manifestos, contributors work to answer these questions, generating through theory and practice new ways of understanding how queer theatre and performance have contributed more broadly to the political and social development of LGBT2Q communities in Canada.

The Q2Q conference was the first event of its kind in Canada, and its belatedness, like the long overdue appearance of this anthology, is a residue of what the eminent scholar of queer Canadian theatre, Robert Wallace, identified in 1989 as the twinned historical marginalization of theatre and queer communities in this country. Wallace issued his diagnosis of the relationship between performance and the Canadian public sphere when the state of independent not-for-profit theatre in English Canada looked to be as economically precarious as the social and creative sustainability of a queer community suffering devastating personal and professional losses as a result of the AIDS pandemic. Thirty years later, it would appear his pronouncement "that the marginal positioning of theatre within Canadian culture—like the marginal positioning of women and gay men inside the dominant culture of patriarchy—can be resisted and, eventually, overcome" has indeed come to pass (*Producing* 29). Of course, there are always additional processes of marginalization within any marginal culture. The 2016 intervention of Black Lives Matter at Toronto Pride to protest police presence and a perceived culture of "anti-Blackness" among event organizers attests to this, as does the continued under-representation of the voices of queer women and queer artists of colour on Canadian stages. The post-1967 nationalist narrative of Canadian theatre studies, as Wallace and several other critics have noted, has long tended to militate against a parallel entrenchment of more "particularist" (i.e., "queer" or "feminist" or "post-colonial" or "Indigenized") readings of performance and theatre in this country (see Wallace, *Producing* 10–12). In the same way that Laura Levin and Marlis Schweitzer's recent suggestion that performance studies' association "with the study of 'non-theatrical' or 'extra-theatrical' events" accounts in some respects for its slow disciplinary institutionalization in many Canadian post-secondary institutions (14), queer theatre and performance, encompassing everything from drag acts in bars to pop-up street actions and political protests, frequently fall outside of the bounds of what has traditionally been defined as legitimate—and legitimately Canadian—theatre.

A consequence of this has been the necessarily local, ephemeral, and personal archiving of queer performance in Canada, its history residing in the embodied memories, material collections, and affective lineages of those who have produced and consumed it. This is something that Cameron Crookston, drawing on the work of Ann Cvetkovich and others, brings out in his contribution, using interviews and oral histories with drag queens in Halifax, Toronto, and Vancouver to explore the notion of chosen queer and aesthetic families. It was with a performative reconstruction of the embodied micro-history of Vancouver queer performance that the Q2Q conference officially opened in 2016. David C. Jones, in consultation with Kevin Dale McKeown, put together a cabaret retrospective called *Out on Stage in Lotusland* (available to view on the conference website) that was as hilariously instructive for local attendees as it was for out-of-town guests, tracing the evolution of queer live arts in the city from early drag troupes like the Waitresses, the Facettes, and the Bovines to the twentieth anniversary of **the frank** (formerly Screaming Weenie) as a company, and duly celebrated by three of its past artistic directors.

Alongside the publication of this collection and its accompanying play anthology, one of the goals of the event was to make available as a living archive as many of the conference performances and roundtable conversations as possible. In this respect, even a cursory survey of the participants to those conversations reveals that their combined institutional memory represents not just the very best in queer performance practice (and politics) over the past forty years, but the very best in contemporary Canadian theatre-making *tout court*. Still, in terms of the relationship between identity and aesthetics, it is worth asking what makes this theatre distinctly "queer." As a provisional answer to this question, let us consider three invited Q2Q artists' contributions to three separate roundtables. Each is archived on the Q2Q conference website (https://q2qconference.com), and each grapples with extracting meaning from the conjunction of the words "queer" and "performance."

In his contribution to the Queer Playwright roundtable, Dave Deveau struggles not just with the notion that the label playwright may have become passé in a world of increasingly devised and postdramatic theatre, but that adding the descriptor "queer" is equally problematic. He asks, "Have I failed as 'queer playwright' if I write straight voices?" Moreover, he worries that owning such a label might limit the reception of his writing: "Queer work asking questions about queerness for queer people can at times feel like performing a talent show for your family in your living room." Queer, in this instance, when yoked to performance, acts as a marker of identity, be it in terms of the content of the work or the sexuality of the writer. While excited to see queer voices finding their way onto more and more mainstream national stages in Canada, Deveau understandably chafes against being defined solely as a "queer playwright," both in terms of the boxes it slots him into regarding what he can write about and how this might foreclose on the audiences whom he might hail.

While she could not make it to the conference in person, Donna-Michelle St. Bernard (who is one of the nine featured writers in our accompanying play anthology) did send a powerful provocation entitled "Counter: Offensive" for inclusion in the Queer Real roundtable. In it she defines queer performance—both in content and form—as insistently "radical": "Not an aberration excluded from the conventional[;] not a variant permitted within the conventional[;] but a proposition counter to and questioning of the conventional." Like Evalyn Parry in her contribution to this volume, St. Bernard, in suggesting that queer performance culture is a "prototype" to "expand," "push," and "transgress" boundaries, is asking how we might think of queer as playing with, upsetting, and defying theatrical norms, making the familiar strange, and generally disrupting the expected teleologies of aesthetic production and reception. This carries over to the level of both women's formal production of their documents, with St. Bernard including drawings alongside her prose, and Parry composing her essay as a list-like manifesto. Such experimentation should remind us in turn that one intervention associated with the reclaiming of "queer" in the 1990s, especially among queer theorists in the academy, was to think of the word as much as a transitive verb as a noun: to *queer* something (or someone) as a strategy both of relationality and of quasi-Brechtian alienation or defamiliarization (see Sedgwick, *Tendencies* xii).

Katie Sly, in the statement they submitted to the concluding Queer Theatre and Performance to Come roundtable, would seem to subscribe to this process of "queering" the status quo. They write that "queerness is an act of disruption, it is the tear that forces tissue [. . .] to reassemble itself differently in its wake. Queer performance is an event that leaves its audience questioning what they've assumed is a given. Or at least it can be." Sly, whose *Charisma Furs* (created and developed with Jonathan Seinen) is also included in the *Q2Q* play anthology, goes on to cite some examples of the queer work that excites them, both intellectually and sexually. In doing so, they bring up the fact that queerness is complex, it is messy, it is intersectional, it is transhistorical. Above all, as Sly notes, because queerness is about desire in all its unruliness and non-normativity, it does not respect neat categories of object-choice (that if you present as a cisgender white female, for example, you should desire a cisgendered white male). In other words, Sly reminds us that queer performance—at least in its non-commodified forms—remains unabashedly sexual and rooted in the body.

While by no means exhausting the landscape of what queer performance might mean, especially historically and interculturally, these three distillations of what St. Bernard refers to as "the staged manifestation of this phenomenon"—that is, queer as being a marker of identity/identification (on stage and off), as exploding and making strange traditional modes of presentation, and as a process of storying the sexual body in multiple ways and across multiple communities—permeate the contributions collected here. The book itself sits at the intersection of theatre and performance studies, queer theory and gender studies, artistic practice and social activism. As we learned from our conversations at the Q2Q conference, that can sometimes make for a combustible mix, as generationally, regionally, culturally, economically, and politically our community is as socially diverse as it is geographically and aesthetically dispersed. Thus, midway through the second decade of the twenty-first century, when we are apparently post identity politics and also in the midst of an identity politics resurgence (often linked to and fuelled by the Internet and social media), what aesthetic and political traction is to be gained—if any—in retaining the label "queer" to describe contemporary theatre and performance practice made under the LGBT2Q banner? In a country as regionally, linguistically, and culturally diverse as Canada, can one even adequately account for all the material produced under such a label? And in a performance landscape increasingly crowded with ever more queer idioms (burlesque, cabaret, stand-up), does the gay- or lesbian-themed play seem impossibly quaint? In short, where is *here* now? And is *here* still queer? Our contributors explore these questions in relation to a broad array of topics, which we have loosely constellated around the following porous and overlapping categories.

HISTORY

Despite the important work that has so far been done in gay and lesbian theatre studies in Canada, "the histories of LGBT2Q theatrical production and performance in this country remain largely unaddressed" (Halferty 257). In this respect, queer Canadian theatrical scholarship would do well to follow the historiography being modelled by scholars of feminist performance in this country (see Bird, *Redressing*; Scott). Doing so would place queer performance histories in Canada in critical conversation with performative analyses of queer temporality that have proliferated in recent years in the United States, in which queer futurity remains inseparable from the constant memorial pull of a queer past (see Dinshaw; Freeman, *Time Binds*; Halberstam, *The Queer Art* and *In a Queer Time*; Love, *Feeling*; Muñoz, *Cruising*; and Román, *Performance*). To this end, in her contribution to this volume, Kym Bird draws on the work of Heather Love, and in particular Love's theorization of "redemptive" versus "curative" approaches to queer history. She does so to ask what it might mean to read an unfinalizable archival and biographical project of identifying early Montréal playwright Amy Redpath Roddick as "lesbian" alongside—rather than in opposition to—specific instances of queerly historical experience in Roddick's work. In this process, queer and theatrical histories necessarily converge, to adapt Love, as a mix of desire and need in terms of the ghosted demands of the past (33); that is, reclaiming historical figures, including playwrights, actors, and theatre managers, as queer can never be separated from our sense of who we are (or who we are not) in the present.

This necessarily Janus-faced approach to queer history applies equally to the recent past. In terms of a Canadian genealogy of dramatic responses to the AIDS epidemic, Dirk Gindt demonstrates in his essay that a comparison of recent plays by three of the pre-eminent theatrical chroniclers of AIDS (Michel Tremblay, Brad Fraser, and Sky Gilbert) affords spectators a window on a unique history of the present: gay men aging in a "post-AIDS" era. At the same time, as Gindt notes, the unspooling of this once unthinkable queer future has been coterminous with a homonormative mainstreaming of queer culture more generally, meaning that what these playwrights have to teach us, collectively, about aging as queers (including the importance of a long memory of resistance) risks being subsumed by a narrowly presentist (and consumerist) narrative that equates visibility with liberation. Similarly, in analyzing the responses of his interviewees, Crookston demonstrates in his essay that both the on- and off-stage instruction drag mothers pass on to their drag daughters in different present-day Canadian cities needs to be situated in terms of a much longer history of the evolution of non-biological kinship structures in queer subcultures.

That the staging of queer history might have both a pedagogical and a memorial function and that, moreover, those functions might operate differently according to the generational makeup of a given audience is the subject of Stephen Low's essay. Focusing on two recent award-winning plays, *The Gay Heritage Project* and *The Body Politic*, Low argues that these works, in their melding of fictional and documentary approaches to queer historical events and icons, performatively constitute a cross-generational gay community through two different modes of audience address: one harnesses an older generation's *nostalgia* for the history of queer liberation to which they were witness and the other targets a younger generation *pedagogically* by showing them that this history, while perhaps one to which they feel only remotely or distantly attached, is nevertheless in need of their affective custodianship. This syncretic approach both to the theatricalization of queer Canadian history, and to queer Canadian theatre audiences, is symptomatic of what Moynan King, in her essay, calls the "scrambling" of post-millennial queer feminist performance in this country. Discussing successive iterations of Christina Zeidler's *Rehearsal for an Endurance Performance of the SCUM Manifesto: A Ukulele Concerto in C Major*, King suggests that Zeidler's mash-up of Valerie Solanas's revolutionary text models a progressive queer feminist performance aesthetic and politic that reclaims but does not own "the monstrous elements of its histories"—with monstrous here referring at once to that which mainstream culture disavows as "other" and that which othered communities defiantly hold up as a marker of (un)likeness. Through such scrambling—which in Zeidler's case was effected over time, across different media, and involved an ever-expanding field of collaborators—lesbian identity and its "sticky attachments" are at once locally grounded and transhistorically distributed. Thus, according to King, "contemporary queer performance [in Canada] reorders, refracts, and exceeds the silos of representation"—which in the case of the queer feminist performance artist, who continues to be marked as other even within gay and feminist theatre spaces, becomes a strategic form of monstrous camouflage.

PLACE AND SPACE

Of course, queerness has always hidden in plain sight. This has proven to be a key challenge to the project of queer historiography, Canadian or otherwise. But an additional impediment to a definitive history of Canadian queer performance is the country's de facto geographical, cultural, and linguistic regionalism. Not only does work produced in St. John's rarely tour to Victoria, but scholarly assessments of theatre and its relationship to local queer public spheres can be quite distinct. For example, Québec critics have for the most part resisted the dominant Anglo genealogy of the term "queer," and have largely adopted a sociological and materialist approach to queer theatre and performance in the province (see Rocheleau and Sandford; Turcotte; and Namaste). Sean Metzger explores the confluence of different minoritarian discourses (linguistic, sexual, ethnocultural) at work in the production of a queer Québécois insularity, especially as that idea of an "islanded" identity registers performatively in three different webseries produced and set in contemporary Montréal. At the same time, situating his argument in the context of different social media responses to the Pulse nightclub shootings in Orlando, Florida, Metzger demonstrates how the Internet, as a virtual space, has the potential to connect different insular spaces and communities (be they geographical, gendered, or generational) into an archipelago of shared imagining and cross-identification that might, however fleetingly, exist "outside of established modes and structures of belonging."

Sky Gilbert likewise turns to a recent example of queer Canadian web performance to argue for the *place* of fiction in the constitution of a queer self in relation to a larger queer social imaginary, one in which the truth of a given identity (or identity politics) is only ever as certain as its performative and mediatized elaboration in time and space—of which we may take Jimmy's live conversation with his projected avatar in Sunny Drake's *No Strings (Attached)*, included in the companion play anthology, as paradigmatic. Gilbert's essay is a provocative intervention into ongoing debates about the contingency of gender and the fluidity of sexuality, but it also addresses discourses of realness and fakeness that have overtaken popular media more generally. In this space of rigidly polarized camps for whom truth coheres precisely with belief, Gilbert argues that it behooves queers to remember the axiomatic advice of Oscar Wilde and Michel Foucault, namely that the care of self and community cannot be separated from the place of art-making.

In the case of queer performance culture, the co-extensiveness of place-making and art-making has often been tied to major metropolitan centres. However, in their essay on the Lethbridge queer theatre company Theatre Outré, Jay Whitehead and Richie Wilcox demonstrate that being on the frontier, both geographically and institutionally, can present rich opportunities for new kinds of queer "homesteading" in terms of the kind of work that is produced, where that work is produced, and what audiences it attracts. Whitehead and Wilcox's contestation of traditional centre/margin, urban/rural distinctions in the constitution of both queer and performance cultures resonates with theories of queer diaspora, in which different kinds of transversal migration manifest not as a refusal of home, but rather as replacing the idea of home as origin with one of home as destination (see Pecic 10). According to Sara Ahmed's influential phenomenological reading of how queer bodies form and follow different lines of sexual and social attachment across time and space, this *re*orientation toward feeling *at home* first requires becoming *dis*orientated with/from home (*Queer* 5). The idea of queerness being about how we negotiate and perform the flows of desire between bodies and places resonates with a remarkable number of the plays included in our companion anthology, from the spaces of African, Armenian, Caribbean, and Chinese diaspora that intersect with, help guide, give comfort to, and occasionally oppress the queer characters in works by St. Bernard, lee williams boudakian and Kamee Abrahamian, d'bi.young anitafrika, and Minh Ly, to a play as quintessentially "New Brunswick" as Shawn Wright's *Ghost Light*.

And yet while diaspora has been productively deployed in queer of colour critiques to unsettle queer theory's tendency to entrench universalizing (read: Western) categories of sexuality (see Gopinath), Andrea Smith has noted that diaspora's "deterritorializing" of the (queer) nation not only overwrites questions of Indigenous sovereignty, but also erases the history of Two-Spirit cultural production in the Americas ("Queer Theory" 54–55). This is an issue Jean O'Hara tackles in her essay on Daniel David Moses's *Indian Medicine Shows*, two linked one-act plays that performatively revise the power dynamics inherent in that queerest of frontier relationships: the cowboy and the Indian. As O'Hara demonstrates, Moses works to expose how the colonization of Indigenous sexualities went hand in hand with the unlawful annexation of Indigenous territories and the forced Christian conversion of the First Nations and First Peoples of the Americas. In this scenario, the repression of queer desire in the frontier myth manifests as a coincident and highly aggressive expression of a white supremacist ideology that continues to have repercussions for Two-Spirit people on both sides of the forty-ninth parallel.

FORM

Many queer performance makers and scholars, including several included in this volume, would say that Canadian theatre continues to be governed by repression—and white supremacy (see below). In 2015 Toronto- and London-based theatre artist Jordan Tannahill published a jeremiad against mainstream Canadian theatre, suggesting that it was "risk-averse." He tied this theatrical timidity to a subscription-based model of safe, tried and true programming aimed at putting as many bums in seats as possible. In contrast, Tannahill offered his own Kensington Market storefront performance space Videofag (co-run with William Ellis from 2012 to 2016) as a "micro-economical" model that allows for radical experimentation in terms of both content and form (*Theatre* 71–87). Videofag, in other words, gave many queer (and other differently identified) artists a safe space to fail. The aesthetics and politics of failure have been a recent preoccupation of both performance and queer theory, with the work of Sara Jane Bailes and Jack Halberstam (*The Queer Art*), respectively, achieving prominence. In the Canadian context, Sarah Garton Stanley has been an especially adroit champion of a "failure theatre" that is analogous to a queer style of being premised on the beauty of "belowness" ("Failure Theatre" 12, 13).[2] Tannahill cites from all three theorists/artists, as does Cordula Quint in her own essay in this volume, which analyzes the queer failure aesthetics elaborated in Tannahill's own plays. Focusing in particular on Tannahill's innovative livestreamed web drama *rihannaboi95*, Quint argues that the play's form, in its hypermediating of the very technology protagonist Sunny uses to explore and disseminate his nascent queer sexuality (by posting to YouTube a series of videos showing him dancing and lip-synching to Rihanna songs), reveals "how the performativity of 'failed style' captures the complex inside/outside tensions of queer identity."

It is likewise interesting to note that *rihannaboi95*, constructed as an autobiographical monodrama, shares a similar structure to three of the works included in our companion play anthology: Katie Sly and Jonathan Seinen's *Charisma Furs*, Shawn Wright's *Ghost Light*, and Sunny Drake's *No Strings (Attached)*. This is perhaps to be expected. As Holly Hughes and David Román assert in their landmark anthology *O Solo Homo*, autobiographical solo performance will inevitably remain "an especially popular form for queer writers and performers and for their readers and audiences"; in part this is because the political utility and necessity of "again and again" asserting queer (and feminist and racial minority and sex positive) presence will never be exhausted, no matter the claims toward visibility achieved or aspired to (4). Hence the continued relevance on Canadian stages of works like Nina Arsenault's *Silicone Diaries*, Waawaate Fobister's *Agokwe*, Tawiah M'Carthy's *Obaaberima*, d'bi. young anitafrika's *She Mami Wata & the Pussy WitchHunt*, and the list goes on.

Of course, the realization of claims toward visibility can take other forms, including the queering of resolutely classical forms. For example, in his reading

2 See also Stanley's "Failure Points."

of Minh Ly's *Ga Ting* (also included in our play anthology), Eury Chang asks how this contemporary, queer-themed Asian Canadian play might be seen as renovating or innovating some of the more tired and clichéd tropes of Western tragedy. In answering this question, Chang suggests that the staging of "*tragic communitas*" in Ly's play—that is, the transformation of characters' individual privation into a shared grief that cuts across gender, sexuality, age, and cultural background—does more than just spotlight "the suffering of historically marginal characters"; it also exposes, particularly through the homophobic patriarch Hong, the narcissistic and melancholic heteronormativity at the heart of classical tragedy itself, in which the fractured family unit must be shored up, according to Judith Butler's reading of *Antigone*, at the expense of those "relations that cannot be honored, cannot be openly acknowledged, and cannot therefore be publicly grieved" (*Antigone's Claim* 79). The complicated lines of relationality on view in *Ga Ting*, which works within traditional theatrical forms as it plays with them, is symptomatic of queer forms more generally, according to current Buddies in Bad Times Artistic Director Evalyn Parry. In her "informal set-list of considerations" on her own "polyformal" experiments as a theatre artist, songwriter, curator, artistic director, and community builder, Parry suggests that the container that is queer theatre and performance, like the container she envisions an institution like Buddies to be, is as capacious and expansive as that sometimes more, sometimes less formal set of relations "we call 'queer community.' " Which is also to say that both theatre and queerness are always in a process of being re-formed.

DIVERSITY

Like most in North America and Western Europe, Canadian theatres remain predominantly white and male and able-bodied—both in terms of the folks on stage, and those behind the scenes. As recent statistical reports published by Equity in Theatre (EIT) demonstrate, Indigenous, racial minority, trans, differently abled, and female artists are consistently under-represented in our performance communities (MacArthur). How has queer theatre and performance in Canada responded to the challenge of gender, cultural, and physical diversity? What still needs to be done? And how might the hasty and programmatic institutionalization of a diversity mandate within a given organization end up reproducing historical power structures and reifying categories of identity and difference? Laine Zisman Newman takes up these questions in her essay, framing her discussion of diversity in Canadian queer theatre by recounting the Toronto queer community's racist response to the intervention made by Black Lives Matter Toronto in that city's 2016 Pride Parade. Zisman Newman uses this inequitable spotlighting of difference within queer culture to outline the ways in which whiteness is normalized and universalized in theatre companies' programming by being left unstated, whereas (usually white) artistic directors often go out of their way to call attention to "diversity" within their seasons, sometimes even when it is not really there (as in the #CanStageSoWhite controversy that accompanied Matthew Jocelyn's announcement of Canadian Stage's 2016–17 season). As but one example of how the very category of diversity in queer theatre and performance can perpetuate a binary opposition between invisibilized whiteness and the hypervisibilization of artists of colour, Zisman Newman points to the titles of two collectively devised shows produced by Buddies in Bad Times Theatre: in the case of *The Gay Heritage Project* the race of the white creator-performers is not announced, but with *Black Boys* the title becomes the de facto main focus of attention.

Ryan Cunningham, in his contribution to this volume, talks about another kind of invisibilizing at work in official diversity strategies within the queer theatre community. He argues that adding "2" or "2S" to the umbrella term LGBTQ establishes a false equivalence between queer and Two-Spirit identities that subsumes a complex Indigenous epistemology of gender variance within a contemporary Western idiomatic shorthand for sexual preference and self-expression. As Cunningham notes, such moves, while undertaken in the name of inclusivity, actually risk perpetuating a doubled discriminatory violence for Two-Spirit theatre artists (who may or may not identify as queer) trying to tell their stories on stage: by encouraging Indigenous audience members schooled in the homophobia that accompanied colonization and Christian conversion to dismiss an important part of their history, and by licensing non-Indigenous audience members to absorb that history into a narrative framework with which they think they are already abundantly familiar. Cunningham illustrates the consequences (both expected and surprising) of such "diverse" readings through a discussion of the reception of his remounting of Waawaate Fobister's acclaimed play *Agokwe* at Alberta Aboriginal Performing Arts in Edmonton in 2012.

The interventions by Zisman Newman and Cunningham point to a larger paradox confronting anyone working in the queer theatre community in Canada today: What does it mean to aim for inclusive art-making and performance practices while also acknowledging that our community is defined by diversity both within and without? To put this another way, while it may, on some levels (including but not limited to content), be possible to account for the ways in which the "subculture" of queer theatre-making is distinct from the "super-culture" of so-called straight performance, how do we remain accountable to representing on stage all of the subcultures within queer culture itself? This challenge lies at the heart of T. Berto's essay. Analyzing three recent gay plays—Andrew Kushnir's *Small Axe*, Tim Luscombe's *Pig*, and Michel Marc Bouchard's *Tom at the Farm*—Berto demonstrates how each forces its audience to confront the divisions that exist within the supposedly unified facade of legitimate and legible gay culture. Specifically examining divides rooted in national origin, sexual practice, and rural-urban location, Berto's survey of what potentially unsettling kinds of queer self-expression do and don't find their way onto our stages intersects with ongoing sociopolitical discussions of the new "homonormativity" (see Duggan) and the mainstreaming of queer culture in the name of inclusion. In his contribution to this volume, Spy Dénommé-Welch tackles this idea of the non-conforming, or "productively contrary," aspect of queer theatre and performance by discussing how dissident queer Indigenous performance addresses the ongoing "fissures of colonial violence" by scripting a counterperformative category of the "queered-Queer," or the "othered-Other." Eschewing, like Zisman Newman and Cunningham, tokenistic gestures of inclusion within mainstream LGBTQ forms of cultural expression, Dénommé-Welch argues that creators and presenters of queer theatre and performance in Canada must not think of diversity and Indigenization as an afterthought. Instead, they must strive to embed the work of "deep decolonization" into their very processes of composition and production, a strategy that Dénommé-Welch illustrates through a discussion of his own collaboration with Catherine Magowan on the musical theatre piece *Victorian Secrets*.

In all aspects of the Q2Q project we made a special effort, as principal organizers, to be as diverse and inclusive as possible: in the range of invited presenters, in the list of topics for discussion, in the artistic programming that paralleled the roundtable conversations, and in a by-invitation workshop for queer and trans artists who identify as Indigenous, Black, and of colour that preceded the start of the conference's public events. However, as Sarah Garton Stanley notes in her heartfelt, generous, and ultimately hopeful reflection on her experience of the Q2Q conference, sometimes the best of intentions are doomed to fail. And, as importantly, sometimes the consequences of that failure register very differently depending on the diverse subject positions of a given project's various stakeholders. As Stanley recounts, and as the archived video footage on the Q2Q website attests, by no means did the conference achieve consensus on what queer theatre and performance in Canada is, nor on what it could or even should be. On the one hand, Q2Q—both the live conference event and its documentation here and in our companion play anthology—would seem to confirm what Miranda Joseph, based in part on her own ethnographic observations of the pioneering San Francisco gay and lesbian nonprofit company Theatre Rhinoceros, has identified as the romantic chimera of community. That is, the existence of a queer (performance) community in Canada is not only co-extensive with its performative exclusions, but is also—via its various entrepreneurial claims to be speaking "in the name of" *this* but maybe not *that* constituency—necessarily embedded within the structures of capitalism (vii–xviii). Stanley notes by way of Q2Q conference attendee Brad Fraser that neoliberal capitalism thrives on sectoring markets and pitting them against each other. But as anyone who has lived through the cue to cue of a technical rehearsal well knows, amidst the discord of competing voices, abruptly interrupted speeches, and general tedium of being trapped together in a single room for hours upon end, we can only survive such a process and remain committed collaborators with an infinite amount of patience and love. Knowing that is still not nearly enough, we nevertheless offer this book to the world in the spirit of both.

NO BLOOD ON THE SHEETS: LESBIAN HISTORY AND IDENTITY IN THE LIFE AND THEATRE OF AMY REDPATH RODDICK

KYM BIRD

In her article "Spoiled Identity," queer theorist Heather Love sets up an opposition between two kinds of history: one is redemptive or affirmative and "shore[s] up identity in the present . . . by searching for moments of pride or resistance in the past"; the other is curative and undercuts the problems or limits of identity that Love associates with redemptive history. Foucauldian in its conception and posed as queer in its approach, curative history "seeks out the 'discontinuities' in the past in order to disrupt the stability or taken-for-granted quality of the present," a quality that underpins heteronormativity (523).[1] Like queer philosopher Frances Latchford, whose article "Un/Identified Remains" critiques as unnecessary the opposition between queer theory and identity politics, I suggest curative and redemptive approaches to history are both valuable and need not be treated as mutually exclusive or oppositional. Indeed, a curative approach can be enlisted precisely to redeem the possibility of lesbians and gays having access to figures in the past with whom they can identify *or* queers having access to prior lifestyles that illustrate the multiform paths that desire, sexuality, and gender can take—and this is true even if such historical figures never identified as lesbian or gay or consciously pursued "queer" experience.

The literary text on which I focus to demonstrate the appropriateness of a doubled approach that is redemptive *and* curative is the closet drama *The Romance of a Princess*, by early twentieth-century Canadian playwright

1 Queer refers here to a fluid, anti-identitarian subject position that interrupts identity via the pursuit of new experiences, sensations, pleasures, affects, and intensities.

Amy Redpath Roddick, about the daughter of a king who renounces her royalty, legacy, and life as she knows it for the love of a commoner. When coupled with her biography and poetry, this play facilitates an interpretation with which lesbian feminists might identify *or* that can be read as "queer" or "genderqueer" in the sexual and gender transgressions that its female hero enacts. Moreover, because there is little to no early Canadian theatre history that either affirms lesbian identity or elicits depictions of female queerness, both projects, identitarian *and* queer, retain value for the liberation of contemporary lesbians and queers alike.[2]

There is no "blood on the sheets," no ocular proof that Roddick (1868–1954), the wealthy granddaughter of two of Montréal's most influential nineteenth-century patriarchs, and Mary Rose Shallow (1870–1943), her Newfoundland housekeeper, were having a sexual affair.[3] There is, however, innuendo, rumour, and poetic palimpsests that can elicit a queer feeling (i.e., affect) or lesbian meaning in Roddick's life and works. To better elucidate Roddick's biography and works relative to what is queer or lesbian, this essay already assumes two things: it takes for granted Ernst Van Alphen's claim that "affects . . . can be transmitted . . . by an artwork or a (literary) text" (23) and Ann Cvetkovich's position that "the queer and the lesbian . . . are [not] mutually exclusive," a position that thwarts totalizing renditions of either "the queer . . . [a]s the undoing of the identity politics signified by the category lesbian, or . . . lesbian culture [a]s hostile to queer formations" (11). These assumptions are necessary insofar as the lesbian is construed to be at odds with what is queer. Within queer theory, lesbian histories, identities,

2 I have argued in the past that Sarah Anne Curzon's *Sweet Girl Graduate* can be read as the exception here. But, because there was nothing "queer" about Curzon's life, it is difficult to be entirely convinced that her cross-dressed boy-dating-girl is little more than a narrative device. See "Leaping into the Breeches."

3 Roddick was the paternal granddaughter of the wealthy Montréal financier and sugar magnate John Redpath (1796–1869). Her maternal grandfather was John Easton Mills (1796–1847), often called the "martyr major of Montreal," because during his short political tenure, he died of typhus while endeavouring to stem the outbreak there in 1847. See "John Easton Mills."

sexual practices, and experiences are neglected or marginal at best; that is, it is taken for granted that lesbian realities as such are generally irrelevant to gay men and queers, whereas the reverse is not true at all. David Halperin and Valerie Traub capture this when they ask, "Why is it that gay male identities, histories, and sexual practices seem so good for so many lesbians to think with? And what is it about lesbian identities, histories, and sexual practices that might limit their use-value for other conceptual problems and other groups?" (36). Foucault's influence and "the assimilation of lesbian/gay studies to 'queer theory' " undoubtedly play parts in this troublesome outcome in queer theory: *it is* preoccupied with queer styles of life that, in the main, centre on gay and queer-masculine, not lesbian or queer-femme, styles of life (Halperin and Traub 17, 35–36). In effect, part of the work yet to be done in queer theory *is* the historical recuperation and analyses of lesbian styles of life *for* queers, as opposed to just lesbians. And, insofar as "affective and relational virtualities," thanks to Foucault, are central windows onto queerness, female affective virtualities that occur in texts like Roddick's *are* worthy of queer theory's attention and not merely that of lesbian theory's (Foucault, qtd. in Latchford 21).

More than fifty years after Roddick's death, her grandniece, Linda Roddick, admitted a family story that Amy took Rose to bed on her wedding night instead of her husband, Dr. Thomas Roddick (1946–1923). Although this story is apocryphal, there is real, circumstantial evidence that the two women shared a profound intimacy that, to my mind, was very like that of lovers: Shallow did accompany the Roddicks on their extended honeymoon and on many of the couple's subsequent journeys thereafter, often summering with them in Europe and in later years wintering in Florida (Redpath).[4] Furthermore, when Dr. Roddick, twenty-two years his wife's senior, died in

4 Hilda Ridley contends that "they were on the continent before the outbreak of hostilities in 1914" and only with great difficulty were able to get back to Canada. See also Roddick's "Diaries." Lady Roddick and the doctor toured widely in Europe and the United States. They also travelled out West and down East in Canada; they stayed regularly in Florida and visited Cuba. Roddick continued to travel with Shallow after the doctor died.

1923, Shallow continued to live with Amy in her Sherbrooke Street mansion for another twenty years until Shallow's death in 1943. Amy also made substantial and lasting provisions for Shallow in a will she drew up in the winter of 1925 in which she provided her with twelve hundred dollars annually and the appearance, if not the purse, of the upper class she had come to occupy by also bequeathing her all her clothes ("Last Will"). As fate would have it, however, Rose died first. It is in the facts surrounding Shallow's death that the case for lesbian identification or queer feeling is most evocative. According to historian Mary Anne Poutanen, a year after Roddick buried Shallow in Notre-Dame-des-Neiges [Catholic] Cemetery, she had her body exhumed and reinterred with her husband (and later herself) in the Redpath family plot in Mount Royal [Protestant] Cemetery. On the reverse side of their communal headstone she inscribed the following epitaph: "Mary Rose Shallow 1870–1943 beloved companion of Lady Roddick." That she would go to such lengths to lie beside Rose in death suggests to me she was likely to have done so in life.

This brief sketch of Roddick's life serves as an affirmative history of a figure from whom lesbians can learn, and with whom they can identify, feel empowered, and connect to ongoing lesbian and feminist politics and thought in the present. Her life and her work, as we will see, form a piece of lesbian history. At the same time, Roddick's biography and works serve history projects that are queer, because the life she arranged for herself and the passions about which she wrote transgressed the norms of female gender and sexuality and served the liberation of her passions and desires.

Roddick and Shallow enjoyed something akin to a "Boston Marriage," which Lillian Faderman long ago reclaimed as lesbian. Women in these relationships were socially elevated, usually upper-class, educated, and progressive thinking. They were New Women. Their lives together were grounded in "culture and in social betterment" (Faderman, *Surpassing* 190). In this sense, Roddick and Shallow's relationship can be read, at least in part, as lesbian. They lived together for forty-three years and were financially independent, Roddick through inheritance and Shallow through her connection to Roddick. Roddick was unquestionably liberated for her age: she was interested in women's politics, particularly suffrage, and expressed a desire to vote.[5] She sought to empower other women, like her nieces, whose independence she attempted to insure when she stipulated in her will that bequests "not enter into any community of property . . . with any husband but . . . [be] held by the legatee as her own property . . . as if she had remained single" ("Last Will"). Roddick held membership in a host of organizations, including the Montréal branch of the Canadian Authors Association. She also took a particular interest in the welfare of the Kahnawake First Nation, was honoured with the status of Kahnawake princess, and paid to erect their longhouse. She was, at one time or another, a member of the Women's Canadian Club, an honorary member of the McGill Alumnae and the Art Association of Montreal, and "a patron of the Women's Council of Canada" ("Lady Amy Redpath Roddick").[6] She possessed sufficient money not to have to seek paid employment and the time and inclination to pen ten plays and five books of poetry.[7] Roddick embodied the cultural elitism of her age. She studied the English classics on her own and with McGill professors; she spoke, read, and wrote in what were considered the most important European languages of the day, including German, Italian, and French; she availed herself of the theatre in Montréal, as well as outdoor winter sports like snowshoeing and skating; and, like other

5 On 28 February 1917 Roddick writes in her diary that she and Rose "took the cars . . . to the Capitol [Washington] and spent an hour and a half in the gallery of the House of Representatives and half an hour in the gallery of the Senate listening to the debate. We noticed Miss Rankin, of course, the first woman to be a member of the house." On 3 March they "drove to the National Suffrage Headquarters on Rhode Island Avenue. The house is beautiful and most artistic. I just loved seeing Miss Anthony's Room. It makes a fine memorial" ("Diaries" MS 659/9).

6 She was also a governor of the Montreal General Hospital and president of the Montréal branch of the Labrador Medical Mission. See "Lady Amy Redpath Roddick, Poetess, Philanthropist, Dies."

7 Roddick's ten plays include *The Birth of Montreal* (1921), *The Key That Unlocks* (1921), *The Romance of a Princess* (1922), *The Seekers: An Indian Mystery Play* (1920), *In a Venetian Garden* (1926), *St. Ursula* (1926), *An Old Bologna Tale* (1927), *Tharbis: A Poetic Drama* (1937), *The Tomahawk: A Playlet and Other Poems* (1938), and *A Chance Meeting Play* (1939).

adventurous women of her era, she learned the new art of bicycle riding. She travelled to the great European capitals, toured their churches and their galleries, and kept copious notes describing their most famous artworks. Her writing was based on a certain, educated intimacy with the Christian Bible, European history and literature, Greek myth, and First Nations lore, which she endeavoured in various ways to incorporate into her fiction.

Shallow was a fisherman's daughter, from another country than Roddick's, with another accent and a remarkably different set of cultural references. She applied to the Redpath household in 1901 for the job of "housekeeper." Her education could only have been rudimentary, and at thirty-one years old she had probably never left her small fishing village of Fermeuse in Newfoundland, never mind having any acquaintance with a metropolis like Montréal. Her wildly different class, education, religion, and culture must have played out in the women's relationship, but to what extent she came to regard Roddick as a peer, particularly over time, is difficult to say. Clearly, Shallow never undertook literary work or sat on the boards of associations or had memberships in societies; she didn't marry a doctor, or become a lady or an Indian princess, all things that Roddick did do. Yet, over forty years she became a "beloved companion," a different order of affection than her sister, Margaret Shallow Coleman, with whom she shared the same grave, and whose epitaph of "housekeeper and friend" Roddick had carved into the same gravestone. Set in such close proximity, Shallow's description as "beloved companion" seems to signal an order of equality, a love, an intimacy, and partnership like that of a Boston Marriage.

However, Roddick's life also serves as an early example of queer practice or a queer style of existence. Her history lends itself to this reading because lesbian identity was not—indeed, could not—be her project, although a life stylized to secure personal freedom and passion was something she clearly pursued. While Faderman intends to recover lesbian histories specifically, she nevertheless can be understood to shed light on how and why Roddick's life speaks to a queer sensibility. For reasons of religion, medicine, and respect for individual freedom, same-sex attraction between women in early twentieth century contexts, including in "popular stories," was often treated "without self-consciousness or awareness that such relationships were 'unhealthy' or 'immoral' " (Faderman, *Surpassing* 298).[8]

In an era when "women were not given the freedom of their sex drive," generally speaking, people either did not notice or did not believe that sexual relations between women were even possible (Faderman, *Surpassing* 313). Perhaps for this reason Roddick was able to live a queer life, one in which she was surprisingly unconcealed and unselfconscious regarding her affections and desires, as appears in her poetic writing. The narrator of "In A Train" (1918), for example, talks of a woman "Who clears my thoughts of wintry gloom" and "coax[es] summer flowers to bloom!"; "The Parson's Daughter" (1919) is penned to "My little love, my Mary!"; "Her Face" (1921) opens, "You say you do not love, Sweet, then why / Those tell-tale blushes?" and ends, "You liked me from the first you now confess / Ah Love! 'twas large writ on your truthful face"; "Where Willows Intertwine" (1919) is about unrequited love in which the speaker laments, "She treats me as a singing bird / That chirrups at her call, / And if with tears my eyes are blurred / She answers not at all." At the same time, the queer affects that Roddick's poetry convey also invite lesbian identifications with her same-sex desire, especially when one discovers "Sappho in Exile," a poem whose title is a kind of shorthand for any initiated lesbian.

8 According to Faderman, America may have been slower than Europe to be impressed by the taboos against same-sex love for several reasons: (1) Without a predominant Catholic mentality the country was less fascinated with "sin" and therefore less obsessed with the potential of sex between women; (2) by virtue of distance, America was not so influenced by the German medical establishment as other countries were, such as France and Italy and, to a lesser extent, England; (3) there was less clear-cut hostility, or rather there was more ambivalence, to women's freedom in a land which in principle was dedicated to tolerance of individual freedom. Therefore, romantic friendship was possible in America well into the second decade of the twentieth century, and, for those women who were born and raised Victorians and remained impervious to the new attitudes, even beyond it. In America, it took the phenomenal growth of female autonomy during and after World War I and the American popularization of the most influential of the European sexologists, Sigmund Freud, to cast the widespread suspicions on love between women that had already been prevalent in Europe. See Faderman, *Surpassing* 298.

Roddick did not identify as lesbian or even as a marginalized subject, but she was transgressive in the confidence she expressed in resisting the otherwise heteronormative demands imposed on her as a "woman," including heterosexuality, a timely marriage, and children. It is true she enjoyed access to liberties not afforded most women, for reasons having to do with her patrician class, her palatial mansion, and her single status—her mother and two of her brothers having died by 1902. But plenty of women with similar opportunities did not abandon their gender roles in the ways that Roddick did, especially at the turn of the twentieth century, when women's association with domesticity and maternalism relegated them to the home even more powerfully than in earlier generations. Thus, Roddick's gender, evidenced by her biography and arguably in her works, is another important factor in rendering her a lesbian touchstone and a source of queer feeling. Rich, handsome, well-schooled in literature, conversant in several languages, and an observant Christian, by any standards she would have made a fine, sophisticated match for a contemporary man of means. Yet, in the diaries she kept between 1897 and 1926, there is not a single mention of romantic feeling, a date, a crush, or a flutter of the heart. She was an undeniably "odd" woman in her age and time. And while Roddick likely intended to maintain the *appearance* of heterosexuality and the gender roles expected of a woman of her class, her attempts to do so were decidedly unusual and certainly on her own terms. This is evident in her 1906 marriage at the comparatively advanced age of thirty-eight to Thomas Roddick, who was twenty-two years her senior. Dean of the McGill Faculty of Medicine (1901–1908) and a conservative member of the federal parliament who was later knighted by King George V for introducing antiseptic methods into Canadian hospitals, Roddick bestowed upon his wife a social pedigree independent of her birth. As a result, at forty-six she became Lady Roddick and no doubt at that very moment all of her subsequent social choices, including her decision to continue to live with her female companion after Thomas's death in 1923, were placed further above suspicion.

At first glance, Roddick's choices may not appear to challenge heteronormativity nor to map onto contemporary notions of lesbian identity or queerness simply because she married a man. Yet, somewhat perversely, even for the time, she married a man who was an entire generation older, a father figure of sorts, a long-time family friend, and the family physician. The oddity, or the convenience, of her nuptials is reinforced by the likelihood that it was *she* who initiated the arrangement, as well as by her descendants' rumour that, in exchange for the marriage, she agreed to pay off Roddick's accumulated debt (Redpath). Of course, there is a genuine sense of desperation in the letters from Amy to Thomas throughout the summer preceding the marriage, as though she feared he would not come to marry her, but her panic is strangely devoid of romantic passion. In fact, my suspicion is that Roddick may have deposited the only truth there may be of her erotic life within her plays and poetry precisely because she was something like a lesbian or queer. She did so slyly, under the cover of her uncle's press, John Dougall and Son, which additionally ran the influential and conservative Protestant newspaper *The Montreal Witness*; had her relations recognized what arguably is the same-sex meaning that attends her masculine female and feminine male characters as a reflection of her inverted sentiments, they would surely never have published them but would have found them immoral and blasphemous.[9] Roddick's transgressions with respect to the social expectations of gender, coupled with her lower-class female intimate, the exhumation and reburial of Rose's Catholic body in the Protestant family plot, the "beloved" epitaph, her late marriage to the elderly man she chose, even the deception implicit in her choice of publishers are all non-normative acts that, minimally, represent a queer mode of being, if not a subjectivity "that if [she] had lived today . . . would have been described as falling somewhere on what Adrienne Rich has called the 'lesbian continuum' " (Faderman, *Odd Girls* 23).

Roddick's 1922 verse drama *The Romance of a Princess* is recoverable as neither lesbian nor queer on the surface; yet it leaves the reader with a queer feeling, especially when it is considered in light of the life and poetry I have

9 *The Montreal Witness* "repeatedly ran articles condemning fiction," and there is no indication that after John Dougall died in 1888 his sons, Roddick's cousins, who took over the press, were any more progressive. In fact, to his sister Elizabeth Dougall in 1877, James Dougall "said in a letter, 'the reading of ordinary novels or the skimming over of any book does not cultivate the imagination but rather depresses and weakens' " (Dean 36).

discussed thus far. This particular exegesis of the play text bequeaths a fragment of Canadian theatrical history to lesbians and queer women. Read as a displacement of Roddick's feelings respecting what I suspect was her real and illicit affair with Shallow onto an equally forbidden heterosexual romance, this mythic tale of two ninth-century lovers is about forbidden attraction, sexual secrets, and moral stains.

Inspired to some extent by *La Chanson de Roland*, a twelfth-century French epic poem, *Romance of a Princess* is a poetic drama that centres on the king's daughter, Emma, who, as the tale begins, is having a furtive love affair with her father's closest advisor, Eginhardt.[10] When their love is exposed, the king banishes each separately. They rather magically find each other and, with remarkable speed and conviction, enact a solemn if crude wedding ritual in which they consecrate their own vows. As the final act opens, we are to imagine that six years have elapsed, Emma and Eginhardt are in their log hut, poor but happy and independent, when their young son brings home a man he has met by chance in the woods who turns out to be the repentant king. Strangely contrite and apologetic, the king invites the couple to return home despite their sexual transgressions.

Like so many texts already recovered for an affirmative gay and lesbian history, Roddick's play is premised on the idea that "each soul has got some stain, some hidden mystery" (4). It recounts the scorn and disappointment of the father and the shame, rejection, and banishment of the forbidden lovers. But unlike the vast majority of early texts with characters who are lesbian, gay, or genderqueers, wherein the authors kill off these characters so that their story may be told at all, *The Romance of a Princess* redeems its heroine-lover.[11]

Despite Emma's disobedience to her father and her love of a man beneath her social class, she is virtuous and principled and understands her affection,

---

10 *The Romance of a Princess* shares with *La Chanson de Roland* the character of Eginhardt and the themes of transgressive sexuality and class in a medieval Christian society. Roddick certainly had read the French poem, as Naomi Moses notes.

11 The lesbian and gay pulp novels of the 1940s, 1950s, and 1960s are obvious examples.

as does Eginhardt, as a sacred seal, impossible to break (38). Like the protagonist of *La Chanson de Roland*, Emma is protected and abetted by the relics of saints, in this case sacred silks given to her by her father, who believes that "none but her is pure enough to shelter them" (6). Even though she could, like her mother before her, use magic to bend her obstinate father to her will, Emma will not "defile her soul" in this manner. Cast out by the king, she is an oddity *as* a woman in her *absolute* refusal to feel ignominy for who she is and whom she loves; with almost uncanny confidence she rejects the king's assertion that morality lies in her (gendered) obedience and passivity, exclaiming, "I'll take . . . this silk, 'twas given me last night to guard and am I different? My place in life may be; but not myself" (22). As the inheritor of the sacred relics, Emma is protected by God, even after she leaves the security of the castle for the dangers of the forest.

But if Emma's queer confidence, at odds with her sex, has not yet convinced you Roddick's play is worth taking up as a lesbian *or* queer play, consider that in both her essay on *Roland* and in the play itself, Roddick argues that it is not whom one loves but loyalty within their union that distinguishes the virtuous; thus, when the charcoal-burner's wife implores Eginhardt to break free from Emma, he refuses because he and she believe that immorality is not the result of an unsanctioned union but the denial of genuinely held passions.[12] To prove the moral righteousness of the lovers and their forbidden love, it is the king who wanders the land for six years in search of the couple and he who begs their forgiveness, whereas Emma and Eginhardt neither repent nor regret their affair or their elopement. To demonstrate to the king God's sanction, Emma presents him with the holy silk, exclaiming, "See Father, I have guarded it—no harm has come to us in this old pagan grove" (78). The play ends with the king's pronouncement that within their forest home he sees the germ of "the City of God on earth, an Empire as St. Augustine once visioned"—St. Augustine, appropriately, being the most sexual

12 See *The Romance of a Princess* 38–40. To prove the holy nature of their love, Emma and Eginhardt make a cross from sticks, drape it with the holy silk, and exchange wedding vows. When Emma's pet dove appears at that moment, the couple interprets it as a divine sign that their union has been sanctioned.

of saints (prior to his conversion at least, although chastity, arguably, is a kind of sexual choice and act too) (79).

Emma disrupts normative notions of sexuality because she embodies a gender identity that is antithetical to her sex.[13] When her lover is trapped in the palace, it is she who saves him from being discovered by carrying him on her back across the palace courtyard to prevent any evidence of his footprints in the newly fallen snow. Despite her six-year banishment, her separation from kith and kin, she repents nothing and, in the end, she does not conform to the demands of society, but it is society, in the figure of the king, that conforms to her: the king accepts her on her own terms, with her self-fashioned husband and new family.

Emma embodies a transgressively active female sexuality and Eginhardt forsakes stereotypical masculinity, making both obvious genderqueers. Heteronormativity demands that feminine females desire masculine males and *vice versa*, whereas Emma is a female who desires a feminine male and Eginhardt is a male who desires a masculine female. As a result, there is a real sense in which the difference between their sexes is neutralized, or rendered equivalent, when it is juxtaposed against the meanings of their embodied genders. Even if sex, gender, and sexuality have been teased apart and isolated within theory, the meaning of gender is nevertheless entwined with the meaning of sex in the context of desire: for instance, if and when a character's gender is or can be read as a stand-in for that character's sex. Both Emma and Eginhardt can be read to suggest something that is queer *and/or* lesbian—or gay, for that matter—a conclusion in line with Robert Wallace's rhetorical question, "[a]re . . . plays 'gay' because they depict 'gay' characters?" to which the answer is obviously "no" (*Making Out* 20). In effect, it doesn't matter if Emma and Eginhardt are categorically queer, lesbian, or gay. What matters is that the contradiction in the sex and gender of each elicits a meaning that readily allows for a (covert) queer or lesbian reading of the desire between them *as* same-sex.

---

13 For example, she is the play's active hero and as such fails at conventional femininity. She also rejects the king's assertion that morality lies in obedience and passivity.

Redemptive history, as I am using it here, is premised upon a notion of a coherent lesbian identity that is transhistorical, transcultural, and rooted in a beguiling essence that begins with Sappho and courses through to today. It is not just a beautiful fiction. It is a political act to restore, repair, and regenerate a lonely, shamed, isolated, and illegitimized group for a contemporary culture. In it lies the promise (which need not necessarily be a surety of community or a consciousness of oneself as part of a community) of heritages, mythologies, and traditions that inspire and heal those who have suffered from erasure, regardless of whether they are lesbian or queer. It offers an arsenal of stories with which one can resist silence and the heteronormative status quo.

Curative history is set up by Heather Love and others as the opposite: it is anti-identitarian. It looks for the fissures in identity and schisms in the homogeneous facade of history. It looks for the disruptions, the pauses, the suspensions in identity: the things that do not fit, that do not make sense, that one cannot celebrate, in this way agitating the stability of the identity that a redemptive history seeks. Indeed, the cultural critic Aurora Levins Morales describes curative history as "re-creat[ing] the shattered knowledge of our humanity [by] retelling the stories of victimization, recasting our roles from subhuman scapegoats to beings full of dignity and courage" (13). Morales also calls curative history a "radical" or "medicinal history" and claims that it *can* distill "a legacy of pride, hope and rebellion from ordinary people's lives" (13). It can do so because it, too, is about rewriting and retelling stories about cultures of inequality which, one must never forget, are wrought from "pain, confusion, alienation, a sense of the unreality of our own experience and that of others, an inability to name the abuses we experience, perpetuate and witness on a daily basis" (13).

As a result, redemptive and curative history are alike, at least in their intent to tell stories like Roddick's. By doing so, we give possible meanings to lesbian, gay, and queer lives, whether those meanings manifest as an identity or experience. To recover Roddick, therefore, is to recover an *other* past one that, nevertheless, signals to us in the present how marginal lives have and do become livable for lesbians and queers. There are many identifications and affective virtualities yet to be revealed in recuperative projects like this one, because lives and works like these are not only worthy of our attention but benefit us. As a history, Roddick's life and work is as intriguing as it is strange, and it benefits us as a morality tale of passions that we as lesbians or queers refuse to deny.

THE QUEER FUTURE THAT DARED NOT BE IMAGINED: AGING AND "POST-AIDS" THEATRE

DIRK GINDT[1]

In spite of significant pharmaceutical breakthroughs and new methods of treatment and prevention, the medical, political, social, and cultural challenges posed by HIV and AIDS are far from resolved, as theatre artists and activists all over the world continue to show (Campbell and Gindt). My current research project, of which this essay forms a part, focuses on the myriad intersections of HIV and AIDS with queer theatre and performance in Canada, taking into consideration both historical perspectives and contemporary challenges, including the stigmatization of people living with HIV, the criminalization of HIV non-disclosure, and the financial interests of both the pharmaceutical and cultural industries. While doing research, I was surprised and intrigued to discover how forcefully and innovatively three well-established playwrights—all of whom have, to varying degrees, addressed the impact of HIV and AIDS on gay and queer communities—have recently written about their own aging processes and the prospect of a death not caused by AIDS-related illnesses.[2]

---

1 I would like to express my gratitude to Peter Dickinson, Linda Morra, and John Potvin for valuable feedback and suggestions, Ed Roy for graciously sharing a video recording of the production of *A Few Brittle Leaves*, and Sky Gilbert for his unfailing generosity and for allowing me to quote from the unpublished script of his play.

2 An estimated ten percent of the 36.7 million people living with HIV worldwide are aged fifty years or older. Due to the unequal distribution of and access to prevention and treatment, this number is significantly higher in the Global North, where one third of adults living with HIV are fifty years or over (UNAIDS). People living with HIV who are on antiretroviral treatment have a longer life expectancy compared to the first decade and a half of the AIDS epidemic. Nevertheless, long-time HIV infections risk causing numerous

One of the challenges I attend to here is the question of aging in the "post-AIDS" era for a generation of urban gay men who have long been confronted with the brutal reality of dying, often prematurely.[3] Posed as a question, this essay asks: How do gay playwrights who lived through and survived the AIDS crisis in the 1980s and early- to mid-1990s explore the topic of aging and the prospect of death that is not caused by AIDS-related illnesses? To tackle this question, the essay analyzes selected examples from three acclaimed playwrights who have each in their own way left a decisive mark on gay male and queer theatre in Canada: Michel Tremblay, Brad Fraser, and Sky Gilbert.[4] In recent stage works, each confronts the challenges of aging, including the death of a parent, cancer, Alzheimer's disease, fears of abandonment, and, not least, the insidious mechanisms of homophobia and misogyny that also affect elderly queers. Without pretending to engage in a universalizing discussion about queer people and aging, my specific interest here is to tease out contemporary tendencies in plays published and staged by a generation of gay male playwrights who now grapple with the issue of aging in a "post-AIDS" era—a prospect that many did not dare to imagine only a few decades ago.

---

medical conditions that accelerate the aging process, including some forms of cancer, lymphoma, diabetes, cardiovascular diseases, liver and kidney diseases, bone loss, hepatitis, chronic inflammations, as well as neurocognitive disorders and dementia, to say nothing of the psychological stress caused by the ongoing stigmatization of HIV. Women living with HIV may also experience early menopause and have an increased risk of developing osteoporosis (Canadian AIDS Society; "Aging with HIV").

3 Performance scholar David Román first suggested the term "post-AIDS" in 2000 to identify the cultural shifts that happened after the introduction of highly active antiretroviral therapy in 1996 ("Not-About-AIDS"). While new treatments turned the focus from dying of AIDS-related illnesses to living with HIV as a manageable medical condition for some privileged social constituencies, Román also warned of new inequalities structured along racialized and income lines. Moreover, I wish to add that the notion of "post-AIDS" is a false and illusory privilege afforded to the Global North, making it seem as if the epidemic is either "over" or "over there," as in Africa and other parts of the Global South.

4 Although the focus is on gay male playwrights, I attend to dramatic characters and conflicts located outside of the narrow confines of heteronormativity, which is why I find it appropriate to use the term "queer theatre" throughout the essay.

As gerontologist Brian de Vries and sexuality studies scholar Gil Herdt argue, until recently, the very idea of gay men aging seemed unintelligible because of HIV and AIDS:

> Not long ago these two terms [aging and gay] were thought to be at best incongruous and at worst incompatible. The incongruity derived from ageist notions of homosexual culture; the incompatibility derived from linking AIDS with homosexuality, in which the presence of the disease precluded a future. (de Vries and Herdt 85)[5]

Ever since the invention of the homosexual as an identity category in the second half of the nineteenth century (see Foucault, *The History of Sexuality*), a number of historical disasters, ranging from the pathologization and criminalization of same-sex desire and trans people to the onslaught of HIV and AIDS, coupled with the silencing effects of the closet, have prevented many queers from being allowed to deal with the experience of aging in cultural representation. It is exactly against this backdrop that this essay seeks to make an important intervention. My premise is that the present, so-called "post-AIDS" era signifies a key, and unprecedented, moment in theatre history since it marks the first time openly gay playwrights are able to write about the process of aging *as* gay men.[6]

---

5 De Vries and Catherine Croghan together published an article in a special issue of the *Journal of Homosexuality* devoted to the question of aging within LGBT communities and debating a number of challenges that are particular for queer people growing older, amongst them, a lack of caregiving and support networks, reduced income levels and poorer health in comparison with straight populations, HIV-related illnesses, discrimination based on homo- and transphobia, and, not least, a life-long experience of stigmatization (de Vries and Croghan 10–11). For a distinctly Canadian perspective, see Brotman et al.; and Daley.

6 This is not to suggest that playwrights have not previously written about elderly or dying gay characters. See, for example, Peter Eliot Weiss's *Remembering Shanghai* (1996), in which a gay man takes care of his elderly former lover dying from AIDS-related illnesses.

My methodological approach is influenced by notions of queer temporalities. As J. Jack Halberstam argues, "Queer time perhaps emerges most spectacularly, at the end of the twentieth century, from within those gay communities whose horizons of possibility have been severely diminished by the AIDS epidemic" (2). It was in a time of crisis and urgency that new understandings of and relations to time manifested themselves for queers. On the one hand, queer lives were filled with despair and expectations of lacking a future; on the other, queer ways of arranging and experiencing time also had the potential to offer new forms of hope and the option of "life unscripted by the conventions of family, inheritance, and child rearing" (*In a Queer Time* 2). In other words, queer temporalities propose a non-normative way of organizing not only sexuality, but also the attempt to try and stand outside of re/productive capitalism (see also Edelman, *No Future*). Queer temporalities also, importantly, allow us to critically explore some implications of the "post-AIDS" moment and the social changes that have led to new forms of homonormativity, including increased access to marriage, military service, and neoliberal modes of consumption (Duggan), coupled with cultural amnesia of past forms of queer and AIDS activism that occurred as soon as new combinations of antiretroviral treatments became available in 1996 (Castiglia and Reed).

In her valuable study of how fiction shapes gay identities and how narratives about HIV and AIDS in turn create gay subjectivities and communities, literature scholar Monica Pearl identifies two major shifts that have occurred in gay male fiction since the "pharmaceutical threshold" of new treatments (2). The first of these is the move away from disease and death to survival and, as a consequence, "this surprised apprehension, that surviving AIDS—which seemed so impossible at the time—did not save one from mortality" (120). The second theme Pearl identifies as defining gay literature "post-AIDS" is the critical scrutinizing of "marriage as an entity, an institution—a possibility" (129). In this essay, I demonstrate how all three playwrights under review here scrutinize the institution of marriage, albeit in very different ways. What sets them apart from their colleagues south of the border, who form the subject of Pearl's book, is that they do not ponder the pros and cons of same-sex marriage at all, but instead subject heterosexual marriage to critical analysis. In the process, all three offer an important critique of heteronormativity and the social organization of sexuality and relationships in a "post-AIDS" moment. Moreover, all three seek alternatives to normative ways of conceptualizing a lifespan by setting loose queer temporalities that either threaten to destroy or promise to liberate their dramatic characters. Tremblay shows the implosion of a traditional marriage and charts the emotional damages caused by hegemonic masculinity;[7] Fraser dissects the expectations on and constraints of straight marriage by allowing his dramatic characters to imagine and start pursuing alternative life paths to heteronormative and monogamous coupledom; and, finally, Gilbert lets a couple of single, aging sisters face the social stigma of *not* being married, and thus not conforming to heteronormative feminine standards, to explore potentially new forms of gender performativity beyond the illusion of wedded bliss.

MICHEL TREMBLAY: *L'ORATORIO DE NOËL*

As one of the first openly gay authors in Canada to write about queer issues, not least in his acclaimed play *Hosanna* (1973), Tremblay hesitated a long time before he wrote about HIV and AIDS. In 1993 he published the novel *Le Cœur éclaté*, in which Jean-Marc (a recurring character in Tremblay's oeuvre) escapes from Montréal to Key West to come to terms with his long-time partner Luc's death from AIDS-related illnesses. Among the *dramatis personae* of his play *Messe solennelle pour une pleine lune d'été* (1996) is a middle-aged gay couple trying to cope with the knowledge that one of them is dying of AIDS-related conditions. Years later, Tremblay explained in an interview with *The Lesbian and Gay Review Worldwide* why he had been initially reluctant to write about the epidemic: "I didn't want to talk about AIDS until it was

7 Hegemonic masculinity is an analytical concept suggested by Australian sociologist Raewyn, a.k.a. Robert, Connell to identify the culturally and economically most privileged way of performing masculinity in a given time period and to study the subordination of both women and other masculinities.

clearer. We didn't know enough about it then to be objective. [. . .] I was too scared about writing about AIDS. You can't write out of fear" (qtd. in Hays).

In 2012, Tremblay, who has survived a brain tumour and throat cancer, addressed the topic of Alzheimer's disease, which has become an increasingly urgent health concern for the baby-boomer generation, in a play called *L'Oratorio de Noël*. While promoting his new work, he made frequent comparisons between Alzheimer's and AIDS. To the *Montreal Gazette*, he explained "[i]t's like AIDS 20 years ago. After 10 years, everybody knew somebody who died. It's the same with Alzheimer's now" (qtd. in Donnelly). A similar statement was repeated in *La Presse*: "Ça rappelle notre impuissance devant le sida au début des années 80, alors qu'on n'avait pas d'information sur la maladie" (qtd. in Boulanger).[8] While interesting, these comparisons between Alzheimer's disease and HIV and AIDS are also problematic. Alzheimer's is not an infectious disease that can be transmitted via sexual or blood-to-blood contact and it does not have the same stigma attached to it that HIV and AIDS continue to have. Nevertheless, what makes the play interesting for my analysis here is how Tremblay explicitly anchors the topic of aging and Alzheimer's in a "post-AIDS" moment and mercilessly depicts the decline of brain functions and the collapse of the nuclear family.

The first production of *L'Oratorio de Noël* was directed by Serge Denoncourt, who lost his mother to Alzheimer's, and opened on 5 February 2012 at the Théâtre Jean Duceppe in Montréal. The title of the play takes its inspiration from Johann Sebastian Bach's *Weihnachtsoratorium* (1734), which is played as the curtain opens. However, while Bach's oratorio celebrates the birth of Christ, the main character in Tremblay's play is a distinguished brain surgeon called Noël who has developed Alzheimer's and is represented lying in a private hospital room, waiting to die. Without any delay, he addresses the audience to describe his medical condition:

8 "It reminds us of our helplessness about AIDS in the early 1980s when we had no information on the disease" (my translation).

> Vous avez compris que chuis atteint de la maudite maladie au nom si laid et qui fait encore plus peur que le cancer parce qu'on sait que ça peut durer longtemps, des années, que ça gruge lentement, qu'on a amplement le temps de s'en rendre compte, parce que même si on perd des grands morceaux, on reste assez conscient pour sentir le mal se développer. (Tremblay, *L'Oratorio* 11)[9]

L'Oratorio de Noël is thus not simply a play about aging—it is a play about dying. As a doctor, Noël knows exactly what awaits him, including the loss of memory, the loss of control over bodily functions, and the eventual loss of dignity. Tremblay avoids any melodrama, however, and evokes little compassion for his protagonist who, as we learn over the course of the play, was a very selfish man. Noël receives visits from three family members: his estranged former wife, Jacqueline, who divorced him twenty years earlier because of his indifference toward her and his multiple extramarital affairs; his daughter, Isabelle, a successful painter whose talent Noël refuses to acknowledge, let alone compliment; and his son, Jean-Sébastien, who has followed in his father's footsteps even though Noël, out of sheer envy of his son's skills, questions his professional dedication and qualifications.

What at first seems like a deceptively simple plot soon reveals itself to be driven by a complex dramatic composition. Apart from these actual visits, Noël's brain conjures two additional, younger versions of each family member. Each character is thus tripled—a physical manifestation of the chaos in Noël's deteriorating brain, all of which results in a compelling dramatic structure that continuously merges seemingly realistic representation with embodied memories and hallucinations. Eschewing both melodramatic pathos and the linear logic of realistic conventions, Tremblay conjures a cacophony of voices and characters that result in a temporal dissonance and represent what queer

---

9 "You've understood that I'm suffering from the damned illness with that ugly name and that is even more frightful than cancer, because we know that it can continue for a long time, for years, that it slowly eats away, that we have ample time to be made aware of it, because even if we lose big pieces, we remain conscious enough to feel how the malady is developing" (my translation).

theorist Elizabeth Freeman calls "the pull of the past on the present," a concept I discuss in more detail below (*Time* 62).

This elasticity of time is one of the symptoms of Alzheimer's, as many patients find themselves stuck in a temporal vortex that makes it difficult to separate past events from present ones. Noël is, however, painfully aware of how the disease manifests itself and how it progresses. He knows and understands that his visitors are memories turned into flesh, but he can no longer differentiate between these visitors from the past and the family members as they are in the present. *L'Oratorio de Noël* is reminiscent of the strategy of ghosting that Canadian playwrights frequently used in the 1990s as a means of resistance to grant the queer subject a voice and presence even after their death from AIDS-related diseases (Gindt, "Queer Embodied"). In Tremblay's play, however, the family members are vengeful ghosts who appear out of nowhere and replay scenes from the past to confront and blame Noël for his failures as a husband, father, and human being. In the process, accusations are repeated over and over again—"C'est pas parce que les choses ont été exprimées une fois qu'elles sont réglées!" (64)[10]—as the youngest version of Jacqueline snaps. It remains ambiguous to what extent the nine visitors are manifestations of Noël's progressing neurodegeneration or are products of his guilty conscience for having prioritized his career at the expense of his family.

While there are no queer characters in *L'Oratorio de Noël*, I claim it as a queer play. The queer project, after all, is not just about inserting queers into dominant narratives, but also about critically dissecting heteronormativity. *L'Oratorio de Noël* is a play depicting the dissolution of the heterosexual nuclear family, and mercilessly reveals the disappointments, emotional distances, lies, hypocrisies, and false expectations attached to it. It also reveals the failure of hegemonic masculinity: the celebrated brain surgeon, who claims to live on in the memory of the patients whose lives he saved, can no longer control the workings of his own brain, and the patriarch who ruthlessly imposed his will on his wife and children can no longer manipulate his family members, who now seem to multiply. As the past and present merge,

10 "Things aren't settled just because they've been expressed once" (my translation).

Noël cannot maintain any rational command over temporalities that elude him more and more. On the threshold of death, he is confronted with the collapse of what Freeman identifies as chrononormativity and "the use of time to organize individual human bodies toward maximum productivity" (*Time* 3). For Freeman, chrononormativity is the joint result of the breakthrough of industrial capitalism and the birth of the sexual deviant, both of which emerge in the second half of the nineteenth century. It is an internalized way of organizing time that follows the logics and demands of capitalism as well as the narrow path of heteronormativity. Freeman emphasizes that chrononormativity and chronobiopolitics extend "beyond individual anatomies to encompass the management of entire populations," as various state apparatuses conspire to implement and naturalize "teleological schemes of events or strategies for living such as marriage, accumulation of health and wealth for the future, reproduction, childrearing, and death and its attendant rituals" (*Time* 4). In a cruel twist of fate, Tremblay's white patriarch sees the very chrononormativity on which he built his entire life fall apart as his neurological functions fail him. In a last attempt to impose some form of control over his actions, he swallows a fatal dose of sleeping pills.[11] The other characters, whether real or imagined, withdraw one by one until Noël finds himself alone in the hospital bed, crying for help while an absent choir sings a long-drawn-out "Amen" (Tremblay, *L'Oratorio* 80), an allusion to the previously mentioned play *Messe solennelle pour une pleine lune d'été* that ends with all of the characters singing slowly "A . . . men . . . " (119).

---

11 In a recent issue of *Modern Drama* devoted to aging and theatre, Margaret Morganroth Gullette analyzes a play about Alzheimer's by Tony Kushner and criticizes the playwright for letting his protagonist commit suicide at the end, which she argues corresponds to the inhumane demands of a failing social security net, where sick people pose an emotional and financial burden. This critique is particularly salient if we compare *L'Oratorio de Noël* to plays that were conceived at the height of the AIDS crisis and often underlined the importance of community solidarity and networks of support. I am, however, inclined to see the ending of Tremblay's play as a political statement to signify the self-admitted defeat of an old patriarch.

Tremblay's play subverts chrononormativity in order to mercilessly confront the sick and aging patriarch Noël with the emotional damage his hegemonic masculinity caused his family members before he finally dies, all alone. Aging, the pursuit of alternative temporalities, and the dissolution of a straight marriage and nuclear family are also key themes pursued in Brad Fraser's 2009 play *True Love Lies*, which subverts the supposed stability of heteronormative kinship constellations.

BRAD FRASER: *TRUE LOVE LIES*

In a column written for *Daily Xtra* in 2013, Brad Fraser recalls the many friends and acquaintances he saw die during the worst years of the AIDS crisis, "a decade of abject fear, crippling paranoia and functional despair," which only came to a temporary halt with the introduction of new treatments.

> Then people I knew started to die of cancer and heart ailments at an alarming rate. It was happening with my queer friends but not at the same levels it seemed to be happening with my straight friends. Both communities were decimated, but it seemed the theatre world, with its mingling of all types, was the hardest hit of all. Now it's rare for a month to go by without some person I'm in some way connected to shuffling off this mortal coil—which I suppose is natural at middle-age. ("Releasing")

The physiological and psychological trials of middle age have become a central concern for Fraser in a number of recent plays. *Five @ Fifty* (2011), written specifically for female actors for whom interesting parts become fewer and fewer as they age, is a play about a group of middle-aged women staging an intervention for their alcoholic friend and her codependent lesbian lover. *Kill Me Now* (2015) depicts the futile struggle of a single father to come to terms with a rare disease that eventually paralyzes him while he simultaneously tries to raise a teenage son living with a physical disability.

With *True Love Lies* Fraser resurrects David McMillan, who is a central character in his popular and critical breakthrough *Unidentified Human Remains and the True Nature of Love* (1989, later retitled *Love and Human Remains*). In this early play, AIDS only lurks as a shadow figure whose danger David does not yet fully realize. However, the impact of the epidemic on queer communities becomes a central concern in the acclaimed *Poor Super Man* (1994) and its follow up *Martin Yesterday* (1998), both of which feature David as a protagonist. Over the years, David has become a "literary doppelganger" of the playwright, who explains:

> When I write a David McMillan play it's because something has happened in my life that I want to write about . . . In *Poor Super Man* he's about to turn 30, wanting a partner and to settle down, which totally reflected my feelings as well at the time. Now he's 50, dealing with aging and how hard it is. (qtd. in LaRiviere)

Directed by Fraser's frequent collaborator Braham Murray, *True Love Lies* opened on 2 February 2009 at the Royal Exchange Theatre in Manchester, where it played for three weeks. After having been away for two decades, David returns to Edmonton and opens a restaurant. One of the people applying for a job as a waiter is a young woman named Madison who, it turns out, is the daughter of David's former boyfriend Kane (another character from *Love and Human Remains*). David, returning to town, carries the past into the present as the various characters start imagining alternative temporalities and find themselves wondering how different choices in the past might have led to a happier life in the present. Madison and her brother Royce find out that they could have been rich if their father's parents, whom they believed to be dead, had not disowned their son because he was once in a relationship with another man. David, meanwhile, sleeps with Madison, who reminds him of Kane, to whom he continues to be sexually attracted.

Kane is also still drawn to David but worries what his children will think of him now that they have found out about his past. Open-minded Madison states that labels no longer matter—"[i]t's all just sex" (73)—leading *The*

Guardian to make the celebratory statement that Fraser's play is "notable for the depiction of a post-AIDS generation for whom sexuality has become an increasingly fluid concept" (Hickling). This naive assumption is, however, brutally contradicted by Royce's violent homophobia, which manifests itself when he finds out that his father is "a fudgepacker" (11); this hurtful remark reminds us that homophobia is still a brutal, living reality. Furthermore, in a brief yet telling comment, David points out the harsh realities of urban gay culture and explains how his social life and friendship networks have been affected by the intersecting problems of HIV and AIDS and drug culture: "Between substance abuse and AIDS they're all pretty much drunk, crazy or dead" (36). This line not only draws attention to the temporal disruption that AIDS has caused in queer communities, but also serves as a poignant reminder that not everything is bright in this "post-AIDS" moment.[12]

Although David's own issues with aging are briefly addressed, his character remains in the background and acts as a catalyst that sets a number of developments in motion that lead to the collapse of Kane's already fragile nuclear family. Freeman's influential notion of " 'temporal drag,' with all the associations that the word 'drag' has with retrogression, delay, and the pull of the past on the present," is instructive here (*Time* 62). First and foremost, the temporal dragging back into the past instigated by the unexpected reunion with their old friend sharpens Kane and his wife Carolyn's awareness of how much they have physically aged.[13] In order to prepare for a dinner party with David, Kane covers his grey hair and Carolyn treats herself to "a mini makeover" (31). Second, they make a concerted effort to have sex more regularly—and louder—to reassure themselves of their own sexual appeal (and heterosexuality). Kane cannot deny his attraction to his old boyfriend and Carolyn is forced to confront her desperate attempts to convince herself that

12 For a study of the combined effects of crystal meth, unsafe sex, long-term trauma, or loneliness caused by the closet and fear of rejection on gay men's physical, mental, and emotional health, see Hobbes.

13 David is astonished by how much Kane, who has grown a belly, seems to have aged and sarcastically comments that "time works differently in the straight world" (29).

"Kane's whole thing with David wasn't real" (40), i.e. that her husband was never deviating from the straight and narrow path of chrononormativity. In spite of their efforts to act civilized, the unexpected reunion with David and the temporal drag exercised by Kane's bisexual desires put a lot of strain on their marriage and, eventually, they both realize that they are feeling trapped. The elusive promise of wedded bliss and chrononormativity to offer happiness and fulfillment has failed them: "The nuclear family. One day it just blows up. [. . .] Everyone's become body parts in a mushroom cloud. The only thing that holds them together anymore is the fallout" (95–96). As regrets and feelings of guilt over choices made in the past become more palpable, Carolyn starts imagining alternative temporalities. When she suspects, and eventually uncovers, that her husband continued to sleep with David while she was pregnant with their first child, she can no longer ignore her own unhappiness and initiates a separation. The revelation about an event in the past thus allows for the exploration of an alternative future, at least for Carolyn.

While Tremblay's play dealt with the anguish caused by the prospect of death and regrets about the past, *True Love Lies*, though far from offering a happy ending, hints at the possibility of a more fulfilled future for the aging characters beyond the narrow confines of heteronormative relationships. Fraser's play therefore constitutes another example of chrononormativity being disrupted, not by a self-imploding hegemonic masculinity, but by queer feelings and desires that are at odds with the expectations placed on traditional marriage. My final case study, Sky Gilbert's *A Few Brittle Leaves* from 2013, offers insight into queer aging as it unfolds outside of normative temporalities and the institution of marriage.

SKY GILBERT: *A FEW BRITTLE LEAVES*

AIDS runs as a leitmotif throughout Sky Gilbert's dramatic and literary oeuvre, in plays such as *Drag Queens on Trial* (1985), *The Bewitching of Max Gunter* (2001), *I Have AIDS!* (2009), and *Hamilton Bus Stop* (2010), as well as in the novel *I am Casper Klotz* (2001), to name only a few examples. Like his contemporaries Tremblay and Fraser, Gilbert has, in recent years, increasingly addressed the challenges of his own aging. *The Mommiad*, for example, is a monologue that discusses the loss of his mother and was delivered by his drag alter ego Jane at a special reading organized at Buddies in Bad Times Theatre in Toronto in 2012. The following year, Gilbert directed and performed his metatheatrical play *To Myself at 28*, an extended dialogue between Gilbert and a younger version of himself. In the play, the artist takes stock of professional and personal failures and explains the physiological changes caused by aging, including the agonizing pain stemming from the deterioration of his knees. He also attempts to warn his younger self, who has just come out as a gay man, of the various forms of homophobia he will encounter throughout his life.

As I have argued elsewhere, Gilbert often undermines two of the dominant and irreconcilable modes of representing gay men in popular culture: on the one hand, the well-adapted homonormative citizen and, on the other, the hedonistic party animal who indulges in drugs and unprotected sex. To oppose these two limited ways of representing gay men, Gilbert creates dramatic characters that revel in and celebrate their own excessive performances of gender and sexuality (Gindt, "Your Asshole"). In a column published in the *Globe and Mail* in 2009, Gilbert bemoans the gentrification of previously gay neighbourhoods, the increased representation of desexualised and bourgeois gay couples in popular culture, the various forms of homophobia manifested in both mainstream society and gay communities, and the rise of unsafe sex practices and hardcore drugs like crystal meth. At the end of the letter, he vows to leave gay culture behind:

> I reject the gay world. I have a new identity: I'm an ESP (pronounced ESPIE). That means effeminate sexual person. I'm committed to

> things that are no longer gay: alternative sexual and romantic relationships (promiscuity) and gender play (I prefer my women to act like men and my men to act like women). Don't worry, you can be a butch woman and still be an ESPIE—all you have to do is commit to gender-inappropriate behaviour of any kind and enjoy sex for pleasure alone (please don't do it—yawn—just to beget children). ("If That's")

The ESP, as suggested by Gilbert, represents a clever addition to Eve Kosofsky Sedgwick's seminal definition of queer as "the open mesh of possibilities, gaps, overlaps, dissonances and resonances, lapses and excesses of meaning when the constituent elements of anyone's gender, of anyone's sexuality aren't made (or can't be made) to signify monolithically" (*Tendencies* 8). The ESP constitutes a culturally unintelligible gender that not only falls outside the narrow binary of heteronormative concepts of femininity and masculinity, but also rejects the logics of re/productive capitalism by refusing to become a "good" and assimilated citizen. Equally important, the ESP is a sexually active person and opposes the increasingly desexualizing mechanisms of some parts of gay culture.

While there is no shortage of gender-deviant characters in Gilbert's dramatic world, the ESP, or, more specifically, two aging ESPIES, made their first appearance in *A Few Brittle Leaves*, which ran at Buddies in Bad Times Theatre from 24 April to 5 May 2013, directed by the playwright himself. *A Few Brittle Leaves* is heavily influenced by British sitcoms like *Keeping Up Appearances*. Moreover, it contains traces of Noël Coward, Oscar Wilde, and Joe Orton—all of whom have significantly influenced Gilbert's theatre—as well as British novelist Barbara Pym's social comedies and, as Gilbert explains, her " 'excellent women'—the kind of women who go to church, have tea, frequent jumble sales and never get married" (qtd. in Walker). The two main characters are a pair of unmarried sisters who live in a small village called Upsydownshire, a name seemingly taken straight out of *Alice's Adventures in Wonderland*. Viola Pie is trying to gracefully settle into middle age by having few expectations of real life, instead preferring the imaginative landscapes of her favourite literature and poetry.[14] Significantly less complacent and more outrageous is her sister Penelope (a.k.a. Penny), who refuses to be called a "spinster" (7) and has not yet given up hope of one day finding a suitable husband. Whereas Tremblay and Fraser direct their attention to the dynamics and eventual dissolution of the heterosexual nuclear family, Gilbert builds on a non-normative premise from the start and redefines kinship as a queer relationship. The two spinsters act as if they were a married couple. At one point Penny threatens to file for divorce and yells, in caps, at Viola: "YOU ARE NO LONGER MY SISTER" (32).

The sisters' quiet and regular life is interrupted by a visit from their niece Nora, an aspiring writer, and the almost simultaneous arrival of the new town vicar, Reverend Gupta. Penny immediately develops an interest in the handsome vicar (who is half her age), while Viola tries to encourage Nora (who is not interested) to flirt with him. Reverend Gupta, it turns out, is gay, but this revelation comes too late for Penny, who makes a fool of herself when her sister invites the vicar for dinner. Not only has she coloured her hair orange and plucked and reshaped her eyebrows in a way that makes her look like a clown, she also tries to impress Reverend Gupta by wearing a sari and performing her own bizarre version of an Indian dance. Her tongue loosened by a few drinks and her temper fuelled by jealousy of her younger niece, Penny blatantly exoticizes and insults the vicar. During their first meeting she had already expressed her concerns that he would ask his Anglican parish to "partak[e] in any rituals involving the worship of the bovine" (29). At the unfortunate dinner party, she unmistakenly spells out her apprehensions and accuses him of planning "TO COMMIT ATROCITIES WITH A COW ON THE SACRED ALTAR OF OUR CHURCH" (45; caps in original). *A Few Brittle Leaves* shows to what extent queer persons of colour are subjected to both heterosexism and racism by their supposed peers, often in shockingly casual ways, on a daily basis. Rather than wooing the audience and asking for their approval, Penny is palpably ignorant and hideously racist in her

14 The title of the play is inspired by a line from F. Scott Fitzgerald's *The Great Gatsby* (1925).

interactions with the vicar. Through this character, Gilbert lays bare the false assumption that a queer identity is incompatible with racism.[15]

What gives the play an additional dimension of queer gender transgression is that cisgendered male actors are expected to perform the roles of the two sisters. At Buddies in Bad Times Theatre, Gavin Crawford played the part of Viola and Ed Roy that of Penny. In an interview with *Daily Xtra*, Gilbert explained, "I call it Chekhov in drag . . . But the actors are playing women . . . I have cast this play with fine actors, and they will be playing women, with real emotions, that I hope will move the audience" (qtd. in Walker).[16] In the same article, Crawford, who later won a Dora Mavor Moore Award for best male performance for his portrayal of Viola, elaborated: "It isn't a send-up or a parody of these women . . . I approach characters the same way, male or female: what's the core of this person?" Roy, finally, added, "The consumer society has us all by the short [sic] and curlies, creating the illusion that we'll all be young forever. It's a distorted view of life that causes a lot of unhappiness for people."

In a society that continues to discriminate against women on a daily basis, ageism and body shaming undoubtedly hit women harder than men. There are fewer roles for aging women in theatre, a concern also voiced by Fraser in the foreword to *Five @ Fifty* (iii–viii). Considering the misogynist traditions omnipresent in Western theatre history and historiography, men playing women on stage is not unproblematic and risks being perceived as an expression of misogyny (see Case; Phelan). Moreover, one might argue that casting cisgendered male actors in the roles of Penny and Viola takes away

15 It is worth pointing out that almost every Gilbert play has a jaw-dropping moment that has the potential to make audiences feel extreme discomfort (and confront them with their own prejudices), while also posing a significant challenge for actors by encouraging them to take creative risks (King and Hennessy).

16 This statement is only partially true. Both of the main actors made a subversive statement about the artificiality of gender with their respective performances, albeit in different ways. Crawford approached his character Viola as if he was actually playing a cisgendered woman (as opposed to a drag queen or female impersonator); Roy's performance as Penny, on the other hand, was more indebted to the hyperbolic performativity of drag-queen culture.

potential roles from cisgendered female actors. However, with these concerns in mind, it is important to note that Gilbert is not a gender essentialist and has declared himself a feminist (*Ejaculations*). Rather than reading his casting choices as an expression of misogyny, I suggest that these are yet another way for him to subvert conventional notions of gender and sexuality and explore what happens when age and gender dissidence collide and intersect. By granting a voice and presence to the culturally unintelligible figure of the ESP, or, more precisely, the *aging* effeminate sexual person, *A Few Brittle Leaves* hints at a new direction in queer drama.

It is appropriate here to introduce sexuality historian David Halperin's concept of gay effeminacy, which stands as a "proxy identity" that is directly opposed to and protests normative heterosexual masculinity (*How to Be* 318). It is articulated through melodrama, glamour, role-playing, and other cultural practices that are traditionally identified and often devalued as feminine. This concept helps us to tease out how Gilbert, in his play, celebrates various ways of doing (aging) gay femininity as a potentially exciting new way to organize queer temporalities and gender performativity. Male effeminacy, Halperin argues, must not be conflated with either female impersonation or male homosexuality, but needs to be understood as a particular gender: "[E]ffeminacy deserves to be treated independently because it was for a long time defined as a symptom of an excess of what we would call *heterosexual* as well as homosexual desire. It is therefore a category unto itself" ("How to Do" 92; emphasis in original). Halperin further notes the stigmatization of male femininity, equally motivated by misogyny and (internalized) homophobia, and the concrete risks of abuse and discrimination:

> Any gay man who forsakes the ranks of the privileged gender and the desired gender style, who lowers himself to the undignified, abject status of the effeminate, the fairy, the poof, the bitch, the sissy, the flaming queen, incurs the easy ridicule and cheap contempt of both the straight world and the gay world. (*How to Be* 307)

Viola and Penny are part of a long lineage of marginalized yet purposefully subversive characters that Gilbert has created over the decades to trouble normative gender performances. Throughout the play, Penny alludes to a dark secret that Viola holds, which is eventually revealed in a melodramatic fashion. After Reverend Gupta's dramatic exit, Viola has a couple of drinks herself and reveals that she was not always a spinster. As a young woman she was stuck in a loveless marriage with a soldier who eventually abandoned her. Now, for the first time, she confesses that she "was just a little bit . . . happy" when her husband left (49). The reason that Viola has always been afraid to admit this feeling of relief to anyone is "[b]ecause [. . .] women aren't supposed to like being alone" (50). The dominant gender order continues to define (and rank) women in relation to men; hence the spinster, like the ESP, falls outside of the confines of heteronormativity and becomes culturally and sexually unintelligible. When Viola keeps emphasizing that "we have no way to think about women who want to be alone," even her previously supportive niece Nora starts getting uncomfortable and makes up an excuse to go to bed (51).

In her discussion of queer performance practices, Freeman identifies "the power of anachronism to unsituate viewers from the present tense they think they know, and to illuminate or even prophetically ignite possible futures in light of powerful historical moments" (*Time* 61). Viola, as the queer person aging outside of marriage or a relationship, and Penny, as the queer person aging while trying to look and act young and appealing, are both out of sync with the demands of chrononormativity. They stand in opposition to re/productive capitalism, outside of heteronormative family structures and outside of normative temporalities with their clearly outlined stations of marriage-procreation-death-inheritance. Penny and Viola's concerns about aging, or more precisely aging alone, also constitute a form of "temporal drag," with the implication that the present is dragging along unresolved questions for women and queers after decades of activism and scholarship. Like most of Gilbert's dramatic characters, Penny and Viola represent an intriguing form of queer performativity with potential promises for a queer future as articulated by Leo Bersani's famous call for "*a massive redefining of relationality*" (*Homos* 76; emphasis in original). As spinster ESPIES they represent a potentially exciting new form of gender performativity, "an embodied temporal map, a fleshly warehouse for contingent forms of being and belonging, a closet full of gendered possibilities" (Freeman, *Time* 70–71). One of Penny's last lines, spoken after Reverend Gupta and Nora have left the two sisters, is not an admission of defeat, but rather a liberating prophetically and optimistically queer statement: "When somebody leaves before dinner I suppose that we well—technically speaking, we have been deserted—but in reality, there's simply more dinner for you and for me" (54). For the first time Penny seems to value queer kinship with her aging ESPIE sister over her previous aspirations to enter into a relationship with a man, thereby hinting at the possibility of liberating herself from her own internalized demands of heteronormativity.

CONCLUSION

None of the plays analyzed here explicitly deal with HIV and AIDS, but I believe it is vital to contextualize them as capturing a "post-AIDS" moment in order to truly understand their importance and innovative potential for contemporary gay and queer theatre in Canada. All three playwrights explore questions of aging, illness, regret, dissolving relationships, loneliness, and/or death within contexts not expressly labelled "gay" or "queer," which allows them to leverage a critique against various manifestations of chrononormativity that affect contemporary culture, both queer and straight.

Post-Stonewall, HIV and AIDS have not only negatively affected the prospect of a future for queer and gay communities, but have also severely disrupted a sense of multi-generational legacy and community (Witten 4). This is why, as queer theatre scholars and practitioners, we need to listen and continue to study the work of pioneering playwrights who have survived the AIDS crisis and, confronted with their own aging process, continue to write and produce queer plays in a "post-AIDS" moment—without having recourse to role models or precedents. Despite the undeniable progression in the fields of politics, law, cultural representation, and HIV treatment and prevention, there remain numerous challenges for queer people, including the unresolved question of aging in a "post-AIDS" era. At this stage, it is too early to draw comprehensive conclusions or to make definitive statements.

What is certain, however, is that Tremblay, Fraser, and Gilbert remain relevant playwrights who continue to carve out new directions for queer theatre in Canada by showing and teaching us how to age as queer artists and scholars, all the time remaining critical of old and new forms of normativity.

PASSING THE TORCH SONG: MOTHERS, DAUGHTERS, AND CHOSEN FAMILIES IN THE CANADIAN DRAG COMMUNITY

CAMERON CROOKSTON

Early gay liberationists in the US and Canada intentionally modelled the emergent "gay community" of the 1970s and early 1980s after an ethnic community (Licata 161). However, unlike members of a racial, ethnic, or religious community, queers do not give birth to the next generation. For the most part we are raised by straight people, people who are not members of the queer subculture. So, whereas ethnic communities can use kinship networks and biological lineage to pass down cultural memory and tradition, queers do not learn about their culture from the people that raise them. Queers have instead sought out "chosen families" and other social networks that can replace or supplement bio-legal families of origin to provide support, guidance, and a link to their shared past. One of the most enduring ways queers have accessed history across generations has been and continues to be drag.

Since homosexuality entered public consciousness in the eighteenth century, it has been associated with the performing arts, particularly "female impersonation" or drag, which incidentally emerged as a distinct performance form at roughly the same point in history.[1] As George Chauncey notes, gender presentation and gender "deviance," as opposed to the contemporary concept of sexual object choice, were the primary factors for defining homosexuality

---

1 Arguing for a specific origin point for drag as an artistic practice is always interesting given the long-spanning history of men playing female roles in most cultures. I agree with Peter Ackroyd's starting date of the late 1700s, which is backed up by academics like Laurence Senelick, who acknowledges this period as the birth of female impersonation as its own attraction, rather than a stage convention that necessitated casting men in female roles by virtue of banning women from the stage (Ackroyd 122).

until the 1940s. Because of the long-standing tradition of "cross-dressing" in the performing arts, theatre often provided a loophole for skirting gender dress-code laws, making the stage an attractive option for anyone looking for a "safer" way to perform a queer identity. Similar laws permitted licensed festivals and masquerades to operate despite laws about public dress codes and appearing in disguise. As such, by the turn of the twentieth century, drag balls had become central symbols and rallying points of early queer culture (Chauncey 291). Drag balls were both performative and theatrical, but they did not necessarily require a professional ambition to be a performer, or appeal exclusively to the artistically inclined. As Chauncey describes elsewhere, participation in the drag balls was analogous to participating in cultural celebrations: "[t]he Theatre of the drag balls" functioned "much as ethnic parades and festivals helped establish the solidarity of the ethnic community by bringing people together and constructing a sense of common culture" (297). This is perhaps the earliest historic inkling that queers might be forming a community that resembled that of an ethnic minority, an idea that, as I noted earlier, gay liberationists of the 1960s and '70s would adopt. As such, early pre-war drag's unconscious use of an ethnic-community model was in effect five decades before the Stonewall generation intentionally deployed this strategy.

Because participating in drag culture, whether on the vaudeville circuit, on a nightclub stage, or by walking a ball, required specific artistic skills and knowledge about a formal system of organization and conduct, it became necessary for young queers to seek out guidance and training about how to participate in this world. At the same time, for the majority of queer youth for most of the twentieth century, and for many still today, to come out as queer means to cut ties with your birth family. This is particularly true for drag queens and trans people[2] who, historically, have come from the most

2 While contemporary identity politics tend to place trans women and drag queens as mutually exclusive identities, prior to the mid 1990s these identities were much less defined, with considerably more overlap. Many historic trans activists and public figures self-identified specifically as drag queens, including Marsha P. Johnson, Sylvia Rivera, Miss Major, Candy Darling, and Venus Xtravaganza.

marginalized subcultures of the gay community. As Chauncey, Laurence Senelick, and Susan Stryker each note, prior to Stonewall, the public image of homosexuality (including drag) was represented predominantly by racialized and/or working-class queers. A middle- or upper-class queer could afford to express any gender-variant desires only in private spaces. On the one hand, it is important to note that drag queens were among the most marginalized groups within queer culture. Another way to look at this, however, is that queers who had lost everything were the most likely to defy middle-class normative values and openly express their queer gender identities. Thus drag mothers emerged in a community that was especially vulnerable to isolation.

The problematic relationship between queers and "the family," both personally and politically, has been explored by Kath Weston in *The Families We Choose*. As Weston explains, "[f]or years, and in an amazing variety of contexts, claiming a lesbian or gay identity has been portrayed as a rejection of 'the family' and a departure from kinship" (22). Some scholars have gone so far as to say that homosexuality and family are functionally and conceptually antithetical (Mays, et al.; Strommen; Weston). On a very literal level this was a reflection of the fact that queer youth were frequently disowned upon coming out, so the choice between living an authentic queer life and continuing to be a member of one's birth family became a question of one or the other. The anxiety around disclosing sexuality to one's family and the inherent risk of rejection—which can include disavowal; violence; verbal abuse; and the cutting off of financial, emotional, or medical support—has remained a serious risk to queers throughout the twentieth and into the twenty-first century (D'Augelli, Hershberger, and Pilkington; Mays, et al.; Oswald; Weston). Due to the prevalence of this concern, Ramona Faith Oswald notes that "managing disclosure is discussed in virtually every study of gay and lesbian individuals and family relationships and is often the primary focus of inquiry" (377).

Perhaps in reaction to this trend, early gay liberationists rejected the "nuclear family" as an inherently oppressive institution. As an article from a 1969 issue of *The Rat*, an early gay liberation publication, cited: " 'We expose the institution of marriage, as one of the most insidious and basic sustainers [sic] of the system,' proclaimed the Gay Liberation Front in 1969" (qtd. in

Stacey 1912). Weston also notes that "[i]t is but a short step from positioning lesbians and gay men somewhere beyond 'the family' [. . .] to portray[ing] them as a menace to family and society. A person or group must first be outside and other in order to invade, endanger, and threaten" (23). Thus, in addition to the common personal trauma of being disowned by one's family, both queer youth and adults must live in a community that defines their identity in opposition to the very philosophical and political idea of "the family." Anti-gay organizations and legislation have capitalized on this idea that queers, just by existing, endanger families with slogans and titles like "saving the family" or "protecting children." Public displays of affection or visible queerness are often objected to under the pretext that "this is a family place."

Yet the idea of chosen family, as well as kinship-based rhetoric (referring to peers as queer brothers and sisters, for example) has continuously been used within queer subcultures. Drag mothers and drag families thus can be seen existing within the tradition of the queer chosen family. Stacey notes there is a certain irony that a community that initially defined itself in opposition to traditional family units embraces a familial model when creating their own system of relationality. Stacey also notes that a major conceptual shift in how the gay community understands itself in familial terms occurred as result of the AIDS epidemic. The initial ideological root of gay liberation valued, among other things, a radical break from the hegemony of family and liberation from systemic oppression. However, when faced with AIDS and a total lack of government support, liberation gave way to the fight for rights. Simultaneously, priorities within the community shifted to focus on caregiving and support. As Stacey explains, "the AIDS epidemic subjected gay male sexuality to extraordinary levels of collective scrutiny and debate, and it incited gay men to perform Herculean levels of caretaking outside default mode family forms" (1914). So while AIDS and the public scrutiny that came with it did not necessarily dislodge attitudes that saw traditional families as problematic, it created an opportunity to find new ways of forming non-traditional, non-bio-legal family structures. These kinds of familial support systems, amongst both peers and across generations, have continued long after the worst years of the AIDS epidemic, as the system similarly lends itself to youth and adults alike who have been alienated from their families due to their sex and/or gender identities.

What makes drag families distinct from other queer chosen families is drag's status as an art form. One of the many things that queer culture and theatre share is the problem of how to document the ephemeral. Ann Cvetkovich explains that

> [g]ay and lesbian cultures often leave ephemeral and unusual traces. In the absence of institutionalized documentation or in opposition to official histories, memory becomes a valuable historical resource, and ephemeral and personal collections of objects stand alongside the documents of the dominant culture in order to offer alternative modes of knowledge. (8)

Queer theatre, which, at the risk of generalizing, tends to reject more traditional text-based forms of performance, thus faces double erasure as it exists both outside the normative cultural narratives and outside the normal grasp of text-based performance documentation. While drag has many dramaturgical aspects, the concept of nostalgia and a parodic reverence for the past is a common if not universal feature. Thus, in taking a drag daughter under her wing, a drag mother connects their daughter to cultural artifacts from the art form's history. I don't wish to overstate drag's ties to cultural memory. Drag performances about Stonewall[3] or Marsha P. Johnson are rare, and learning the lyrics to "Somewhere Over the Rainbow" is hardly a complete history lesson on the LGBTQ+ community. Nonetheless, drag, by its very nature, allows its audience access to the cultural practices of previous generations.

Drag's performance of pop cultural artifacts reflects the overall relationship between queer culture and mainstream media that David Halperin has

3 The Yes-Men, a Toronto-based drag king group, did perform a theatrical lip-synch of the Stonewall riot at World Pride in 2014. This is so far the only drag performance inspired by Stonewall that I have seen.

explained as one of the defining aspects of queer cultural practice: "gay men circulate specific bits of mainstream culture among themselves, endowing them in the process with non-standard meanings and consolidating a shared culture and sensibility on that basis" (*How to Be* 18). The deployment of these coded bits of nostalgia serves as the primary dramaturgical basis for a large amount of drag performance. For example, in one number, Toronto queen Miss Conception lip-synchs to ABBA's "Mamma Mia" while dressed as Faye Dunaway's Joan Crawford from *Mommie Dearest*. This number enacts multiple simultaneous levels of parody and satire as Conception evokes Crawford as a pre-Stonewall gay icon, Dunaway's performance in a camp classic, and ABBA's disco as a fixture of queer music canon, despite a total lack of literal homosexual content in any of these sources. The predominantly gay male audience has no trouble instantly decoding the complex multi-layered parody.

Halperin's text, *How to Be Gay*, is largely based on an undergraduate course he taught of the same name. One of Halperin's hypotheses going into both the text and the course was that this practice of "decod[ing] heterosexual artifacts and recod[ing] them with gay meanings," having emerged at a time in which all communication between gays, due to criminalization, was required to be covert, would likely begin to either die out or certainly lose its primacy within the LGBT community as newer generations came of age (18). Halperin was surprised to learn that despite the wealth of out and proud queer literature and film on his syllabus, his millennial students nonetheless vastly preferred recoding and queering mainstream heterosexual culture to engaging with more explicitly LGBT-focused texts (123).

Halperin is uncertain as to why exactly young queers respond so positively to this survival strategy of yesteryear. A possible reason could be that, despite the strides made by both independent queer media and the mainstream's embrace of LGBT content, there remains a fundamental gap between "authentic" queerness and the mainstream. As Halperin explains, many of his examples of authentic queer-authored texts remain entrenched in alternative and/or typically "highbrow" culture and are thus not necessarily as accessible to members of queer culture who crave more mainstream forms of entertainment like Hollywood film or television (123). Hollywood films and network television series featuring gay characters—which have seen an increase since the mid-1990s (such as *To Wong Foo, Thanks for Everything! Julie Newmar*; *The Birdcage*; *Will & Grace*; *Queer Eye for the Straight Guy*; and *Hairspray*)—have conversely been accused of delivering sanitized versions of queers, representing essentially straight characters in gay contexts, or relying on the trope of the "magic queer." In other words, authentic queer media is not mainstream enough and mainstream media is not queer enough. Beyond the sheer creative fun of being in on the joke that straight audiences frequently miss, the tradition of coding straight mainstream media with covert queer meanings allows queers to enjoy the accessibility of mainstream genres while simultaneously revelling, and participating, in authentic queer cultural sensibilities. Thus, despite the rapid changes over the past half century in the lives and rights of queers, queer coding remains a desirable aspect of gay culture. As such, it is perhaps less surprising that drag, an art form predicated on such coding, and which many predicted would die out with in the post-Stonewall era (Halperin 74), has managed not only to survive, but to thrive well into the twenty-first century.

Because of drag's ability to code bits of nostalgic popular culture, and in doing so provide a rare link amongst queers to their community's own origins, drag queens remain one of the strongest links between young queers and the history of the community. However, drag's intrinsic relationship to the past and cultural memory is present not only in its dramaturgic content but also on a structural level. Drag queens, as a community, use a kinship system—much like that of a chosen family—in order to train future generations of performers and pass down artistic and professional knowledge. With drag mothers functioning as professional mentors and links to the past, young and aspiring drag performers encounter a unique opportunity in the queer community: to be "raised" by queers from the generation that preceded them. As such, drag's ability to serve as a conduit to intergenerational communication exists both on a performed and communal level. In the remainder of this essay, I will explore the implications of these kinship systems by discussing interviews I conducted with six queens from across Canada: Lucy Flawless, Dmanda

Tension, Allysin Chaynes, and Farra N. Hyte in Toronto; Raye Sunshine in Vancouver; and Elle Noir in Halifax.

All the queens I interviewed described their impetus for connecting with a drag mother as a desire to learn about some technical or professional aspect of drag. Both Hyte and Sunshine had already begun performing drag in nightclubs before they met their mothers. Their previous careers as a professional dancer and actor, respectively, helped them bridge knowledge gaps in performance, makeup, and costumes. Both queens noted that while being self-taught had served them well initially, "higher standards" and internal politics in the pageant system necessitated guidance about a specific cultural tradition.

Tension and Noir, on the other hand, identified the first queens to put them in drag as their drag mothers. Flawless, who comes from a theatre conservatory background, learned makeup techniques from YouTube and performed largely at local theatre fundraisers in Toronto. In the spring of 2016 Flawless participated in Project Drag Queen, a sort of emerging-artist workshop that Flawless thought would help her integrate into the local professional drag scene. In our interview Flawless referred to the mentors who ran Project Drag Queen as her "foster drag parents."

One trend that emerged from the interviews is that while all queens sought out—or accepted the invitation of—their drag mothers for professional reasons, there is nonetheless a familial element to the dynamic that hinges on the idea of a mother/daughter relationship. All of the queens noted that despite the power dynamic between the new and old queen, for the most part mentoring took the form of suggestions and the sharing of stories or techniques, as opposed to coaching or instructing, which tend to involve more strict directives. Hyte, who currently has five drag daughters that make up the "Hyte" family, stressed that being a drag mother was not about imposing her own aesthetics or artistic vision on someone to create tiny versions of herself. Hyte explains that she often approaches aspiring queens when she recognizes a similar artistic spirit—members of the House of Hyte tend to come from a dance background and, generally, tend to affect a glamorous aesthetic—so that rather than trying to impose her artistic aims on a young queen, she instead looks for queens who might naturally wish to engage with the same aspects of drag as she does. However, as Hyte emphasizes, beyond that spark of recognition, she encourages her queens to explore and express their own sense of self through drag, offering advice and guidance rather than narrow instructions. A general attitude of respect for the young queen's sense of self and artistic practice as self-expression is paramount to the mother/daughter relationship.

However, the term *mother* is more than just a metaphoric term for a feminine mentor. In addition to the practical mentoring they offer, drag mothers and families do tend to function as actual families. All participants talked about the fact that their drag family's activities extended beyond their work as drag queens and into their personal lives. Drag families frequently celebrate holidays together, as well as commemorate personal milestones like anniversaries and birthdays. Hyte explains that the long-time partner of one of her drag daughters is incorporated into the family as her "drag son," despite having never performed or appeared in drag.

Drag mothers also frequently offer guidance on life issues that tend to parallel their chosen artistic practice. For example, Hyte and Noir are both trans women who began transitioning after they started performing as drag queens. Hyte explains that her drag mother, whom she met at pageant in the US, also identified as trans and was thus also able to offer her guidance and support as she began to transition. Noir notes that as an out trans woman of colour and a drag queen, she is approached by many of her drag daughters because of a shared investment in that experience of intersectionality.

I would like to close by talking about how drag has changed in Canada over the past decade and the effect of drag's mainstream success on drag families. The most conspicuous influence on drag's recent surge in popularity has been *RuPaul's Drag Race*, which in addition to turning the art form into mainstream entertainment, has led to a "baby boom" of aspiring queens. However, *Drag Race* and its sleeper-hit popularity ride on the shoulders of some subtler influences. Despite the widespread belief in the 1970s that drag was on its last legs, the 1990s saw mainstream culture taking an interest in drag through such films as *The Adventures of Priscilla, Queen of the Dessert*; *The Birdcage*; *To Wong Foo, Thanks for Everything! Julie Newmar*; and the documentary *Paris is Burning*, which has had enduring popularity. Soon afterward, drag went from being a dirty little secret to a mainstream novelty, and social media granted access and the possibility of documentation to a previously underground ephemeral art form. Trade secrets like creating the illusion of "feminine features" with makeup contouring or the practical question of where to buy a size fourteen heel had previously been passed by word of mouth between daughters and mothers. But now they are available to anyone with an Internet connection. This increase in drag's popularity and accessibility had similar ramifications in the Canada. Hyte, who began her drag career in the early 2000s, and Sunshine, who began his soon afterward, each note that drag in Toronto and Vancouver followed similar patterns to those of the States. Canadian cities saw an increase in both audiences and sheer number of performances throughout the first decade of the new millennium.

Many queens were invigorated by the explosion of interest in drag and saw it as an exciting time to be practising the art form. A few did voice concerns over some of the effects on the community. Tension, who began performing just before the boom hit, notes that there has been a drastic shift in the expectations of audiences and managers in Toronto: "A queen used to be able to show up and do four numbers. Now everyone is expected to do twenty." She referred to this as "marathon drag." Hyte also voiced concern that *Drag Race*'s power and influence projects a more processed version of drag, which disconnects the "reality" show from the actual art form.

Going into the interviews, I had a pessimistic theory that the recent explosion of "all-access drag" would start to erode the figure of the drag mother. I am happy to report that, as far as the six queens interviewed are concerned, this does not seem to be the case. The overall trend in drag communities in Canada seems to remain that, despite a sharp increase in online access to practical training, young queens seek out drag mothers. At this point in my research it is a little early for me to be drawing definitive conclusions, so instead I will offer a few thoughts that might suggest why a kinship system endures in drag.

First, while homosexuality and gender play may be far more accepted today than they were twenty years ago, queer youth, particularly those whose gender expression is outside the hegemonic norm, continue to face high levels of rejection from their biological families and the broader queer community. It is possible that more than being a system for perpetuating its survival, family and connection are part of what attracts young queens to the art form. On the other hand, many queens seek out drag mothers despite having a strong and positive connection to their birth families. Hyte, Sunshine, and Flawless all maintain active relationships with their parents, but nonetheless have sought out drag mothers. Anna Muraco noted similar results in her study, reporting that two thirds of those surveyed about their chosen queer families reported no significant issues or estrangement from their bio-legal families. Muraco concludes that even if the concept of the chosen queer family originates from rejection and the need to survive, this is no longer the sole reason queers seek out fictive kinships with friends that are modelled on familial structures (1320).

Aside from the obvious practical training that queens gain from acquiring a drag mother as a mentor, connecting to a drag family offers the young queen a connection to the history not only of the art form but of the LGBT community at large. As was mentioned earlier, gay men and women are, historically, raised by straight parents and thus outside of the queer culture they may wish to engage with as adults. Even the most accepting straight parents are typically ill-equipped to teach their queer children about the history and culture of the LGBT community. Drag mothers are typically older than their drag daughters, so there is the possibility of a traditional passing down of knowledge from "elders" to youth; at the same time, many drag mothers are less than a full generation ahead of their daughters. Nevertheless, drag is an art form largely based on nostalgia and, as I have mentioned, the queering and recoding of generally outdated pieces of heterosexual media. From Old Hollywood to John Waters, drag queens possess an encyclopedic knowledge of popular culture from past eras and the interaction between the mainstream and gay culture. Thus, drag mothers can supply their daughters with multiple links to the shared queer past that are likely inaccessible to birth parents.

Furthermore, drag mothers are part of the culture they perpetuate and are often represented in mainstream representations of drag. From *Paris is*

Burning's Dorian Corey to Mama Ru herself, the image of the wise, sassy drag mother is a celebrated and exotified symbol in queer culture. Aspiring queens who want the full drag experience may seek out drag mothers in order to complete the image of drag presented to them in the media.

Lastly, the long-standing ethos of "don't dream it, be it" that echoes in drag culture, from the plot of *The Rocky Horror Picture Show* to RuPaul's multiple autobiographies, has helped define drag in the last forty years as an expression of an idealized self. This concept of an artistic, living self-portrait exists in stark contrast to the pre-Stonewall definition of drag as predicated on mimicry and impersonation. This concept, which is fundamental to contemporary drag, can be applied to the creation of the drag family. Muraco, still citing the creation of chosen families in the absence of rejection from birth families, explains that "[f]amily, as a cultural construct, is idealized to such an extent that many familial relationships are likely to fall short of the desire for them to fulfill all social, instrumental, and emotional needs" (1320). As such, chosen queer families may be sought out to supplement rather than replace. Just as a drag persona mixes authentic self-expression with an artistic recreation of one's identity, so too can drag mothers and families function as an almost utopian creation of this idealized family.

So, while drag mothers, much like other forms of queer chosen families, may have originated out of survival, be it personal survival or the survival of an art form, what I have taken away from these interviews is that they, like drag itself, have evolved from the days of struggling to survive. In an age in which many may not have to worry about survival or access to practical skills, the emotional and cultural function of drag mothers seems as strong as ever in Canadian cities. And much like drag itself, it does not seem like they are going away any time soon.

CONSTITUTING COMMUNITY: *THE GAY HERITAGE PROJECT*, *BODY POLITIC*, AND THE PERFORMATIVE POWER OF THEATRE

STEPHEN LOW

In *The Gay Heritage Project*, developed and performed by Damien Atkins, Andrew Kushnir, and Paul Dunn, Atkins performs a scene in which "HIV/AIDS" is put on trial and convicted of the murder of one hundred million people. Even though he is not HIV-positive, nor has had a loved one die of AIDS, Atkins declares: "[W]hile I'm very glad that you've been convicted of one hundred million counts of murder, I would like to add another charge to that list. I would like to add theft. I can't even really be sure what you stole from me. But I know that you did." In this scene, Atkins expresses a sense of grief, not just for the many people who tragically died of HIV/AIDS, but for the wealth of knowledge about gay historical events and figures that disappeared with them. In this scene, one of many vignettes that make up the ninety-minute play, Atkins gestures toward a chasm between an older generation of gays and lesbians who are familiar with historical events and icons that are central to the gay community—and specifically in this case to events related to the HIV epidemic—and a younger generation who are potentially disconnected from a communal gay history. *Body Politic*, by Nick Green, dramatizes the same chasm through a narrative memory play. The work tells the story of an older man, who belonged to the *Body Politic* collective, recounting stories of the rise and fall of the Toronto LGBT political newspaper of the same name to a young man whom he has invited to his home for a sexual encounter. Both plays were programmed by Buddies in Bad Times Theatre for their 2015–2016 season, which centred on "personal and collective histories." The following essay argues that both of these plays have the capacity to performatively constitute community by telling the history of the gay community in Canada in live performance to an audience often divided along generational lines.

This argument aligns with scholarship that outlines how the theatrical event can bring together strangers to form community. In *Utopia in Performance: Finding Hope at the Theater*, feminist theatre scholar and critic Jill Dolan "investigates the potential of different kinds of performance to inspire moments in which audiences feel themselves allied with each other, and with a broader, more capacious sense of a public" (2). Dolan applies anthropologist Victor Turner's term "communitas," which, as she explains, "describes the moments in a theater event or a ritual in which audiences or participants feel themselves become part of the whole in an organic, nearly spiritual way; spectators' individuality becomes finely attuned to those around them, and a cohesive if fleeting feeling of belonging to the group bathes the audience" (11). Theatre scholar David Román echoes Dolan (and Turner) when he writes, "Performance proves an especially effective means to engage the contemporary in that artists and audiences are constituted and composed as a provisional collective in a particular temporal moment and in a specific localized space" (*Performance* 1). Not only do *The Gay Heritage Project* and *Body Politic* constitute the temporary community in the moment of the theatrical event that Dolan and Román describe, but these plays bind their audience to a larger, more permanent sense of community outside of the theatre and the particular moment of performance through two different theatrical approaches to history: one pedagogical, and one representational. These strategies appeal to two different demographics. One follows from Buddies in Bad Times Artistic Director Evalyn Parry's quotation of Gertrude Stein in the season program: "Let me recite what history teaches. History teaches"; it attends to a young generation *pedagogically* by teaching them gay history. The other strategy appeals to an older generation *by performing the past* through the representation of events from Canadian gay history on stage, drawing on the personal connection these audience members might have to these events.

Atkins's short scene in *The Gay Heritage Project* described above performs both these strategies simultaneously. In the scene, Atkins performs the role of the younger generation, stating that he is unaware of what was lost in the HIV/AIDS epidemic of the eighties and early nineties. Atkins teaches that younger generation about the scope and tragedy of the loss in his emotional delivery of the text. At the same time, by identifying the great loss of life caused by the epidemic, even if he "can't even really be sure" what was stolen from him, Atkins also honours the tragedy and sorrow of what was lost for an audience partly made up of those who lived through it. Green's *Body Politic* functions in a similar way. Focusing on the political events that the newspaper covered, such as the bathhouse raids of 1981, *Body Politic* teaches an audience that may have been unaware of this part of Canadian gay history, while simultaneously representing these events and institutions to audience members who may have lived them. In such moments these plays performatively constitute gay community and, in the process, attempt to bridge some of the generational fissures that continue to divide this community. Of course, it is impossible to determine what each member of the audience experienced witnessing these plays; this paper's analysis aims only to outline the *potential* of the scripts and their performances to constitute community performatively through pedagogical and representational modes.

The conception of gay community appealed to here cannot be defined as a collective of individuals who identify as gay. After all, the members of the audience who are constellated into a "gay community" through the performative exercise of witnessing one or both of these two plays may not necessarily identify as gay. The concept of community appealed to here is both local and discursive, akin to, but fundamentally different from, Michael Warner's concept of public. In *Publics and Counterpublics,* Warner defines public as "a space of discourse organized by nothing other than discourse itself" (67), and one that is addressed to an indefinite number of strangers (74). I differentiate community from the more general concept of public insofar as community is not indeterminate—its members can be enumerated. In this formulation, community is defined as a group of people who share a geographic location, race, ethnicity, sexual orientation, language, politics, or, as is the case with these two plays, a shared history.[1] Though often formed because a group of people share a similar identity, communities can coalesce around shared history that may not necessarily be expressed as an identity category: an individual may, after living in a particular city for some time, belong to the community of that municipality but still not express their identity as such. For example, I have lived in Ithaca on and off for five years, and feel that I belong to the Ithaca community, but I do not identify as Ithacan.

Community as employed here also engages Miranda Joseph's monograph *Against the Romance of Community*, which critiques communities determined and defined by shared identity. In the introduction, Joseph narrates her ethnographic experience working with Theatre Rhinoceros, a "gay" theatre formed in San Francisco in the early- to mid-seventies. In the early nineties, as part of her research, Joseph attended a company retreat at which "gay community" was assumed to be "by, for, [. . .] and of" gay-identified individuals in a neighbourhood populated by those individuals (xiii). This discussion revealed that the company was invested in a definition of community that "enact[s] and produce[s] identity, unity, communion, and purity" (xvii–xix). Community as articulated at the Theatre Rhinoceros retreat was "conservative, disciplining, and exclusionary" because it necessarily excluded heterosexuals, queers, trans, and bisexual individuals (xviii). When two individuals challenged this assumption they

> stood in stark contrast to the dominant vision of the theatre as a ritual or healing space or as a mechanism for affirming and documenting the history of a knowable and coherent community, a vision that imagined the theater to be the site at which communal crises and changes were processed and subordinated to an ongoing identity and unity. (xv)

Unlike the concept of community recorded in Joseph's ethnographic field work, the grounds upon which it is constituted in the theatre for this paper

---

1 Identity can fashion itself to an individual, while community emerges when a *group of people* come together.

is inclusive because it is not organized around a shared identity. Through the experience of witnessing *The Gay Heritage Project* and *Body Politic*, audience members, though they may not identify as gay, are invited to become a part of a gay community by accessing and sharing a common history through live performance.

LEARNING TOGETHER: PERFORMATIVE PEDAGOGICAL CONSTITUTION OF COMMUNITY IN *THE GAY HERITAGE PROJECT*

The audience is immediately interpellated as a community when they enter the theatre for *The Gay Heritage Project*. As performed at Buddies in Bad Times Theatre when it premiered, and as stated in the as-yet unpublished script, "[T]he three performers—Damien, Paul, and Andrew—greet [the audience], going up and down the aisles, shaking hands, and chatting with the patrons" (4). With a "Hello!" or more suitably a "Hey, girl!" that echoes Louis Althusser's iconic performative interpellative speech act "Hey you!" spectators are welcomed into the theatrical space as audience-subjects. The division between the stage space and the audience space is collapsed as the performers "[go] up and down the aisles," greeting the spectators. The performers—whom the audience learns constitute a community unto themselves when they discover that Damien, Paul, and Andrew have been friends for many years[2]—extend their personal community to the audience in the moment they speak to the patrons as they speak to each other. Even before the performance begins, the audience and actors are established as a collective, a community.

The play opens with two vignettes that further establish a sense of collectivity. In the first, Atkins re-enacts his childhood ritual of performing Brian Orser's 1988 World Figure Skating Championships long program, which prompts his sister to ask, "Why do you like Brian Orser so much?!"

2 The audience learns this in one of the opening scenes of the play, when each of the performers declares how long they have been friends (9).

(5, 6). Atkins responds, "I don't know. I just feel like . . . like he's cool, and like . . . maybe it would be fun to hang out because like, maybe we would have something in common" (7). As the audience enjoys Atkins's humorous re-enactment, either chuckling in recognition of gay icon celebrity worship or merely laughing at the ridiculousness of performing a figure-skating long program in a living room, the audience is having "fun" hanging out with Atkins and each other. Through this mutual enjoyment, expressed through laughter, the audience establishes something in common with Atkins, just like Atkins intuited he would have something in common with Brian Orser. After being interpellated with a "Hello!" as they entered the theatre, the audience continues to be constituted into community through a shared sense of enjoyment and recognition of gay celebrity worship.

The vignette that immediately follows echoes the performative community established through rituals of nationalism, but with a gay twist. All three in harmony sing Madonna's "Like a Prayer"—recognizable as a "gay anthem"—with a waving rainbow flag projected in the background, evoking the performative ritual of singing the national anthem at sporting events (7). Just as singing the national anthem offers a performance of belonging to a nation-state, this anthem-singing positions the performers and their audience, which is very likely aware of Madonna's appeal to the gay community and status as a gay icon, as members of something like a queer nation.

The play moves on to present a collage of small scenes which often mention cultural and historical references, from Leonardo da Vinci to Lady Gaga, that are identifiable to an audience acquainted with gay cultural phenomena. The performers ensure the audience is aware such references are associated with gay culture—or, in other words, the play *teaches* the audience about gay cultural phenomena—when a list of "gay people, images, and icons in history" is projected on a screen up stage early in the play (18). As short scenes are performed one after another, the audience understands themselves as having a common place in a gay community when laughter, or silence, or tears are heard in the dark space of the auditorium. The representation of gay cultural phenomena performatively constitutes community either by audience members learning that these icons and images are meaningful to members of the gay community or by members who are part of the gay community recognizing that this collection of icons and images is meaningful. In both cases, the audience, whether they be young or old or familiar or unfamiliar with gay culture, is potentially mobilized into community based upon new-found or well-established shared cultural appreciation (17).

The brief cultural and historical references throughout *The Gay Heritage Project* have the capacity to constitute community pedagogically as well. For example, a series of scenes in which two children play with their "Gay Canadian Action Heroes" tells the audience the story of some of Canada's most important LGBTQ activists. In these scenes, a younger Canadian audience is informed of an important part of their history they otherwise would not have known about, which in turn connects them to an older generation who survived those tumultuous times. By *learning* together in the theatre, and learning material that older audience members are likely already familiar with through reactions that suggest recognition, younger audience members are welcomed into a community through the pedagogical modes subtending the play. After witnessing *The Gay Heritage Project*, an audience member who is not familiar with gay culture would learn how gay meanings are attributed to certain cultural phenomena—such as Joan Crawford, *The Golden Girls*, and Madonna's heteronormative pop anthems—and consequently be incorporated into gay community.[3]

The Gay Heritage Project not only teaches its audience about gay history, but also about queer theory. The engagement with queer theory is not purely pedagogical, but rather challenges some widely accepted scholarly ideas from an affective, personal, and theatrical perspective. In other words, *The Gay Heritage Project* asks: How do we *feel* about the arguments presented by queer theory? In a scene that revises the story of *The Wizard of Oz* and places the search for gay heritage as the central problem of the story instead of Dorothy's quest for home, Michel Foucault is exposed as the Wizard who masterminds the project of queer theory. Exposing Foucault and his theories—which limit

3 For more on the process by which mainstream cultural phenomenon is attributed with queer meaning, see *How to Be Gay* by David Halperin.

the possibility of gay history[4]—as covertly directing the development of queer theory writ large, *The Gay Heritage Project* suggests that there is something else behind these ideas that inhibits us from connecting to a history. Though the arguments of queer theory and those of Foucault specifically are accepted as persuasive in most academic circles, they are resisted in the play on the grounds that such arguments deny the individual a sense of belonging to something beyond themselves in their current historical moment. In a short conversation after the show, Andrew Kushnir, speaking to the play's treatment of Foucault's theory, admitted that the "numbers add up," but continued that "they don't feel right." As Kushnir noted, *The Gay Heritage Project* demands, in terms of queer theory, that we examine *how we feel* to determine if the arguments presented can enact the political, social, and cultural effects that would make our lives better.

Alongside engaging, then challenging, seminal works of queer theory, there are several other instances in which the actors perform the act of learning. In one scene, Paul Dunn "runs" through history, learning how gay men were discharged from the Canadian military for being homosexual, were considered a threat to the nation during the Cold War, and were subject to police surveillance and violence during the bathhouse raids. In each instance, Dunn re-enacts an encounter with a military officer, a government psychiatrist, and a cop respectively. After "running" from one scene of violence and oppression to the other, Dunn is stopped by his friend Mark, who asks him, "You okay? How was the reference library?" In this scene, Dunn dramatizes both

---

4 In *The History of Sexuality Volume One*, Foucault contends that the "homosexual" was a modern invention. He writes, "The nineteenth-century homosexual became a personage, a past, a case history, and a childhood, in addition to being a type of life, a life form, a morphology" (43). In other words, the homosexual was an identity, in contrast to the act of same-sex love, sodomy, which "was a category of forbidden acts" (43). Foucault's distinction between the practice of sodomy and the homosexual suggests it is incorrect to describe figures who lived before the late nineteenth century as "gay." Consequently, it is incorrect to categorize parts of history as "gay" because no individual or community coalesced around a common identity that describes a shared sexual orientation until the second half of the nineteenth century.

the history he learned through his time at the library, but also the horror he felt from reading this history. The performance of learning staged by Dunn teaches an uninformed audience member by taking them on his own journey of learning, but also honours the violence and oppression that the gay community faced in the past for older members of the audience.

Another through line in the play features Kushnir searching for evidence of—and later learning about—gay life and culture in Ukraine. As a Ukrainian Canadian who was told by his mother when he came out that "[t]here were no people like you where we came from. There's no such thing as a Gay Ukrainian" (12), Kushnir is compelled to locate a gay lineage in his cultural heritage. The opening scene in this series, in which he is researching "Gay Ukrainians" at the Toronto Reference Library, ends with Kushnir discovering he needs to find his gay Ukrainian brethren by travelling there himself. In Ukraine, Kushnir interviews two gay Ukrainian men he meets on a train, Rostik and Sasha. After interviewing them for *The Gay Heritage Project*, Kushnir concludes, "I'm not exactly gay in the same way you're gay, am I?"

> **ROSTIK:** Our lives are very different, Andrew.
> **ANDREW:** And I'm not Ukrainian, in the same way that you're Ukrainian.
> **SASHA:** No.
> **ANDREW:** And, so why was it so important to me for us to be exactly the same?
> **ROSTIK:** For *droojel'yoobovnist*, probably.
> **ANDREW:** Oh, I don't know that word.
>
> [. . .]
>
> **SASHA:** Belonging.
> **ANDREW:** Belonging. Yeah.
> **ROSTIK:** But you can still make belonging with us, if you like, Andrew.
> **ANDREW:** I guess. But at this point, we'd just be making it up.
> **SASHA:** Perhaps all belonging is just made up, no?

Rather than appealing to certain cultural, historical, or political commonalities, Kushnir appeals to a feeling of belonging to connect with these two men. His desire can be understood as dramatizing a "[longing that] produces modes of belonging and 'being long,' or persisting over time," as articulated by Elizabeth Freeman in her monograph *Time Binds* (13). Kushnir, in terms of Freeman's conception of "belonging," feels a desire that "is a form of belief in the referential object that the subject feels [he] lacks and that would make him [. . .] whole" (13). Though Kushnir's feeling is predicated on a "form of belief," or an imagined similarity, it can function as the basis on which connection and community can be established, or "made up."

The idea that belonging, to either gay culture or Ukrainian culture, can be "made up" suggests that it is performative: it is not what you are, but what you *do* that constitutes belonging. And the theatre, as a site of performance, brings people together in community *despite* their differences. Kushnir and the two Ukrainian men share a cultural heritage, language, and sexual orientation, but these facts are not sufficient for them to have enough in common to establish a shared identity. Yet through the active process of making belonging, they can create community. The conception of community Kushnir dramatizes avoids the "conservative, disciplining, and exclusionary" power of community articulated by Joseph in *Against the Romance of Community*. By taking this journey *with* Kushnir, the audience has been incorporated into the active process of making belonging. Kushnir begins his search with a question: Who else in the world is also both gay and Ukrainian? As the audience travels with Kushnir from the Toronto Reference Library to Ukraine, they learn both the answer to that question and the fact that the question can only be answered through the active process of making belonging. What constitutes "making belonging"? For Kushnir, it means first learning that belonging must supersede identity; second, that belonging is an active process; and third, that belonging requires learning about ourselves and others. Over the course of *The Gay Heritage Project* the audience learns about themselves and others, either through gaining knowledge about the past or understanding what the three performers feel about contemporary issues and debates in identity politics. Through the performativity of witnessing performance, they actively make belonging.

BODY POLITIC: LEARNING AND REMEMBERING TOGETHER TO CONSTITUTE COMMUNITY

Like *The Gay Heritage Project*, *Body Politic* has the capacity to performatively constitute community through pedagogy and the representation of history. These modes are metaphorically anchored in the play by the older man, Phillip, who nostalgically recounts his memories of his time as a writer and collective organizer for the LGBT political newspaper *Body Politic* to the younger man, Josh, whom he has invited to his home for sex. When recounting the stories of the bust on the *Body Politic* collective after the publication of an article on man-boy love and the infamous bathhouse raids and ensuing protests in 1981, Phillip, at times without being aware of it (especially while high), teaches a history of Canadian LGBT activism to Josh. An audience member who remembers these events and the general social, political, and cultural life attending them could, through identification with Phillip, also participate in remembering this time of struggle. Conversely, Josh and those members of the audience who are too young to have lived through these events are pedagogically engaging with the past by learning about these events through Phillip's stories.

Late in Act One, Phillip proclaims that his generation "started the conversation," to which Josh replies, "Yeah. And here we are. Having it" (56). When Phillip concurs—"Right. Yes Josh. Here we are"—his words spill over from the world of the play into the metatheatrical: not only are he and Josh having the conversation, but the audience is a part of that conversation too. When Phillip declares, "Here we are," his words could be understood as meaning both here we are having the conversation in my apartment and here we are in the theatre. Josh echoes the two modes of community constitution when, while trying to seduce the older man, he asks, "Are you going to make me do all the work?" Phillip replies: "Yes." Josh is, indeed, going to do the "work" in the sense that pedagogy is a kind of labour—effort is required to understand events and issues from the past that may not be familiar to an individual's lived experience in the contemporary moment. In contrast, Phillip, who declares that he won't do any labour in this seduction, is disavowing "work" and indulging in pleasure; Phillip lived through the events and issues from the past he is telling Josh about and, consequently, he requires less effort, if any at all, to understand them. Though it is necessary for Phillip to remember the stories in the act of sharing them with Josh, the acts that he is remembering have been performed before and don't require the historiographic work, or labour, of sense-making that is demanded of Josh. Consequently, Phillip is performatively constituting community with Josh through remembrance, but this act of remembering is not work or labour. Both young and old, and those on stage and those in the audience, are potentially constituted into community through the stories, both within the play and in the theatre, that are being shared.

Body Politic, both the play and the magazine, are performatively constituted as part of this process. Early in the play, when Phillip is remembering the birth of the political magazine in a staged flashback, its purpose is directly asserted. Phillip begins, "The Body Politic is a Gay Liberation newspaper published in Toronto by The Body Politic Editorial Collective. Our Purpose is threefold." Steven continues: "To inform the gay community about news, events involving the gay liberation movement." This declaration is a goal of the play as well. Calvin then adds, "To provide a forum for individuals to express their views on sexual politics." Though these views may be ventriloquized through the mouths of live actors, this declaration mirrors how the play also provides a platform for views on sexual politics to be articulated. And Deb concludes, "To publish prose, poetry, book and film reviews, and graphics relevant to gay liberation" (20). Though the play does not formally publish anything, it is an artistic work relevant to gay liberation that is disseminated publicly in and through the theatre, thus aligning with the concluding declaration. Echoing Kushnir's discovery when seeking out community with his gay Ukrainian brethren, Phillip summarizes: "Gay community is what you make it. We welcome your contributions" (20). The community of *Body Politic*, both the magazine in print and the play in performance, depends upon action, either the act of writing and publishing or the act of live performance. The actions that bring *Body Politic* into being are the expression and dissemination of news concerning gay activism, views on sexual politics, and the artistic and cultural production of members of the gay community. Through these actions, which are repeated in each volume published or performance performed, both bring their audiences together into community. In short, gay community is performative insofar as it is made through repeated and communal acts and not an assumed extension of gay identity.

At the beginning of the play, the text interpellates the audience to identify with either Phillip or Josh. It begins with Josh walking to a door and hesitating before opening it. Though the audience may not share Josh's hesitancy, they, like him, are entering the world of the play. This entrance that metaphorically mirrors the audience's "entrance" is recognized when Phillip says "Hi" to Josh (1). As the play proceeds, and Josh's physical youth is matched by his ignorance of local gay history, those in the audience who learn alongside him will identify with Josh. An older gay generation who lived in Toronto in the eighties and nineties would have likely known about the magazine. It is likely, then, that the older members of the audience will identify with Phillip. The opening moments metaphorically enact the older generation meeting the younger generation: Phillip, as the point of identification for an older audience, welcomes Josh, the point of identification for a younger audience, into the world of the play, which is a world of memory and history.

Even before the play begins, the audience is interpellated as members of the gay community, who are central to the story. In the production at Buddies in Bad Times Theatre, the audience entered through a corridor in which old analogue phone handsets hung from the ceiling. At the beginning of the corridor was a placard with an explanation of what a "phone tree" was—a means of contacting a great number of people before the age of the Internet. One person would call someone, spread information regarding a demonstration or protest, and that person would then begin to call all the others she knew who would be interested, instructing those people she called to do the same. Eventually the number of people who were also calling others would proliferate, allowing the greatest number of people to receive the information. As the audience walks down the corridor after reading the placard, they are invited to pick up one of the handsets and listen to a voice explain how phone trees functioned. This embodied act, picking up a handset just like the demonstrators who protested the bathhouse arrests in 1981, invites the audience to participate in that event across time, once again echoing Freeman's concept of belonging as "being long, or persisting over time" (13). The invitation to listen to the handsets positions the audience as members of a gay community that heeds the call from the phone tree and protests on the streets of Toronto.

When the events of the protest that followed the bathhouse raids in 1981 are recounted, the audience is incorporated into the world of the play, further constituting audience members into community. Standing atop a bed and facing the audience directly, the lesbian character, Deb, recounts her story of leading the protest. As she rallies the protesters, she speaks directly to the audience and rallies them as well. This staging strategy situates the audience as the "sea of people" she saw as she stood atop a car, and, as a consequence, theatrically interpellates the audience as the gay community of protesters. They are bound, not just to each other as a "cluster" or "crowd" that is witnessing the play, but to those in the past that made up the "sea of people" Deb is describing. Across time, community is constituted through the performative act of witnessing—the audience in the present is constituted as a community by being addressed as an audience in the past.

Like the audience, which is not made up solely of gay men, the concept of community that is articulated in the play is not based upon common sexual orientation, or even gender identity, but common political goals. Reeling from the injustice of the bathhouse raids, Brian, whose boyfriend was arrested and beaten, tells Deb that "[she's] making this all about [herself]" and she has no place in this struggle because "[t]his is about the raids" and she can't fight for "[her] right to have gay sex" because she is a woman. Deb argues that "[w]e're all of us fucked, Brian! All of us. Together" (76). Deb is particularly energized to protest the injustice and declares they should "work like it's the most important thing that's ever happened to our community" (77). Considering that Deb is one of the ringleaders of the massive demonstration that follows, the audience witnesses that gay community is not based upon gender or sexual orientation, but is constituted through active engagement with political, social, and cultural production. A conception of gay community not founded on gay identity is evident in Deb's use of the first-person plural pronoun ("we") in her declaration quoted above, but also in her speech during the protest when she yells to the crowd:

> The entire community is now being beaten together. [. . . } Last night as they forced their way into the baths they forced their way into *us*. They came into *our* rooms, *our* showers, *our* lives. *We* offered them the keys to *our* lockers, but they used crowbars instead. They made a mistake. As they pulled *us* out they broke the hinges. They tore off the locks. They pulled *us* out and threw *us* in one pile on the ground, and now there is no way, there is no way ever, that *we're* going back in. (82; emphasis mine)

The constant refrain of the first-person plural pronouns refuses that gay community be bound to identity, and defines it instead by common investments in civil rights and sexual freedom. These are presumably the same values that those who would attend a play at Buddies in Bad Times Theatre share. It is important to note that the bathhouse raids that provided the grounds upon which Deb delivers this speech were not isolated. Deb and her fellow protestors are energized by a *history* of persecution. That history, just like the history documented by *Body Politic*, and being documented and shared by the play of the same name, is also the foundation upon which community emerges.

The final scene of the play also binds the audience together as a community in the present by connecting them to a community in the past. In the last moment of the play, the collective members of the *Body Politic* say "goodbye" to Phillip, who has just sent Josh home. Although the members of the collective from Phillip's past indicate that they are leaving by saying "goodbye," they do not depart, but stand in door frames at various places on the set. Josh joins the collective at the threshold of a door framed by light to also say "goodbye." Because it is the last moment of the play, the word "goodbye" can be understood as being both directed to Phillip within the play and to the audience. Like the members of the collective who say "goodbye" but don't leave, the past, in the form of the momentous events of Canadian history depicted in the play, remains with both Phillip and the play's audience. The past, and the people who inhabit it, are always gone but not gone, always at the threshold of the exit. The fact that Josh is also included in this last moment, saying "goodbye" but not leaving, signifies that a more recent past remains with Phillip and the play's audience as well. For Phillip, within the play, Josh embodies the most recent past, and for the audience, the play that they just witnessed is the most recent past. Both these recent pasts stick with Phillip and the audience respectively. Because the audience must reckon with both pasts—*Body Politic* as a political newspaper that documented Canadian LGBT history, and *Body Politic* as a play that was just witnessed—they share a common experience. Whether that experience is engaged with pedagogically or nostalgically it nevertheless performatively constitutes them into a community. Both an older audience member and a younger one constitute community through their connection to history that is a "mode [. . .] of belonging and 'being long,' or persisting over time" (Freeman, *Time* 13).

Even though the generation gap is apparent early in the play, such as when Josh doesn't recognize, or even know, who Bette Davis was (5), or when Phillip mistakes a J.K. Rowling quote for T.S. Eliot (8), the pedagogical performative constitution of community does not just occur when the older generation teaches the younger. In one of the final scenes of the play, Phillip accuses Josh of assuming "everything is great, right? Which is why all gays seem to hate everything that makes them gay. Which is why you're all getting married. Why HIV is still fucking rampant. Because you don't have to listen to *this* shit" (89). Here, Phillip accuses Josh of not being interested in the history of the gay community, or what he sarcastically refers to as "this shit," and suggests that because Josh's generation is uninterested in their history, they are doomed to repeat it. He explicitly declares, "IT WAS TERRIBLE, JOSH. You fuck like you haven't read a history book" and that "[y]ou fuck like you've never considered fucking dangerous. Without context. You fuck without fucking context." In doing so, Philip implies that Josh is "ignoring that the last 25 years even happened" (90). He concludes his tirade, yelling, "DO YOU KNOW HOW MANY OF MY FRIENDS DIED!?" (91). Following this, Josh confesses that he is HIV positive and consequently aware of the risks involved in gay sex. Josh tells Phillip that "you pretty much don't know anything about me" after he confesses this intimate detail. Following the vectors of identification that are set up in the play, this is arguably true of many of the older generation in the audience who are unaware of the complications of young gay life. In this moment, the general dynamic of the play is flipped, and the older generation is bound to a younger through pedagogical modes. This moment exposes that the older generation, though most likely having a more in-depth knowledge of gay history and the experience of gay life in the past, can still have much to learn about what it means to be young and gay in the present: they can learn from the younger generation what it means to be young and gay in the age of PrEP, Grindr, and gay marriage.

The Gay Heritage Project also performs the flipped dynamic dramatized in this moment of *Body Politic*. In the scene from *The Gay Heritage Project* described at the beginning of this essay, Atkins declares that while he's "very glad that [HIV/AIDS has] been convicted of one hundred million counts of murder, I would like to add another charge to that list. I would like to add theft. I can't even really be sure what you stole from me. But I know that you did." As evidenced in Atkins's scene, *The Gay Heritage Project* teaches the older members of the gay community that younger members feel that HIV/AIDS has stolen a connection. Consequently, *The Gay Heritage Project* teaches an older generation that younger members of the gay community desire a connection to a gay cultural history and that the lack of this connection is a source of sadness and anxiety. Though much of *The Gay Heritage Project* involves re-presenting gay cultural history, which would be familiar to many older members of the audience, Atkins, Dunn, and Kushnir also perform a desire to *connect* to gay cultural history, which may be unfamiliar to an older audience member.

I attended performances of *Body Politic* and *The Gay Heritage Project* with an eighty-two-year-old friend of mine whom my partner met at the Y on College Street in Toronto. As I sat next to him at both performances, I had a very palpable sense of divide between the performance of memory and the pedagogical effects of these plays. Over the course of our friendship, my friend had taught me so much about the history of gay life in Toronto as he reminisced about his past. After *Body Politic*, he remarked that the political newspaper was like "someone had opened a door open wide," and that the gay community was forever changed. His engagement with the past at the theatre, an experience that reminded him of when a newspaper threw the doors wide open for the gay community, was likewise a pedagogical experience that threw the doors wide open for me, as a member of a gay community.[5]

5 This essay is dedicated to Kenneth Druce.

SCRAMBLING SCUM

MOYNAN KING

The performance discussed in this paper was the inspiration for a theoretical model that became the foundation of my Ph.D. dissertation, entitled "Queer Performance in the Post-Millennial Scramble." When I first encountered this performance, Christina Zeidler's *Rehearsal for an Endurance Performance of the SCUM Manifesto: A Ukulele Concerto in C Major*, and then encountered it again, and then again, in a second and third iteration, it caused me to ponder the ways that contemporary queer feminist performance can challenge the stagnant periodization of our so-called post-feminist and post-queer moment by scrambling histories, attachments, and ideas of gender, temporality, identity and form:

> By glitching older forms, by trying on identities, by not saying unequivocally "This is who I am," the scramble of post-millennial queer performance offers a rich ground for the theorization of queer feminist performance in Canada now. As a temporal phenomenon it is about reclaiming but not owning; it is a syncretic temporal mash-up that celebrates the very pleasure in scrambling. (King, "Queer Performance")

Zeidler's re-uptake of the *SCUM Manifesto* by Valerie Solanas is representative of how the scramble of post-millennial queer performance positions feminism as a vital and integral aspect of progressive queer ideologies by reclaiming, but not owning, even the monstrous elements of its histories—histories that are ongoing and still going on. While Zeidler's performance was a foundational example of the theoretical model I am developing to discuss queer feminist performance in Canada now, it is also one of the case studies that have since been elbowed out of the actual dissertation project. Yet it hovers, like a ghost, always nudging me, calling me back to the challenge of its dissonant recollection and harmonic recollation, to grapple with a work whose citational foundation still bears the heat of a highly controversial politic. Like Zeidler's project, this paper is composed in iterations. It began with an analysis of Zeidler's *Rehearsal for an Endurance Performance of the SCUM Manifesto*, transformed into a concentrated attempt to analyze the formal aspects of the *SCUM Manifesto* itself, and then became (as it becomes now) this paper. I thus begin with a brief critical introduction to the original manifesto and then analyze some of the ways that Zeidler's project scrambles its elements into a post-millennial performance that is timely, out of time, and composed of the time of its own iterations and rehearsals.

I don't remember exactly how or when I first learned about the *SCUM Manifesto*. But Christina Zeidler, who heard about it from Toronto writer and performance artist Christie Cameron in the early 1990s says, "It's always a lesbian who tells you about it."

SCUM

The *SCUM Manifesto*, according to Solanas, is a call to "civic-minded, responsible, thrill seeking females" to "overthrow the government, eliminate the money system, institute complete automation and destroy the male sex" (35). "Maybe," as Avital Ronell suggests in her introduction to the recent republication of Solanas's text, "the Solanas tract was payback; it was clocked to strike the time of response to all shameless woman-hating manifestoes and their counterparts, the universalizers. No matter how you cut it, universal—whether common or communist—meant 'man' " (5). In an essay I wrote for an online culture journal based in Montréal called *nomorepotlucks*, I theorized the formal structure of the *SCUM Manifesto* as an act of binary terror, "a transgressive inversion of gender roles that drives head-on into the traffic of the one-way street that constitutes historical gender binary oppression" ("Revenge"). Rebecca Schneider defines binary terror as the fear "that accompanies the dissolution of a binary habit of sense-making and self-fashioning" (*The Explicit Body* 13). As a manifesto, I suggested,

> *SCUM*'s intention is to make manifest, to render perceptible, a new order of ideas. Derived from the Latin manifestus (apparent, palpable), whose etymological roots are mannus (hand) and festus (struck), the manifesto is an apt, if not ideal, form for Solanas's revenge-styled counter-hegemonic text. Solanas inverts the psychoanalytic model of feminine identity by deploying precisely the tactics of historical misogyny, resulting in an act of binary terror that converts female penis envy to the male's envy of the female's free wheeling individuality. The *SCUM Manifesto* takes aim at, while simultaneously (and blatantly) revealing its genesis in, misogynistic polemics throughout history. ("Revenge")

As is a polemic against polemic, the *SCUM Manifesto* renders Solanas herself the scourge of feminism by forgoing her own utopian vision of the female function being "to create a magic world," and to do so "all with love" (Solanas 47).

Historically, Solanas's body of work is overshadowed (or simply brought into view) by her shooting of pop icon Andy Warhol. The bullet that pierced Warhol's flesh was the critical juncture that mobilized her image as the terrifying feminist icon for an anti-feminist agenda (as if her action proved that "by god, the feminists really are trying to kill us!"). Simultaneously, that same bullet was marked as a pivotal gesture of heroism by the radical feminist movement that followed her, while Solanas's gunfire provided a citable excuse for the exclusion of queer women from the mainstream feminist movement of the '60s and '70s. The citational history of Solanas's tract variously and completely embodies the negative aspects of her life (because clearly it's wrong to go around shooting people), but, in so doing, this history disavows the complex critique of capitalism that is the nucleus of her manifesto.

The *SCUM Manifesto* is of ongoing interest to contemporary cultural theorists and artists. Sara Warner considers it part of "a retrogressive repertoire of corporeal gestures and civic performances" (26). She argues that performances like the *SCUM Manifesto*, which "blur the boundary between legitimate and illegitimate, normal and abnormal, justice and injustice, provide a forum in which we can imagine, if not enact, alternative structures of feelings and alternative ways of being in the world" (8). J. Jack Halberstam frames Solanas as the poster child for what they call "shadow feminisms," which "take the form not of becoming, being, and doing but of shady, murky modes of undoing, unbecoming, and violating," a position with which feminism is certainly familiar (*The Queer Art* 4). Meanwhile Sara Ahmed, in her recent development of "A Killjoy Manifesto" in *Living a Feminist Life*, invokes Solanas in ways similar to my deconstruction of the manifesto, saying that "[t]o render a new order of ideas perceptible is simultaneously a disordering of ideas; manifestos often enact what they call for in surprising and shocking ways given how they expose the violence of an order" (251). These contemporary ruminations on Solanas, when considered alongside Halberstam's discussion of the "disloyal historiography of homosexuality" in *The Queer Art of Failure* as "not so much an identity stretching across time as a shifting set of relations between politics, eros, and power" (171); Elizabeth Freeman's theorization of temporal drag's "associations of retrogression, delay and the pull of the past on the present" ("Packing History" 728); and Ahmed's idea that the meanings of "sticky signs" are generated not by cutting them off from previous contexts but by preserving them together (*The Cultural Politics* 90–91), produce a theoretical frame for Zeidler's *Rehearsal*. Zeidler's performative re-uptake of the Solanas tract is part of a larger ongoing investigation of scummy feminist histories, identities, and rehearsals whose sticky attachments are felt even today.

SCRAMBLING SCUM

Christina Zeidler is a Toronto-based artist who identifies primarily as a creative collaborator. The spirit of collaboration, and of hybrid artistic practices, has influenced her paintings, films, performances, songs, and entrepreneurial endeavours since the mid-1990s. In 2012 she embarked on a performance project based on Solanas's *SCUM Manifesto* that evolved through three stages (and stagings) as *Rehearsal for an Endurance Performance of the SCUM Manifesto: A Ukulele Concerto in C Major*. I am interested in the ways that the *SCUM Manifesto* performs over time and how Zeidler takes up this performance in a post-radical feminist, post-Valerie culture. My inquiry into Solanas's manifesto (a performative gender inversion of a patriarchal speech act) and Zeidler's reperformance of *SCUM* (a form of lesbian drag) investigates binary essentialism and the tactics of disidentification in the process of revisioning and reframing a difficult feminist lesbian icon. Zeidler's project is "Deep Lez" in that it delves into herstory to "create new ways of thinking while simultaneously clinging to more radical politics that have already happened but definitely aren't over yet" (Mitchell, "Deep Lez"). From here, right now in 2017, Solanas's manifesto summons a dark misandry that, according to blogger Mira Bellwether, "undermines our CURRENT social goals and the strength of our communities, because it is an expression of an outmoded, sexist, and frankly dehumanizing nightmare vision of the world that scarcely deserves to be mentioned in the same breath as feminism." And yet, from here, feminism continues to be haunted by Solanas's monstrous branding. *SCUM* is sticky. Why we "attempt to resurrect such cringe-worthy performances in order to re-animate a disavowed structure of feeling" is because, as Warner has said, "this mode of archivalism sheds light on how our construction of the past dictates political and performative possibilities in the present" (26).

Zeidler's artistic practice incorporates the awkwardness and originality of an artistic identity always in process, and revels in the discomfort and humour of negotiating her own self-performance as a contemporary queer feminist haunted by multiple queer/lesbian/feminist pasts. In her many and varied collaborations she has drawn simultaneously on feminist theory, punk rock and riot grrrl energy, and DIY processes. For example, her long-standing collaboration with Allyson Mitchell as Freeshow Seymour saw the production of a number of short films, events (such as feminist art show-and-tell brunches), and live performances incorporating craft, spectacle, and music. Likewise, her collaboration with Celina Carroll led to the creation of the faux Euro-pop diva duo Ina unt Ina, a spectacle-based musical act tied to Zeidler and Carroll's queer identities, visual arts backgrounds, and interests in audio experimentation. When Zeidler took on the *SCUM Manifesto*, she did it alone, a process that she describes as initially "terrifying," having "never ever performed solo before." Reflecting on Solanas's status as outsider, even from the burgeoning feminist movement that surrounded her in New York in the mid-1960s, it is interesting to consider that Zeidler's attempt to embody and deconstruct *SCUM* began by working outside of her regular collaborative process.

The first phase of Zeidler's performative embodiment, in February 2012, was at the Art Gallery of Peterborough, where her video work was being shown. In an effort to engage the community, the gallery hosted a performance night as part of the exhibition. Zeidler tried out a short section of the *SCUM Manifesto* on a ukulele with the words projected behind her. I deliberately stated, just now, that Zeidler "tried out" a section of the *SCUM Manifesto*, not "performed," as I am prompted by the intention of the work embodied in its title as always and forever being a rehearsal. As "rehearsal," the work prompts the audience to imagine a future "performance," a final performance that, in the case of *Rehearsal for an Endurance Performance of the SCUM Manifesto*, will never come to pass (except, perhaps, in the mind of the spectator). The project will have a future—it will morph and change while responding to its various audiences as ongoing collaborators. Zeidler's effort to go "solo" was compromised at the outset of this project; she had unwittingly built a collaborative component into the very title.

SINGING SCUM

In *Queer Voices*, Freya Jarman-Ivens considers the singing voice a mechanism for "linking two bodies together." As the voice leaves the singer it "takes a part of [her] body with it—the sound of its own production; and as it enters [the listener] it tickles [her] tympanum and disrupts the tiny hairs in [her] ears' " (2). This process, as an image, is easily sexualized—the aural penetration of one's ears by another's voice—and makes palpable the enduring intimacy of live vocal performance. When the vocal productions emanating from one body penetrate another body, sound becomes waves that "exist at some point in this no man's land . . . and acquire the power to roam at will and launch [themselves] into another body, forcing [themselves] into the passive, waiting ears, and [becoming] invader, intruder . . . contagion" (Jarman-Ivens 3). The no-man's land of Solanas's manifesto, where it has hovered as a wave of phobic lesbian representation for almost fifty years, is rendered vibrant by Zeidler, producing a temporal condition that is present but is not of the present; it is a conflation of time: the now is in dialogue with the past. Or, to reinvoke visual artist and women's studies scholar Allyson Mitchell's words, it has "already happened but definitely [isn't] over yet" ("Deep Lez").

When Zeidler took the stage dressed in her Valerie Solanas drag (men's fur-lined, collared coat and newsboy cap) at the Art Gallery of Peterborough, she began by telling the audience, in a joking tone, that "when I sing the part about destroying the male sex you don't have to take it too seriously." She then began to strum her ukulele and sing an excerpt of *SCUM* (see Appendix A). By giving the *SCUM Manifesto* a voice, Zeidler embodied the raw human physicality of Solanas's words—an embodiment that emanated from her individual corporeal vocal production, "[becoming] invader, intruder" (Jarman-Ivens 3) to the equally raw corporeality of her audience hearing a melodic version of Solanas's radical feminist theory—becoming, then, a sort of idea-probe forcing itself into the audience's waiting ears. It is in this contrast to her lighthearted introduction, the easy melody of her ukulele, and Zeidler's physical presence, which, costume pieces notwithstanding, is nothing like Solanas's, that *SCUM* takes the stage. Zeidler's pitching of the *Manifesto* in C major scrambles the rhythms, and therefore the reception, of the work, making it strangely palatable—not to be taken "too seriously."

By identifying Zeidler's performance as a form of drag, I am drawing attention to the work's ethos of parody (imbued with irony) and inserting it into an established tradition of queer performativity. The object of drag is to perform, to try on, and to rehearse an identity while maintaining a critical distance from the original. Drag acknowledges a third space between original text or performance and the new performance into which that text or performance is incorporated. Inside this third space is an active space for the construction of queer, where we find irony, analysis, and a personal disidentification that links performer to performed, while simultaneously maintaining a critical distance between performer and performed. The object of *Rehearsal for an Endurance Performance of the SCUM Manifesto* is not to realize Solanas's performative text but to take it apart, while at the same time hailing a historicized lesbian stereotype. Zeidler is not just dragging across gender; she is dragging a provocative version of female masculinity across time. Her feminist drag instigates a powerful and subtle medium for social critique, and self-critique, along with a more current and expansive stage for gender performativity without the heterosexual normativity of traditional drag. The kind of acts that Elizabeth Freeman has tagged "temporal drag" (728) form a "constitutive part of subjectivity exteriorized as a mode of embodiment [that] may offer a way of connecting queer performativity to disavowed political history" ("Packing" 729). Zeidler's disidentification with Solanas allows her to make new space for an "other" that is always aware of its own peformativity. This type of drag cites an authority composed of historical models of gender identities that are neither authentic nor parodic. Such performances cling to a binary essentialism—such as that implicit in Solanas's *SCUM Manifesto* and its investment in binary terror—at the very core of their ontology to stage an identity that is both relic and sticky icon. Through a process of temporal "inter(in)animation" (Schneider, *Performing Remains* 7), Zeidler is both revealing historical meaning and making new meaning while being written by, and while writing on, her own cultural signifiers. Imagining, revisiting and re-presenting a queer past always has ramifications in the present and, concomitantly, in the future. A transtemporal trajectory can be observed in the shifting qualities of Zeidler's project across its three instalments. Indeed, this temporal trajectory is embedded in the project's title, with its future promise and historical associations.

When I spoke with Zeidler about her inspiration to perform the *SCUM Manifesto*, she said, "The whole idea is sort of absurd, to take her writing, which is this very intense, driving stream of consciousness, and to slow it down. I think of it as a kind of drag." The theatrical process of "trying on" a persona, of "trying out" historical representations, is at the heart of the malleable and unstable identity formation known as queer. Zeidler's *Rehearsal for an Endurance Performance of the SCUM Manifesto* is a drag embodiment that attempts not to redeem Solanas's existential negativity but to confront it by throwing herself into the critique "and sharing the experience of trying this thing on." Acknowledging the sticky attachment of Solanas, Zeidler's disidentification "with [this] damaged stereotype recycles [her] as a powerful and seductive site of self-creation." Disidentification, according to José Esteban Muñoz, "is meant to be descriptive of the survival strategies the minority subject practices in order to negotiate a phobic majoritarian public sphere that continuously elides or punishes the existence of subjects who do not conform to the phantasm of normative citizenship" (Muñoz 4). Zeidler's re-uptake of Solanas works like Muñoz's concept of disidentification in so much as it enables fluid reconfiguration of a normalized fantasy of the lesbian subject as essentially dangerous.

SINGING TO THE CHOIR

The second instalment of Zeidler's project took place at an event entitled *Explain Yourself*, produced by Toronto's queer performance collective Hardworkin' Homosexuals. Performers at *Explain Yourself* were asked to situate their performances within a context of practising queer theory—a directive that instigated, for Zeidler, a deeper engagement with her own drag appropriation of the *SCUM Manifesto* and resulted in a serendipitous reinsertion of collaboration into the work via the queer audience for whom she would perform. At this stage Zeidler added a new cross-disciplinary element to her ongoing Valerie drag project: she created an ink portrait painting of herself as Valerie Solanas (see Fig. 1). In it, Zeidler is portrayed in the iconic posture of Solanas, with coat and cap, and, in a process of "inter(in)animation," she added her ukulele. Rebecca Schneider, citing Fred Moten's use of the term "inter(in)animation," elaborates on this process as the ways "live art and media of mechanical and technological reproduction, such as photography, cross-identify, and more radically, cross constitute and 'improvise' each other" (*Performing Remains* 7). The inter(in)animation captured in Zeidler's self-portrait-as-Solanas points to Schneider's suggestion that "any time-based art encounters its most interesting aspect in the fold: the double, the copy, the clone, the uncanny, the againness of (re)enactment" (6). The addition of the self-portrait to Zeidler's overall project enacts an embodiment of a phobic representation of her lesbian self. It suggests that even though the artist is nothing and never like Solanas at all, Solanas is hovering always just at the edge of all lesbian representation since the penning of *SCUM*.

At *Explain Yourself*, Zeidler once again projected the text as she sang an excerpt of the *SCUM Manifesto* in her Valerie drag with her ukulele. What altered not only the act but also the course of the future of her project was the presence of a queer/trans/lesbian/gay/genderqueer audience who, familiar with the tactics of disidentification (if not the theoretical terminology) and willing to be seduced by the incongruous logic of humour, were able to hurl themselves into

Fig. 1. Christina Zeidler as Valerie Solanas. Provided courtesy of Christina Zeidler.

the critique along with Zeidler and understand intuitively not to "take it too seriously" (Zeidler). Of this performance experience Zeidler says, "What changed so much at *Explain Yourself* was, without prompting, or with a tiny prompting, but I just said it as a joke, like 'everybody,' the whole audience, joined in and became a choir—that was the inspiration for the choir in the next version at Nuit Blanche." For a moment Zeidler's transtemporal drag netted us all, "reenacted, reenactor, original, copy, event, re-event, bypassed, and passer-by in a knotty and porous relationship to time" (Schneider, *Performing Remains* 9). This netting, this binding together of past and present, event and spectator, original and copy, through the collective action of singing, along with the distribution of her portrait as Valerie Solanas, had an enduring impact on the project, and on Zeidler, who subsequently integrated a video version of a choir into the next iteration of *Rehearsal for an Endurance Performance of the SCUM Manifesto: A Ukulele Concerto in C Major.*

AUTOMATING REHEARSAL/REHEARSING AUTOMATION

When Zeidler was invited by curator Lisa Myers to participate in the OCAD University programming for Nuit Blanche, she was both intrigued and disturbed by the event's potential as a venue for her project. Nuit Blanche, a franchised performance event sponsored by Scotiabank that takes place annually across the city of Toronto for a full night, from seven in the evening until seven the following morning, was, to Zeidler (referencing Solanas's assertion that culture provides a sop for the egos of the incomplete), the ultimate "turd fest" (see Fig. 2). Indeed, Nuit Blanche is a perfect example of what Guillermo Gómez-Peña has called "the mainstream bizarre," where " 'alternative' thought, fringe 'subcultures,' and so-called 'radical' behaviors as we knew them have actually become the mainstream. Spectacle has replaced content; form gets heightened, more stylized than ever, as 'meaning' (remember meaning?) evaporates, or rather, fades out, and everybody searches for the next 'extreme' image or 'interactive experience' " (13).

Fig. 2. Turd Posters at Nuit Blanche Iteration. Photo provided courtesy of Christina Zeidler.

The obvious solution to the challenge of Nuit Blanche's twelve-hour performance framework might have been, given the endurance aspect built into Zeidler's project, to take on an actual live endurance performance of the *SCUM Manifesto*, and, as Zeidler says, if she had been "interested in the element of humiliation as part of the goal then it would have been a great venue for that." She was *not* interested in humiliation as a performance goal, but she was intrigued by the potential of installing the work into OCAD as an institution, and taking an anti-capitalist voice and "positioning it as authoritative, and have it validated by the institution itself" (Zeidler). As the project moved away from Zeidler's live body into a technologized performative installation, it zeroed in on Solanas's scathing critique of capitalism, which would simultaneously constitute a critique of the very audience for which it was designed (see Appendix B). What Solanas's manifesto always wants to render perceptible is a systemic manipulation of power and how power is attained "by the manipulation of money and everything controlled by money, in other words, of everything and everybody" (Solanas 41).

In the development of the video installation, Zeidler worked with one of her regular collaborators, Sarena Sairan, from her feminist emo band Mintz, and queer Toronto-based musician Susan Gale, to create a three-instrument multi-vocal arrangement based on the original ukulele version of the song. Additionally, she decided, in the vein of Solanas's directive to "institute complete automation" (Solanas 35), to create an environmental video installation that used nine projectors and ten projection surfaces. Six of the projection surfaces were made from black Plexiglas (see Fig. 3) that reflected the images projected onto them back onto a larger projection surface (see Fig. 4) to create a ghostly composite image and to facilitate a visual effect that surrounded and encompassed the audience. This composite image broke the frame of its projection surface to make the women (the musicians and choir) fill the space like "feminist lesbian monsters" (Zeidler). The effect was that of a music video broken into its various parts. During the installation we witnessed not only the musical performances but also, at times, the projected text, and images of women waiting around to play or sing their various parts. The installation was an exercise in simultaneous performance and rehearsal. The maintenance of the rehearsal aspect, even in this slick technologically mediated production, was important to Zeidler, who suggests that "the rehearsal is a feminist construct—and we're still rehearsing our lives and our performances and who we are all the time." In the absence of the live body, the work's title continued to support the project as a performance by reminding the audience of its always unfinished quality, one that maintained a future promise of a deconstruction that, though unravelling in the space before us, never culminated in conclusion.

Rehearsal for an Endurance Performance of the SCUM Manifesto is a project composed of repetition: from Solanas through Zeidler's solo song, self-portrait, and collective musical performance, to a video installation created to perform the quality of a rehearsal and talk back to a new audience, the performance and the rehearsal are always happening simultaneously, are always reflecting the condition of queer in a transtemporal dance of identity construction and meaning-making.

Fig. 3. Black Plexiglas Reflective Projections. Photo provided courtesy of Christina Zeidler.

Fig. 4. Ghostly Composite of Sarena Sairan, Susan Gale, and Christina Zeidler. Photo provided courtesy of Christina Zeidler.

SCRAMBLING STICKY STUFF

As individuals whose experiences continue to be marked by shame and stigma, queer women often distribute knowledge through the exchange of rumour, gossip, and hearsay. We identify each other by such exchanges and rely on these modes of knowledge distribution to expand and improvise our individual identities. While our difference, as queers, is informed by prevalent attitudes of our time, these attitudes are always subject to a transtemporal identity formation that is revised and enriched by dialogues in the social and cultural spheres. Queer women are innately aware of their own gender performativity because they embody desires that are always relegated to the borders of the heteronormative social structures that shape and define its aesthetic. The effectiveness of *SCUM* as a topic in the contemporary sphere (and likewise its effectiveness in the overall ontology of Zeidler's project) lies in its activation of ideas that "the language of feminist 'waves' and queer 'generations' sometimes effaces: the mutually disruptive energy of moments that are not yet past and yet are not entirely present either" (Freeman, "Packing History" 742).

Queer identities are formed collaboratively and cross-temporally. The trajectory of Zeidler's *SCUM* project can be seen as a microcosm of this formation, which begins with an individual inquiry, embodies a collective invitation, and results, in its final version, in an attempt to "effectively camouflage content-as-experience" (Gómez-Peña 14). Zeidler's drag performance points to a condition of queer feminist identity as one that is constantly being improvised through an embrace of the scrambled reckoning offered by the post-millennial everythingness of now. Now, for the queer feminist, this is all we have, as the queer performances of the post-millennial scramble often fall between the established folds of disciplinary divides and arts-institution mandates. The queer feminist is marked as other even within politically identified institutions such as gay theatres and feminist theatres. The scramble of contemporary queer performance reorders, refracts, and exceeds the silos of representation. Zeidler's drag performance of Solanas points to the condition of queer feminist identity as one that is constantly in flux, *and yet* one that can also imperceptibly calcify; one that is self-made in iterations and repetitions; *and* one that is burdened by the monstrous auras, like that of Solanas, that it can never seem to shake. Scrambling *SCUM* is an attempt to shake down one of the sticky attachments of the monstrous elements of historical lesbianism and hope that someday its monstrosity will land in a different and more complex overall configuration of queer feminist representation.

Appendix A

Excerpt from the *SCUM Manifesto* used in the live version of *Rehearsal for an Endurance Performance of the SCUM Manifesto.*

Life in this society being, at best, an utter bore and no aspect of society being at all relevant to women, there remains to civic-minded, responsible, thrill-seeking females only to overthrow the government, eliminate the money system, institute complete automation and destroy the male sex.

There is no human reason for money or for anyone to work more than two or three hours a week at the very most. All non-creative jobs (practically all jobs now being done) could have been automated long ago, and in a moneyless society everyone can have as much of the best of everything as she wants. But there are non-human, male reasons for wanting to maintain the money system.

And excerpts of the following:

Appreciating is the sole diversion of the "cultivated"; passive and incompetent, lacking imagination and wit, they must try to make do with that; unable to create their own diversions, to create a little world of their own, to affect in the smallest way their environments, they must accept what's given; unable to create or relate, they spectate. Absorbing "culture" is a desperate, frantic attempt to groove in an ungroovy world, to escape the horror of a sterile, mindless, existence. "Culture" provides a sop to the egos of the incompetent, a means of rationalizing passive spectating; they can pride themselves on their ability to appreciate the "finer" things, to see a jewel where this is only a turd (they want to be admired for admiring). Lacking faith in their ability to change anything, resigned to the status quo, they *have* to see beauty in turds because, so far as they can see, turds are all they'll ever have.

Appendix B

Excerpt from the *SCUM Manifesto* used in the Nuit Blanche version of *Rehearsal for an Endurance Performance of the SCUM Manifesto.*

Appreciating is the sole diversion of the "cultivated"; passive and incompetent, lacking imagination and wit, they must try to make do with that; unable to create their own diversions, to create a little world of their own, to affect in the smallest way their environments, they must accept what's given; unable to create or relate, they spectate. Absorbing "culture" is a desperate, frantic attempt to groove in an ungroovy world, to escape the horror of a sterile, mindless, existence. "Culture" provides a sop to the egos of the incompetent, a means of rationalizing passive spectating; they can pride themselves on their ability to appreciate the "finer" things, to see a jewel where this is only a turd (they want to be admired for admiring). Lacking faith in their ability to change anything, resigned to the status quo, they *have* to see beauty in turds because, so far as they can see, turds are all they'll ever have.

QUEER INSULARITY: ON QUÉBEC, WEBSERIES, AND PERFORMANCES OF COMMUNITY

SEAN METZGER

Live performance is widely understood as contingent; placing some strain on this assertion, scholarly writing about performance usually attempts to erase the traces of its development and rehearsal. In the case of my writing for and responding to Q2Q: A Symposium on Queer Theatre and Performance in Canada, I have chosen to move away from that academic convention to turn attention to the event suggested in the very term "symposium" (etymologically referring to fellow drinkers), and to highlight the conditions of possibility for communities to come together or to explode and fragment. Although new media, to varying degrees, evade the contingencies of specific times and places by creating networks across vast distances, screen cultures also help to construct localities at particular moments. Three webseries set in Montréal—one following a gay male protagonist and his encounters with various urbanites, one featuring a pair of men on a date, and one focusing on a group of lesbians—form the crux of my analysis. Although online narratives might seem an awkward choice for a book primarily about theatre, I turn to this platform for two reasons: first, at UCLA, several of my students now develop projects in this medium because of the low financial barriers to entry; second, the web potentially offers a more democratic space than commercial theatre or cinema for the exhibition of cultural production in the sense of not requiring established producers or other forms of highly trained on- and off-screen talent. I contextualize these digital productions with three discursive frames pertinent to the genesis of this essay—my work in minoritarian performance, the mass shooting at a gay nightclub that was roughly coincident with the Q2Q symposium, and the conference itself—that might shift the import of these otherwise specific stories. In this, my essay's structure mirrors the queerness of new media, where interlinked phenomena—including the adjacency of search terms, browser histories, and corporate opportunism—shape the experience of any web user. These elements offer different portals that have shaped my thinking on queer communities, virtual and otherwise, in and also beyond the provincial.

QUÉBEC, CANADA, AND MINORITARIAN DISCOURSE

What critique does the constellation of terms "queer, Québec, and performance" enable? My assemblage brings into focus notions of insularity (the sense of feeling islanded experienced both as isolation and as a kind of archipelagic interconnectedness) and belonging articulated through new media. My thinking overlaps to a degree with the editors of a colloquium on "Queer in Québec," who, in my reading, locate queer's interventions in affect (in the sense of socially produced emotional responses that happen within, but that also connect, individual bodies) and historiography (Batson and Provencher). These emphases facilitate wide-ranging explorations of how Québec's particular queer formations might link to other spaces in Canada and elsewhere. Such assemblages neither depend on, nor do they necessarily ignore, other characteristics often associated with Québec, such as the use of language like the vernacular of *joual*. Furthermore, they have the potential to destabilize the easy equation of queer Québécois and whiteness.

To destabilize is, of course, not to undo. Scholar Jeffery Vacante's work establishes an interesting base from which to evaluate the evolution of gay male sexuality specifically as he links the ongoing iteration of Québécois, heterosexual, white masculinity to the Catholic Church, rural domesticity, the increasing political power of women, and the movements for sovereignty, among other issues (see Vacante, "Quebec"; and "Evolving"). "Queer, Québec, and performance" as a constellation enables one to think against, or at least alongside, Québec's insistent "national narrative," in which historical writing marshals heterosexual manhood as a means to implant a teleology toward independence (Vacante, "Writing the History" 45). That "national project," as Erin Hurley has demonstrated, has taken shape through many performance platforms and frequently subsumes difference *within* the province under the difference *of* the province in relation to the rest of Canada; as she writes, in Québec, "the nation remains a signal pole for identity-formation" (3, 9).

Such formations appear to lie far outside of my main scholarly preoccupations on circulations of Chineseness, or even my larger orbit of work in Asian American, Caribbean, film, performance, and sexuality studies. However, the ongoing negotiation of majoritarian and minoritarian discourses that suffuse Québec sustains my continuing investment in that space. What Hurley calls "québécité (Quebec-ness)" is a powerful ideology that can function in the mode of minoritarian cultural production (québécité in relation to the rest of the country and the world) but also as majoritarian (québécité iterated within the province itself, usually manifesting in the privileging of the Francophone) (4). My desire to participate in the Q2Q symposium stemmed from my thinking about how various media platforms might facilitate processes of identification at different scales from local to provincial to national to transnational.

As an event, most of the symposium drew heavily on discourses of the national, but also evoking First Nations as well as visible-minority rhetoric. In the United States, the compounding effects of corollary structures of difference are often theorized through intersectional analysis and queer of colour critique. Participants mentioned those frameworks less often than I expected, and I suspect this elision resulted from the training of many folks in the room as theatre and performance practitioners rather than scholars of ethnic and cultural studies. My own profile as a performance-studies scholar who specializes in comparative analyses of race and sexuality, then, may have had repercussions in the way my work, and perhaps my subject position, registered (or failed to register) in the conference as a whole. Before turning to the framing of the symposium, however, I turn to a different event that also informed and shaped the genealogy of my thought in relation to this Canadian iteration of my scholarship.

BELONGING AND AFFILIATION: PULSE AND OTHER QUEER SPECTACLES

The spectacle of homophobic violence at the Pulse nightclub in Florida on 12 June 2016 left me wondering about the political possibilities of queer performance. I found myself dwelling on the renewed import given to quotidian activities from clubbing to texting, as well as the sort of affective and, in some cases, material support offered in the forms of "We Are Orlando" hashtags and Facebook-profile backgrounds, the recording of "What the World Needs Now is Love," and other displays of affiliation.[1] As a caveat, I do not mean to equate the webseries discussed later in my paper with the contemporary events around Q2Q (notwithstanding the fact that explicit linkages did occur). Instead, I hope the latter might facilitate thinking differently about the former.

In the wake of (yet again) a number of fatal shootings in the US, I returned to Elspeth Probyn's exploration of belonging. Written from the perspective of a lesbian feminist scholar then situated in Montréal, she writes of the "transversal connections between individuals" as quotidian experience (*Outside* 6). This idea of transversal emphasizes shallow connections and parallel desires articulated across space. For this reason, it provides an interesting model to track the networked expressions of affect that have followed the homicides at Pulse. Probyn's book, *Outside Belongings*, works through "the desire that individuals have to belong, a tenacious and fragile desire that is . . . increasingly performed . . . with the fear that the stability of belonging and the sanctity of belonging are forever past" (8). She provides a cognitive and material mapping of the "outside," which moves understandings of social relations to considerations of surface and proximity (11).[2] I am struck by these ideas partly because Probyn wrote at a moment when "queer" named an emergent discourse, one that signalled both possibility and disappointment. In the former register, Probyn argued, following Eve Kosofsky Sedgwick, that queer animates the

1 The recording can be streamed online and is available on broadwayrecords.com to support the GLBT Community Center of Central Florida. See Velez.

2 Probyn explicitly offers an elaboration of Michel Foucault's writings on heterotopias.

potential of new forms of spatial relationships: how space means, how space divides, and how space joins.[3]

As we bear witness to the queer assemblage of bodies following the multiple murders at Pulse, the now notorious nightclub in Orlando, such provocations seem all the more pressing. Nightlife venues have long been associated with social dynamics in process; indeed, Celeste Delgado and José Muñoz's 1997 book *Everynight Life: Culture and Dance in Latin/o America* reveals how cruising and dancing have rendered possible self-fashioning and collective movements (physical, political, etc.). The locations that facilitate these activities produce intimacy, what Lauren Berlant calls "mobile processes of attachment" (284). Part of the club's allure is the ways it brings people seeking hookups, one-night stands, and relationships of different sorts into proximity. However, in obscuring divisions between private and public, it also generates waves of anxiety about these sorts of togetherness that frequently cross class and racial lines. In inviting and constructing intimacy, nightlife venues elicit not only pleasure and excitement, but also fear and outrage. Queer communities have long been subject to policing in regard to the latter but forms of individually perpetrated violence (which is not state-sanctioned like law enforcement) also feature prominently in this history. The shootings at Pulse recall this lineage.

However, as much as clubs might serve as loci of violence, they also offer hope. Shortly following the Pulse murders, the novelist Justin Torres published a short opinion piece called "In Praise of Latin Night at the Queer Club."[4] I quote Torres at length to think again about Probyn's notion of "outside belonging":

> You know what the opposite of Latin Night at the Queer Club is? Another Day in Straight White America. So when you walk into the club, if you're lucky, it feels expansive. "Safe space" is a cliché,

3 This line of thinking might be traced through a diverse body of work situated within queer studies—José Esteban Muñoz's *Cruising Utopia* and Sara Ahmed's *Queer Phenomenology*—as well as intersecting that field—Giuliana Bruno's *Surface* and my *The Chinese Atlantic*.

4 Torres's writing suggests José Muñoz's materialist utopian discourse (adapted from the work of Ernst Bloch); see Muñoz, *Cruising Utopia*.

> overused and exhausted in our discourse, but the fact remains that a sense of safety transforms the body, transforms the spirit. So many of us walk through the world without it. So when you walk through the door and it's a salsa beat, and brown bodies, queer bodies, all writhing in some fake smoke and strobing lights, no matter how cool, how detached, how over-it you think you are, Latin Night at the Queer Club breaks your cool. You can't help but smile, this is for you, for us.

Torres feels a sense of belonging inside the club, where he and others live free of whatever constraints exists outside of its walls—at least for a time.[5] Whereas Probyn evokes the outside as a space of encounter in Montréal (in no small part because people can stroll *en plein air* during the summer months and not freeze to death), Torres argues something of the opposite, which, of course, has everything to do with the ways in which different queer communities might negotiate public space.

We could attribute this apparent antinomy to the relative value of whiteness, but I find such an argument to be an oversimplification (since, among many other factors, economic status also matters in spatial encounters). Instead, rather than seeing opposition between these two visions of belonging, I follow Diana Fuss's argument:

> The figure inside/outside cannot be easily or ever finally dispensed with; it can only be worked on and worked over . . . Inside/outside functions as the very figure for signification and the mechanisms of meaning production. It has everything to do with the structures of alienation, splitting, and identification which together produce a self and an other. (1)

5 Torres also seems to reiterate in terms of Latin Night at the club José Muñoz's idea of feeling brown. Muñoz saw "ethnicity as 'a structure of feeling,' as a way of being in the world, a path that does not conform to the conventions of a majoritarian public sphere and the national affect it sponsors"; for Muñoz, this idea of feeling brown calls attention to "the obstacles that must be negotiated within the social for the minoritarian citizen-subject" (Muñoz, "Feeling Brown" 79).

To belong is to produce and participate in structures that construct internal and external elements even as these structures continually evolve, so what is once inside moves outside. Fuss therefore finds figures like the four knot and the Möbius strip useful to illustrate how inside/outside might be conceived.

Tracing these figures also conjures some of the difficulties inherent in thinking about queer now. I have tended to use queer in my own work as a term to mark the anti/normative with the potential to disrupt modes of belonging and identification. This sort of orientation pushes alongside but also sometimes against gay cultural production and critique. For me, "gay" places greater faith in producing difference *within* existing power structures and media forms rather than attempting to fold them on themselves or expose the incoherence of a system of representation.[6] However, technology compels a reconsideration of the normative in a virtual world—not because our online networks do not reproduce normative inscriptions of social life (because they certainly do) but because the vast accessibility of online cultural production means that any number of individuals or groups unversed in particular cultural codes access content, often out of any controllable context. Habitual or otherwise codified understandings that render norms meaningful, therefore, do not always obtain among users of new media platforms.

Our digital age, then, differs significantly from earlier moments in terms of the performance of intimate encounters and their audiences. Disturbing footage from the Pulse attack of survivors huddled with the dead and dying in a bathroom stall exemplifies only one of the ways in which new technology has reconfigured spatial proximity. The perpetrator's Facebook page became a tool of criminal profiling, justifying a swell of Islamophobic comments. The networks of the victims have brought Puerto Rico into focus to suggest that this massacre requires an intersectional analysis—one based specifically on race, ethnicity, and sexuality. Such a concatenation of issues and events exposes the complexity of any structure of belonging, demonstrating links that might otherwise remain invisible. Such connections are conceptual as

6 Here I follow Gregory W. Bredbeck; see his "The New Queer Narrative."

well as material in terms of flows of financial support, and they are electronic in terms of the creation of hyperlinks that create chains of information.

Following these virtual pathways leads me to think about queer performance inside and outside of the digital realm. In this regard, although the Pulse shooting may seem like an odd point of entry into a reflection on queer Québec, I want to suggest that more is at work here than my own obsession and mourning. First, the incident reminds me of the stakes of queer belonging in general. How do queer performances facilitate community formation and/or other forms of sociality? What material collectivities take shape under this rubric? What limits affiliation? Given that Canadian discourse has long been concerned with media saturation (Marshall McLuhan), it is no surprise that direct links between Québec and Florida emerged in the wake of the murders. These connections included live events such as vigils following the violence.[7] But other after-effects continue to ripple precisely because of the networked world in which we live; for example, Arc-en-Ciel d'Afrique (a group concerned with LGBT Afro-Caribbean rights and wellness issues) received a financial boost "after racially-charged hate speech spiked on social media following the shooting at the Pulse nightclub" (Richardson). As an even more blatant illustration, the webseries *Coming Out* posted on its Facebook page an image of solidarity: a ribbon that splices together the stars and stripes with the rainbow flag. Next to the ribbon, the words "We Stand with Orlando" appear. The post states, "Triste journée pour la communauté" (see Fig. 1). What parallels might exist between communities that speak literally or figuratively across the space of North America?

Continuing this line of thought, I wonder how, in the case of Québec in general and Montréal in particular, Probyn's notion of "outside belongings" might usefully be extended for our current historical moment (twenty years after she originally published these ideas)? In terms of the Québécois, this theorization might usefully overlap with the concept of insularity. As I have written elsewhere, in the anthology *Asian Canadian Theatre*, the Francophone capital of North America understands itself as the cultural heart of Canada

7 See Olivier Jean's photo on the website of *La Presse* ("Vigile à Montréal").

Fig. 1. A gesture of affiliation appeared on the Facebook page of *Coming Out*. Image provided courtesy of Mathieu Blanchard.

("*Le Rugissement du Lion*"); this position rests in part on the paradox of Québec seeing itself as islanded from the nation-state to which it formally belongs, notwithstanding the Acadians in New Brunswick and other French-speaking populations scattered throughout the country. The debates around Francophone particularity have swelled at various moments in discussions about the literal island of Montréal, such as the planning policy (2000–2006) designated by the slogan "une île, une ville," that effectively incorporated Anglophone neighbourhoods into the larger metropolis. Critical insularity pivots between seemingly bounded geographic and cultural distinctiveness and expansive interconnectivity (Metzger, Adrián, Crichlow). These cultural debates also take more unusual form within the frame of *les îles Québécoises* as, for example, in the controversies surrounding Anticosti Island's use for modern industrial purposes (fracking) and its maintenance as a hunting ground. In short, insularity reminds us of how certain traditions affirm the context of belonging and the forces that vex those who feel such attachments. The attendant political stakes register differently at various scales of analysis and in terms of belonging's constitutive outside.

This context sets up my specific discussion of how certain forms of gay and/or queer performance might function in *la ville aux cent clochers*, or how the city itself perhaps queers certain mediated performances.[8] The writer Chris Gudgeon has described Montréal as "the sexiest city in North America" (2). His commentary follows his Speedo-attired excursions on the "island" at

8 There has, of course, been a good deal of theatre historiography on gay theatre in Québec, specifically in the period of the 1970s through the early 1990s. See Moss; and Rocheleau and Sandford. More recent work appears in *Québec Studies* 60 (Fall/Winter 2015). Although a project that updates this history from the '90s through today might be useful, that is not my aim here.

Club Crème on Boulevard Saint-Laurent around the old Red-Light District. If one accepts Gudgeon's assessment, then one might expect Montréal, if not Québec as a whole, to lead the country in terms of its production of queer pleasure (and perhaps pain). Certainly Bad Boy Club Montréal, with its signature Black and Blue Party, signals one trajectory of gay performance, one drenched in foam and laden with dollar signs. This iteration seems like a departure from the distinctive Québécois sensibility that drives earlier but perhaps no less theatrical productions. But no linear trajectory connects the worlds inhabited by Michel Tremblay's Duchesse or Hosanna and the soirees that currently occur in the city, despite the fact that drag might offer one way of thinking about their embodied connections across time (Freeman, "Queer Belongings" 309).

Even when turning to representational media, I remain uncertain of what today answers Tremblay's depictions of self-destructive communities, but certainly some of the aesthetic devices he deployed in his more famous works—direct address and extended monologues in *joual*—have become fixtures of queer screen performance. Xavier Dolan's films seem to have earned him a certain notoriety, and their not infrequent narcissistic qualities suggest a self-indulgent (or self-reflexive?) insularity even as he seems to speak to a generation far beyond Québec's borders. Dolan's filmography has brought the occasional play to the screen, as with Michel Marc Bouchard's *Tom à la Ferme*. This adaptation recalls, of course, other Francophone queer theatre developed into cinema, from Tremblay's *Il était une fois dans l'est* (*Once Upon a Time in the East*, André Brassard, 1974) to Bouchard's *Les feluettes* (*Lilies*, John Greyson, 1996) and, if queer expansively includes non-normative kinship relations, Wajdi Mouawad's *Incendies* (Denis Villeneuve, 2010).

The successful dissemination of queer Québec across international screens suggests shared affinities for certain forms of narrative and/or visualization. In a different vein, Elizabeth Freeman provocatively argues that groups which have "come together in more virtual 'spaces' to create ordered social worlds, transmissible over time, have often been predicated upon technological developments increasingly capable of extracting subjectivity from the body" ("Queer Belongings" 302). That context may help to explain the rapid reflection and refraction of the Pulse homicides on Canadian and Québécois social media. Sharing queer sentiment and forms of representation, however, ignores the facets of Pulse that are, from a North American perspective, US-centric. These include the intense Islamophobia attending reporting and criminalization of the shooter and his spouse, as well as the specific ways in which Pulse was marked as a racialized space. In pointing to these particularities I mean to illustrate how the expressions of belonging and affinity that circulated in the aftermath of the homicides depended on certain narrative exclusions, which might have challenged any easy assertion of queer solidarity.

Q2Q: FINDING FELLOW DRINKERS

I participated on a Q2Q panel called "Queer Spaces," and I initially intended to interrogate that rubric by thinking about cyberspace, as well as the specific locations filmed in the webseries discussed below. The Pulse homicides complicated the ways I understood the Internet, as well as queer communities, in constructions of space. But the symposium itself also caused me to rework my incipient ideas.

The demographics of the symposium attendees who were consistently present seemed to divide into two groups: several folks in their twenties and early thirties formed the majority, leaving a seemingly smaller contingent of older folks. Many of the queers of colour were part of the younger demographic, and many of us who identified as such from the older generation (myself, Brad Fraser, etc.) were mixed-race and register unclearly in the national rhetoric of visible minorities. Among the older generation, many if not most of us occupied careers in which we shaped larger programs, be that in the course of developing a season, casting a play, or working through an academic department. In this manner, we differed notably from younger artists looking for or creating venues to give themselves a platform for expression.

I mention this fact because many participants who offered interventions in various discussions began by announcing positionality (e.g., "as a white, cis female, lesbian"). Whether signs of authority or potential trespass, such declarations recalled for me certain strains of identity politics in the US; they tended to frame issues through a subject position. Sometimes this position of the speaker's or the person/group for whom she or he spoke became the political project (e.g., "I want to create a space for this voice to be heard"). In part, I think the debates at the conference involved, if not a lack of knowledge of history of the queer-theatre movement and individuals' places within them, then an articulated desire to make space for "my" voice and perspective. That is an egocentric (placing me and my art at the centre), if not necessarily a self-aggrandizing, move. Whither politics?

For me, that is a generative question as opposed to a condemnation. The symposium reframed my object of study because in two of the three webseries I examined, the point seems to be "look at me; listen to me." In the third, the goal is explicitly commercial: to bring gay tourists to Montréal. Certainly such a call will create certain communities, perhaps more diverse ones. But I left the symposium wondering what the goals of such communities in Canada might be. Given Canada's comparatively robust social system (from my perspective in the US), what might queer do now? Several of my fellow drinkers shared these concerns. For better or for worse, these conversations often involved generational disquiet. Those of us with four or more decades behind us had lived through the height of the AIDS epidemic in North America and several other instances of queer trauma and affiliation. Sky Gilbert had notably fought for the inclusion of queers of colour and trans individuals at the table, and now those groups seemed to be requesting that he relinquish his place there. So the question lingered: What does queer do?

WEBSERIES AND ONLINE CONNECTIONS

Desires for ostensibly clear and equitable representation have frequently permeated political agendas, and these efforts do not necessarily critique the structure of representation itself. The movements for gay marriage illustrate such phenomena, as do some of the more targeted goals of Q2Q participants that I have described. However, I hypothesized that new forms of virtual community through online platforms might produce alternative structures of belonging; my investigation of webseries in Québec aimed to explore such possibilities.

Dynamic representations of exclusion and inclusion occur in several webseries set in Montréal: Mathieu Blanchard's *Coming Out* (consisting of two seasons, beginning with a release in 2013 and ending in 2016 with an official announcement that a third would not be shot); Olivier Labonté LeMoyne's *Montreal Boy: Some Strings Attached* (2014); and Chloé Robichaud's *Féminin/Féminin* (2014). Each webseries consists of episodes ranging from approximately four and a half to twelve and a half minutes. Although the style of each differs, they cohere in their relatively brief duration, their emphases on quotidian relationships in Montréal, their use of popular music, and their tendency to feature actors in their twenties and thirties. The trio also displays an investment in realism, not uncommon to the genre but one that is also consistent with an earlier moment of gay cultural production. The format of this mode of production offers a private viewing experience (me and my laptop), but also the possibilities for fan, interpersonal, and even industrial connections through comments pages, online interviews, and crowdsourcing campaigns.[9] These webseries, therefore, play with insularity in terms of isolation and interactivity.

Mathieu Blanchard has stated that the lack of portrayals "du milieu gai" motivated him to create *Coming Out*. However, he has acknowledged two televised antecedents: the sitcom *Cover-Girl* (2005), a show that focused on drag queens who owned a Montréal club; and the American version of *Queer as Folk* (2000–2005), about the tribulations of a queer circle shot in Toronto, which substituted for an imagined Pittsburgh. Nevertheless, Blanchard suggests that no dramatic series had provided a multi-faceted view of *la vie gai* in Québec through the lens of a gay protagonist (in this case, played by Blanchard himself; here we can see the narcissistic parallel to Dolan). *Coming Out* takes place primarily in French and centres around a somewhat

9 See "Coming Out Saison 2."

promiscuous photographer named (what else but) Mat, in the process of figuring out his relationship with his ex (Ian) and Mat's group of friends and acquaintances. A number of subplots supplement the primary narrative arc: a young addict and gay prostitute who has AIDS; a lesbian couple who lose a baby and work to rebuild their relationship; a young man who steals his co-worker's husband but who eventually attempts to forge a non-traditional extended family. The series highlights white Francophone Montréalais caught up in the drama of everyday life.

The shot and narrative construction of *Coming Out* are perhaps the most normative of the three webseries I consider. Although the last sequence of the first episode crosscuts between a gay bashing and a sex scene, the wesbseries does not innovate at the formal level. The storylines highlight contemporary issues, but followers of similar material, including the aforementioned *Queer as Folk*, will recognize several plot devices and spectacles: scenes of seduction at the bar and office; exposed flesh of same-sex lovers in bedrooms and showers; earnest conversations about relationships. Overall, the topics covered in the online serial drama and its aesthetics seem mundane, even if they aim to titillate. Rather than offering a critique, I suggest that such prosaic concerns are the point. The series renders gay banal.

Can banality yield a progressive political position? Here I am struck by the meaning of series like this one in light of the shootings in Orlando. Certainly, for many marginalized people, conventional desires and quotidian activities can elicit risk and, obviously, can become life-threatening under certain conditions. In these circumstances, communities might queer their affiliations. At its most poignant, perhaps, this is what *Coming Out* demonstrates. Everyday exposure to structural and more targeted forms of violence produce anxiety, terror, and material loss but also creativity, resilience, and improvisatory acts of compassion.

As an illustration, Blanchard offers the story arc of Téo. Ejected from his home after having the courage, as he states, to out himself to his parents, Téo becomes a prostitute who contracts HIV from one of his clients. The lesbian social worker (with no professional boundaries) drops Téo at her friend Mat's to spend the night in safety. The pair of men eventually encounter one another at the threshold of Mat's bathroom, where Téo inadvertently pricks his finger and refuses his temporary host's assistance as he announces, "J'ai SIDA." The shot-reverse-shot sequence contrasts the two bodies in the tight space squeezed between the entry and the bathroom door—one half-naked, with only a few clothes as possessions, the other comparatively privileged with an expression of fear and discomfort. Mat and Téo never again occupy the same frame, although the series later constructs parallels between the former's rejection by his parents and the latter's. Where Blanchard perhaps most succeeds is showing how structures of social reproduction, like the nuclear heterosexual family, maintain norms and facilitate oppression even as individual action and imagination might circumvent or otherwise undo such domination, if only for fleeting moments. Mat's sudden rejection of his HIV-positive house guest and the ways in which this encounter later haunt him with guilt reveal the need to invent new ways of belonging; their connection is, we might say after Probyn, transversal, following a somewhat parallel path within the same urban space. At once critical and hopeful, the shared journey of Mat and Téo, who dies by the end of the first season (a couple hours of screen time), insists that potentially commonplace and relatively superficial encounters have significance and merit attention.

Despite its traffic in well-worn narratives, *Coming Out* nevertheless raises some intriguing questions about contemporary gay representation. For example, the Canadian AIDS Treatment Information Exchange (CATIE) reports statistics from 2011 that one-third of MSM who reported living with HIV are not on treatment. In Blanchard's own assessment, Téo's story addresses the experience of someone avowedly living with HIV but who continues injecting drugs and generally failing to care for his own health.[10] The narrative thus refuses what Alyson Campbell and Dirk Gindt call "cultural amnesia" about HIV and AIDS; even so, this subplot of *Coming Out* falls into a predictable storyline and visualization of AIDS-related symptoms (see Campbell and Gindt). From my perspective of Blanchard's on-screen world, the semiotics of HIV and AIDS return the viewer to an earlier extradiegetic cultural moment.

10 See Blanchard. I thank Mr. Blanchard for his responses as I was writing this essay.

This return produces what Campbell and Gindt have called AIDS nostalgia, but it also provokes an inquiry about what might link a "gay community" over time. This representation relies on an archive of HIV and AIDS performances, suggesting the value in remembering that archive but also a sort of miring within it. Belonging here works through a form of retrospection inclusive of what has passed but exclusive of newer populations affected by the virus and even engagement with current AIDS discourse.

The dynamics of inclusion and exclusion may still facilitate unexpected connections. Blanchard launched a crowdfunding campaign on Indiegogo but ultimately decided against a third season because he felt that a show called *Coming Out* did not speak to the primary concerns of the new generation of individuals who identify as LGBTQ (Blanchard). Like many webseries (and popular cultural productions more generally), the show has already begun to recede into history. Yet the continued availability of the series in whole or in part on DVD as well as on YouTube and Vimeo will continue to provide viewers different experiences of engaging this narrative. Perhaps a more accurate assessment of what has happened to *Coming Out* is that it has become part of what Lucas Hildebrand has called "a culture of the clip," in which content can be recirculated, remixed, and/or recontextualized in service of new forms of media and community (227).

Olivier Labonté LeMoyne's *Montreal Boy: Some Strings Attached* takes the thematic thread of the everyday and indulges in what I would term an aesthetic of the quaint. Having recently broken up with his boyfriend of two years, the protagonist, Stephane (Francis Ducharme), invites a New Yorker named Hugh, with whom he has been chatting online, to Montréal. The six episodes, totalling about thirty minutes, track their weekend together. Like Mat of *Coming Out*, Stephane also seems in recovery from a recent break up (also with a man named Matt). The series ends with the transferring of Stephane's house key from one love interest to another. Here again, the camera caresses white young men, with or without shirts.

However, in this case, Montréal is as much the star as the leading men. Financed by Jimmy Lee, a producer from the LGBT network Logo, in partnership with Tourisme Montréal, the series works like an extended advertisement. After the initial graphics, the opening helicopter shot shows a dramatic cityscape over Le Parc du Mont-Royal. Rue Ste.-Catherine and an array of well-known venues from *le village* and across the metro area also appear. In this manner, the film functions as a kind of travelogue, capturing a number of romantic spots for the gay local or, perhaps, the tourist. Indeed, the conversations occur, for the most part, in English, albeit often with a Francophone accent. The pace of urban life also seems accelerated here as the sheer number of edits lends a dynamic character to the city and its inhabitants. Dialogue spans across scenes without always matching speaker to the image. The soundtrack thus facilitates spectators who might want to project themselves into various scenes.

This series connects two island metropolises—Montréal and Manhattan—with a narrative in which very little out of the ordinary happens. Men meet, eat, drink, dance, have sex, and take bike rides; *Montreal Boy* is perhaps remarkable only for being resolutely unremarkable. Nevertheless, the show also suggests something about the loneliness one might feel on a metropolitan island notwithstanding the relatively high concentration of people, and gay men in particular, in each place. The bonds forged across insular space mitigate these feelings in this web drama.

The brazenly commercial aspect of this project shapes part of the media ecology of our current moment. The casting of Ducharme, known for supporting roles in films including *C.R.A.Z.Y.* (Jean-Marc Vallée, 2005) and *J'ai Tué Ma Mère* (Xavier Dolan, 2009), undoubtedly attempts to capitalize on the actor's gay fan base. This model of using but also potentially furthering the careers of individuals on the brink of breakout success characterizes popular webseries yet also sows the seeds for their demise, since they are largely vehicles to launch on- and off-screen talent to other media platforms. Further evidence of this phenomenon can be witnessed in, for example, the case of Kit Williamson, a former UCLA student. Williamson created the webseries *EastSiders* (2012–present) and later played a supporting role on the last two seasons of AMC's *Mad Men* (2007–2015) even as he continued to produce, write, and perform in *EastSiders*. Williamson's webseries helped elevate to stardom Constance Wu, who left the series to take a lead in ABC's *Fresh Off the Boat* (2015–present). For Williamson, the show has earned him (and his off-screen husband, who also plays a major role in *EastSiders*) recognition within gay media circles, in particular. The pair has now done several online promotions for travel companies seeking to access a gay market. Ducharme's role in *Montreal Boy: Some Strings Attached* is thus not an exception within the new media ecology but indicative of larger trends within an increasingly interwoven network of entertainment companies.

Féminin/Féminin offers the most formal innovations of the three webseries. The work includes structured interviews interspersed with dramatic vignettes that focus on a group of primarily young lesbians in Montréal. Eventually, Robichaud herself appears as the voice behind the camera. The series works to combine an homage to *Go Fish* (Rose Troche, 1994) and *The L Word* (2004–2009) with a self-reflexive record of local lesbian life in Montréal. Occasionally, when characters provide information about themselves, the moving image breaks into a series of stills that provides a photographic compendium of a life. The conversations here flow readily between French and English, with people often code-switching. The interviews include both characters and (apparently) young women whom the director has found around the city. Fiction and reality blur.

The play between documentary and narrative cinema would also seem to reference Jean-Luc Godard's *Masculin/Féminin: 15 Faits Précis* (1966). Although the structure of Godard's film is much more self-reflexive and comments to a much greater degree on the historical moment of its creation, it overlaps with *Féminin/Féminin* in terms of the use of interviews and an emphasis on the quotidian activities of its characters. Robichaud amplifies the lesbian desires in Godard's work to the near exclusion of heterosexuality; in so doing, *Féminin/Féminin* rewrites some of the assumptions that would seem to undergird Godard's exploration of romance and politics.

Each of the eight episodes in Robichaud's webseries tends to focus on one of six couples in a group of friends. Each pair also foregrounds a particular issue from rural small-town life to coming out. The director has expanded the demographics of the cast in comparison to the other webseries; she includes a significant role for a person of colour ("Sam" in a breast-cancer narrative), and she also features a principal role for someone over forty ("Céline" in a cross-generational romance). The locations for each pair vary, but they tend to emphasize interiors. Although a local celebrity (Catherine Renaud) makes a brief cameo, the focus again falls on quotidian experience, both in the narratives and the documentary section. The image that closes the series' first and only season thus far is twelve women assembled in a half circle around the recent grave of one of the character's cats.

Although the medium of the webseries would potentially enable one to discuss almost anything, judging by these examples it would seem to have fostered a niche for artists to portray nothing more than the ordinary. The Québec versions analyzed in this essay join a number of US productions in this project. Webseries portray specific communities who perhaps have not had wide exposure in mainstream media (gay couples on the east side of LA, bears, Asian American lesbians). The Québécois gay and lesbian niche in this growing list, perhaps even more than its counterparts across North America, insists on the mundane as meaningful. The issues encountered here reflect the particularity of the island as much as they suggest similarities with other locales. They emphasize chance encounters and serendipitous community formations.

To create an artistic or political movement, or even a statement, out of these sorts of contingent attachments seems neither the point of any of these works nor necessarily desirable. As a group, the webseries remind viewers all too well of the complicity of community with capitalism, of which Miranda Joseph has written in *Against the Romance of Community*. Yet I am struck that an awareness of the everyday is precisely the sort of reaction engendered by the murders at Pulse nightclub. This event, of course, took place at the beginning of a season of Pride celebrations. The responses included images of same-sex couples kissing posted on the web, and folks going out to dance as a commemoration of those killed who were in the process of doing the same thing. Rather than lambaste these signs of affiliation for being ethically irresponsible or politically inappropriate, perhaps what we learn by thinking about insular performances is precisely that they speak to as-yet unidentified collectivities. Such energies cannot be harnessed to a unified political position but rather are ones in which we might find some flicker of hope for connection in those fleeting moments outside of established modes and structures of belonging.

This point returns me to the symposium and what I perceived as a kind of emphasis on "me." I find myself in a cantankerous role, reproducing a common critique of millennials. Yet my own experience of various social movements and the philosophies that underpin and intersect those movements is that they require continual reconfiguration. What might it mean to embrace outside belonging in order to see how queer might reshape the current moment?

PERFORMING YOUR FICTIONAL IDENTITY: THE TRUE IMAGINARY

SKY GILBERT

Roughly speaking, transgender theory is divided into two opposing camps. Talia Mae Bettcher differentiates between "the traditional wrong-body account of transsexuality (in which gender identity is taken as innate, allegedly determining one's 'real' sex) and the newer, beyond-the-binary vision that emerged with the new transgender politics of the nineteen-nineties" (10.3, para. 1). This debate intersects significantly with wide-ranging and relevant philosophical issues that are contingent on the discussion of what I call "fictional identities."

I wish to introduce the notion of fictional identities as an antidote to the polarization of "fake" identities versus "real" ones. An example of a fake identity would be the recent objections raised against the notion of transgender washrooms in North Carolina. Members of the Christian right routinely object to transgender washrooms, asking, "Would you feel safe with your daughter being in a public restroom with an adult male who is a stranger?" These right-wing critics consider transgender people to be faking their chosen identities; they refuse to recognize any other gender besides those we are all assigned at birth.

I intend to argue here that instead of polarizing the fake and the true, we might accept all identities as fictional. This doesn't mean that we wouldn't challenge people's chosen fictional identities. It means that we must accept all identities as fictional and accept that consequently there is no such thing as a real identity.

It's difficult in the "reality TV" era, where science has to some degree replaced religion, to valorize the fictional. But I wish to resuscitate fiction—that is, to give it some much-needed and well-deserved mouth-to-mouth. I think there is good reason to celebrate fiction, which in philosophical circles, as I intend to prove, has been conflated with misrepresentation, decadence, and lies. Indeed, fiction has been summarily rejected by both postmodernist and "post-theory" philosophers. But the articulation—indeed the romanticization—of the notion of fiction by queer philosophers Oscar Wilde and Michel Foucault offers a potent defence of fictional gender and sexuality identities.

In the mid-twentieth century, the first, most publicized, Western transsexual individuals described themselves as being in the wrong body. As children they looked down at their genitals and were horrified. The earliest publicized American transsexual woman was Christine Jorgensen, who had a sex change in 1951. A BBC news story reported that "as a teenager he [Jorgenson] became convinced he was trapped in the wrong body" (Hadjimatheou). Though medically categorized as male and in possession of a penis, young MTF transsexuals endeavoured to replace male with female genitals, and young FTM individuals tried to make their bodies look like the body of a person assigned a "boy's" identity at birth. After the sex change, their "true" gender identity would be reflected by a material reality.

In the wake of queer theory, transgender theorists and activists have tried to move beyond what they see as the limiting category of transsexual, increasingly questioning categories of male and female, asking whether the gender binary is true in either a spiritual or material way. Kate Bornstein asserts that the transsexual notion of discovering one's true identity is a convenient but intolerable fiction. But the concept of non-binary gender—challenging the traditional notion of categorizing human beings as either male or female—has become increasingly popular in both academic and non-academic circles. The World Health Organization tells us that "it is important to be sensitive to different identities that do not necessarily fit into binary male or female sex categories" ("Gender"). Sam Escobar speaks of non-binary gender in a recent issue of *Esquire* magazine: "The gender binary separates those who identify as male or female, simple as that. Non-binary genders, however, don't fit neatly within these two—they can be a combination of male and female, a fluid back-and-forth, or totally outside of the binary."

Kate Bornstein and Pat Califia represent opposite poles of the transgender theory debate. Bornstein wishes to eradicate gender, an oppressive system of arbitrary categories: "It's safe having a gender. But there's a price for that safety and security within some hard shell. We can't grow anymore . . . And the only thing for it is to come out of that shell, leave it behind us" (55). Califia, on the other hand, argues that the "need to oppress is human" and that jettisoning categories will not eliminate hate or prejudice (246). The battle between Bornstein and Califia has been played out in the context of notions of what is *real*, with justifications sometimes coming from an appeal to empirical evidence. Bornstein is not merely suggesting that there might be no gender in an ideal world; she argues that gender is a toxic lie that has no basis in material reality. Califia's opposing argument also appeals to empiricism, noting that different genders do actually exist; after all, some individuals are born with a specific allocation of X and Y chromosomes, while other individuals are not.

The elephant in the room may be Judith Butler's notion of gender performativity. Butler contends that "gender is a kind of imitation for which there is no original" ("Imitation" 313). This seems to suggest gender is imaginary. She says, "The performance constitutes the appearance of a 'subject' as its effect" (315). While Butler in "Performative Acts and Gender Constitution" states that gender performances in real life can have very real and dangerous consequences, in another essay, "Imitation and Gender Insubordination," she writes that she believes "identity categories tend to be instruments of regulatory regimes" (308). Throughout Butler's work there is what could be seen as an offhand dismissal of gender identity that may stop short of Bornstein's demonization of the binary. Nevertheless, Butler certainly sometimes treats gender and sexuality labels with skepticism. Could Kate Bornstein's distrust of gender categories have its origin in Butler's theories? Undoubtedly the theory of the fictional nature of gender that alienates some transsexual gender essentialists like Califia has been associated with Butler. Theorists like Judith (now Jack) Halberstam, for example, explicitly reference Butler to prove that gender is fictional. But others, such as Jay Prosser, have taken issue with this, stating that the notion of gender as fictional undoes the belief some trans people have that they are "real" men, or "real" women.

So Butler's notion of performativity is a contentious issue in the transgender community. But I wish to defend her ideas because they resonate with contemporary discussions about the nature of reality, debates that have dominated theoretical speculation since the dawn of philosophy. In this essay, I will employ the word "fiction" rather than the word "performativity." "Performativity" is too often misapplied to theatrical performance. Butler intended it to refer to the ongoing creation of the self in daily life (i.e., the repetition of certain gender characteristics to produce identity), not to a theatrical creation. In addition, utilizing the word fiction polarizes the discussion in a good way around a very contentious modern issue: fiction versus the real.

The rejection of fiction (and its corollary, the rejection of "story") is a popular trope in present-day mass culture, and is also reflected in aesthetic theories deemed radical or experimental. The dominance of reality-TV shows over sitcoms on network television, born with MTV's *The Real World* in 1993, is reflected in the mass consumption of YouTube videos that star your next-door neighbours chatting about their own lives or filming their amusing cats, dogs, or children. Of course one could argue that reality-TV shows are not actually very real at all, but are instead plump with invented conflicts and scripted climaxes. But what interests me here is not whether reality TV shows are more real than traditional entertainment, but the degree to which we are obsessed with the notion that our entertainment (and art) must become more "real."

This obsession is not new; the history of the theatre is to some degree a history of those who claim that dramatic art has shifted further from fiction and closer to reality. Each theatrical era claims that the most recent theatrical creations are closest to what is true. Critiques of actors from the eighteenth century onward often rate actors on the basis of the realism of their performances, with each new era offering characterizations free from false and stilted expression or gesture. The apotheosis of this mania for realism would seem to have been Konstantin Stanislavsky in Russia, and the Method in America. Marlon Brando's portrayal of Stanley in *A Streetcar Named Desire* (1947; 1951 film) achieved the status of myth because it represented (for many) the epitome of naturalistic detail. But David Mamet has recently taken the quest for theatrical realism one step further. It is not "real" enough just to portray a character in exhaustive detail; all actors should do is "be themselves." In terms of craft, an actor need only understand the meaning of the lines: "The actor does not need to 'become' the character . . . There *is* no character . . . the audience sees an illusion of a character upon the stage . . . the actor has to undergo nothing whatsoever" (9).

Toronto dramaturgy has lately also moved away from fictional narrative to focus on actors "being themselves" and expressing their own ideas. *Globe and Mail* critic Simon Hayter's review of Canadian Stage's December 2013 production of *Winners and Losers*, created and performed by James Long and Marcus Youssef, asks whether the improvised argument between two friends that constitutes the bulk of the play is real: "The structure is centred on two friends having a lively debate while drinking a bottle of beer . . . But unsettling questions start to arise in the audience's mind. Do they really believe in what they are saying, or does one take the opposing view just to play devil's advocate?" Michael Rubenfeld and Sarah Stanley of Selfconscious Theatre create work in which, as they state in their mandate on their company's website, "we are the protagonists and our personal stories are the entry point into how we explore narrative" ("How"); and in Ravi Jain's hit 2012 play *A Brimful of Asha*, the director and his mother sit on stage and simply chat.

Even the modern novel seems to be reflecting this anti-fiction trend. Karl Ove Knausgaard's much lauded magnum opus *My Struggle* (2013) reports on the mundane details of his own life using the real names of relatives and family members. Knausgaard himself declares: "The only genres I saw value in, which still conferred meaning, were diaries and essays, the types of literature that did not deal with narrative, that were not about anything, but just consisted of a voice, the voice of your own personality, a life, a face, a gaze you could meet" (497). Similarly, ex-novelist David Shields abandoned fiction in his diatribe *Reality Hunger* (2010), a controversial collection of quotations from various authors (including himself) focusing on the fragile and antique mutability of the novel and its increasing lack of relevance in the modern world: "Story seems to say that everything happens for a reason and I want to say, No, it doesn't" (114). Shields is simply rephrasing Oscar Wilde's sentiments in *The*

Importance of Being Earnest: "The good ended happily, and the bad unhappily. That is what Fiction means" (275).

This contemporary preference for reality over fiction sometimes works to invalidate narrative, although personal narrations are rated above fictional stories because they are considered more real. Of course those who celebrate realism seem blind to the fact that the personal stories narrated in the play *Winners and Losers* (and the novel *My Struggle*) may be as fat with invention as a reality-TV show. Nevertheless, I predict that the reality obsession is here to stay. I say this not merely because popular culture and avant-garde theatre are obsessed with reality, but because material truth has become an obsession for philosophers too.

David Hawkes points out in his book *Ideology* that the history of philosophy has been dominated by the debate over the nature of reality. Hawkes is a Marxist philosopher with a very particular point of view. *Ideology* argues that postmodern theory (exemplified by Jean Baudrillard) is nihilistic and ultimately dangerous in its disregard for truth. Baudrillard's theory of the hyperreality can be best understood through his analysis of Operation Desert Storm in his essay "The Gulf War Did Not Take Place" (1991). The Gulf War (1990–1991) consisted of an American intervention in Kuwait to drive out invading Iraqi forces (with the help of the UN). The central assertion of Baudrillard's essay is that the American media manipulated the public into viewing what was essentially a series of American war crimes as a "war." Hyperreality is Baudrillard's conception of the twentieth-century transmogrification of art. According to Baudrillard, art metamorphosed from imitation and representation in the seventeenth century to "production" after the industrial revolution—in other words, the mass reproduction of artistic objects changed the value and meaning of art into a product. Today mass production in the digital world has transformed what was once an easily recognizable material "reality" into an (unreal) state of "hyperreality." Disneyland is significant for Baudrillard as a symbol of an America that has lost touch with material reality. No one knows what America really is anymore; Americans believe America is what Disney tells them it is.

Baudrillard's bland, smooth, unflappable writing style seems, on the surface, to be non-judgmental. But his bald generalizations certainly smack of nihilism: "What lies hidden behind this falsely transparent world? Another kind of intelligence or a terminal lobotomy?" (26). It is this "skeptical relativism of postmodernity" (8) that angers Hawkes, and is so central to his critique of postmodernism. A necessary corollary to Baudrillard's philosophy, according to Hawkes, is that there can be no right and wrong—since nothing is real anymore. Thus, Hawkes claims that postmodernism serves globalism, economic fascism, neoliberalism—what he considers to be the most evil forces of the modern world—by denying that there is good or evil. Since capitalism is essentially amoral (being less concerned with the rules of morality than the rules of the market), "Postmodernism is the ideology of globalization" (10).

Significantly, Hawkes does not disagree with Baudrillard's description of the modern world, only his attitude to it: "There is no doubt that, in the twenty-first century, images really do determine reality, the human subject really is objectified, and the global market really is likely to remain the only significant world power for the foreseeable future. But the market's success does not have to be applauded" (179). But Hawke's analysis of Baudrillard is deeply flawed, because the French philosopher is not applauding anything. Hawkes holds capitalism responsible for our imprisonment in an über-unreality. Though Baudrillard does not overtly blame capitalism in a manner that Hawkes wishes to see, his theory of hyperreality is directly related to Theodor Adorno, Max Horkheimer, and Guy Debord, who do. Central to Hawkes's argument is the idea that Western society has consistently warned against "idols" and asserted that money is the most dangerous idol of all. He quotes Psalm 135: "The idols of heathens are silver and gold, the work of men's hands . . . eyes have they, but they see not" (17). From credit card to Bitcoin, we are being urged these days to deal in an increasingly mythical form of exchange that no longer has a relationship to the gold standard, but is nevertheless the measure of the success of our lives and our self-realization. Money, Hawkes asserts, has—figuratively and literally—become a spectacle that dominates our lives, but has little material reality.

Hawkes agrees with Adorno, Horkheimer, and Debord, who theorize that in capitalism the pursuit of money smothers all of our values and that the commodification of values and discourse (transmitted through the media) has made it impossible to understand the true nature of evil. Hawkes quotes Adorno and Horkeimer:

> That the hygienic shop-floor and everything that goes with it, the Volkswagen or the sportsdrome, leads to an insensitive liquidation of metaphysics, would be irrelevant; but that in the social whole they themselves become a metaphysics, an ideological curtain behind which the real evil is concentrated, is not irrelevant. (133)

Adorno and Horkeimer's "The Culture Industry: Enlightenment as Mass Deception" (1944) argued that Hollywood executives would eventually produce only movies that reflected their own values—to the exclusion of all that was original, challenging, or in any way innovative: "What is new in the phase of mass culture compared to that of late liberalism is the exclusion of the new. The machine is rotating on the spot. While it already determines consumption, it rejects anything untried as a risk" (106).

Adorno and Horkheimer's vision of the future of the entertainment industry was remarkably prescient. We find that there are only a few movies to see these days—despite the plethora of films about comic-book heroes, dinosaurs, car chases, and monsters. Hollywood makes the same movies over and over again because capitalism defines very narrowly not only what we may purchase and view, but how we imagine ourselves. In *The Society of the Spectacle* (1967) Debord asserts that these kind of spectacles eventually change human values and abridge the range of their personal dreams and expectations: we end up thinking about success in capitalist terms, for instance, because of the capitalist spectacle that movies and advertising have become. Hawkes, again, quotes Debord, in describing "the principle of commodity fetishism, the domination of society by 'intangible as well as tangible things,' which reaches its absolute fulfilment in the spectacle, where the tangible world is replaced by a selection of images which exist above it, and which at the same time are recognized as the tangible par excellence" (161).

Hawkes's analysis acknowledges Adorno, Horkheimer, and Debord's critiques of the capitalist spectacle but refuses to acknowledge that Baudrillard shares their views. I would argue that though Baudrillard does not blame capitalism in the same way, his detached, nihilistic description of a modern imaginary inevitably invites us to rebel against it. For example, some have suggested that Baudrillard's theory of the simulacra was the inspiration for the film *The Matrix* (though Baudrillard had nothing to do with the film). In *The Matrix* (1999), the leading character desperately fights his way out of the "unreal" matrix (read: hyperreality) in which he is enmeshed to get to the "real" world. Thus what unites Hawkes, Adorno, Horkheimer, Debord, and Baudrillard is that each writes passionately against a modern inability to perceive a material world veiled by false images. And they all blame capitalism. Hawkes focuses on the "false idol" of the capitalist monetary system, Adorno and Horkheimer on mass culture, Debord on "the spectacle," and Baudrillard on "hyperreality"—but all attack our fetishization of image over the real.

Can I be forgiven for thinking that modern philosophy "has it in" for art?

One might argue that these philosophers are criticizing mediatized images from mass entertainment, not art. I would posit that what is significant is that all of them are extremely suspicious of products of the human imagination. And certainly the process of perceiving and appreciating art is similar to the process of imagining the world through mediatized images that all of these philosophers criticize. On the other hand, Adorno, for one, certainly differentiates between high art and mass culture (which has earned him the label of "elitist") when he writes effusively about Samuel Beckett, asserting that though it is difficult to create art that is meaningful in a post-Holocaust era, it is nevertheless possible and necessary to do so. But Adorno is not the only modern philosopher who defends art. Hawkes ignores two modern theorists who offer spirited defences of the imaginary, and also (I would suggest) a detailed plan for self-realization through fiction: Michel Foucault and Oscar Wilde.

Hawkes does not, strictly speaking, ignore Foucault. Instead, he rejects him—as so many philosophers do—for homophobic reasons. Since Foucault's death from AIDS, James Miller (his last and most controversial biographer) has led a pack of contemporary writers, philosophers, and theorists who can't help interpolating the rumours swirling around Foucault's death into their evaluations of his philosophy. For instance, John Carvalho points out that Miller's biography of Foucault, *The Passion of Michel Foucault*, "paints a lurid picture of a man obsessed by death and drugs, suicide and sadomasochistic sex which Foucault is described as seeking right up until his death in the bath houses in New York and San Francisco." Hawkes dismisses Foucault in the same manner in his differentiation between Adorno and Foucault: "The materialist and superficial culture of Los Angeles seems to have induced in Adorno a political pessimism so deep as to verge on the misanthropic. Foucault, on the other hand, found in San Francisco a hedonistic carnality that he evidently regarded as politically, as well as personally, liberating" (159). Hawkes, with Foucault's imagined sexual excesses at the back of his mind, is hell-bent on classifying Foucault as a materialist, that is, a philosopher who demands physical manifestations of his theories, whether they be manifest in the physical world or simply in occurrences of history.

Hawkes also makes the startling claim that Foucault considered "discourse" (a concept fundamental to his philosophy) to be material: "In order to exist 'for us,' the 'statement' must take on a material form. A 'discourse' is a regular pattern, or 'formation,' of such 'statements.' To all intents and purposes, then, 'discourse' is itself material" (156). However, though Foucault does indeed discuss the materiality of discourse, it is only to clarify that the ideology of certain discourses may have enough power to become a material reality. (One might think perhaps of the concepts of justice, revenge, and punishment as finding their material reality in prisons.) But rather than being a materialist, Foucault is the very opposite: an idealist who—when confronted with the dismaying disorder of reality—makes it his life's work to deconstruct the various fictions that we make about the world, while maintaining a desperate, somewhat wistful obsession over the relationship between truth and lies.

Fiction, art, representation, language—these are all different names for the imaginary central to Foucault's philosophy. His fourth book, *Death and the Labyrinth: The World of Raymond Roussel* (1963) is *literary criticism*—an analysis of the convoluted poetic/semantic puzzle novels of an obscure nineteenth-century writer some see as a precursor to surrealism. Foucault's fifth book, *The Order of Things* (1966), is an attempt to understand "Grammar," the third pillar of education that (along with Rhetoric and Dialectics) formed the medieval classical trivium. In this book, Foucault describes an episteme which declared that the names of objects were intimately connected with the real objects themselves, and that poetry had an inexplicable material reality. For, after all, poetry was considered, in effect, scripture—the word of God. Significantly, Foucault deploys an elegiac tone, seeming sad that this era is gone:

> The primacy of the written word went into abeyance. And that uniform layer, in which the seen and the read, the visible and the expressible, were endlessly interwoven, vanished too. Things and words were to be separated from one another. Discourse was still to have the task of speaking that which is, but it [what is] was no longer to be anything more than what is said. (47)

Because the evidence in much of his work is often anecdotal and sometimes not footnoted, Foucault has been labelled a bad historian. This critique is, I would suggest, irrelevant. Foucault himself did not consider his work to be history or philosophy. Maurice Blanchot says, "Did he not confide to Lucette Finas: 'I am fully aware that I have never written anything other than fictions . . . But I believe it is possible to make fiction function within truth' " (94). The idea that fiction might be truth is fundamental to Foucault's work, and became the focus of his late research. The final volume of *The History of Sexuality* (1988) is concerned with the ancient Greek practice of "the care of the self." When Foucault discusses St. Augustine's *Confessions*, he asserts that part of the care of the self in ancient times was the creation of personhood through writing: "The new form of the experience of the self is to be seen in the first and second centuries, when introspection becomes more and more detailed . . . Attention was paid to nuances of life, mood, and reading, and the experience of self was intensified and widened by virtue of this act of writing" (qtd. in Martin, Gutman, and Hutton 28). Foucault also talks of *parrhesia*, an ancient technique of self-examination, self-creation, and the exploration of truth. An excerpt from a lecture he delivered at Berkeley less than a year before he died (entitled "Discourse and Truth: The Problematization of Parrhesia") explains the practice:

> The one who uses parrhesia, the parrhesiastes, is someone who says everything he has in mind: he does not hide anything, but opens his heart and mind completely to other people through his discourse . . . there is always an exact coincidence between belief and truth.
>
> . . . For not only are these practices supposed to endow the individual with self-knowledge, this self-knowledge in turn is supposed to grant access to truth for further knowledge.

As Alexander Nehamas notes in *The Art of Living*, Foucault "believed that the care of the self was not a process of discovering who one truly is but of invention and improvising who one can be. Foucault's model for the care of the self was the creation of art" (178). Foucault says that when Diogenes confronted Greek citizens with everything that was on his mind (and masturbated in public) he was in the process of creating himself through fiction, and clarifying not only his own private but also a public truth: "They wanted their own lives to be a blazon of essential truths which would then serve as a guideline, or as an example for others to follow. But there is nothing in this Cynic emphasis on philosophy as an art of life which is alien to Greek philosophy" ("Discourse and Truth").

Fiction is, at its essence, a possibility for limitless self-creation, for an imagined self can be anything we want it to be. As James Wood observes about the novel, fiction is "an utterly free space, where anything might be thought, anything uttered" (9). The creator of fiction, like the parrhesiastes, can reveal everything, question everything, and, most importantly, imagine everything, a kind of fiction very much like Wood's description of the novel: "Without God, as Dostoevsky put it, 'everything is permitted' " (12).

Oscar Wilde wrote in much the same way Foucault did about the creation of the self in "The Soul of Man Under Socialism" (1891). Here he speaks of a utopia in which all our physical needs are taken care of, which allows each person to become an artist through development of their own "personality":

> It will be a marvellous thing "the true personality of man" when we see it . . . Its value will not be measured by material things. It will have nothing . . . It will not be always meddling with others, or asking them to be like itself. It will love them because they will be different. And yet while it will not meddle with others, it will help all, as a beautiful thing helps us, by being what it is. The personality of man will be very wonderful. It will be as wonderful as the personality of a child. (26–27)

I see this concept of a playful fiction that constantly intersects with the truth as the future of identity politics. People may identify as gay or straight, male or female, or none of the above, and their identities will be accepted by others as truth or not—because there is no absolute truth in the world of concepts; there never has been any truth other than the fictions we have eternally concocted about ourselves. The danger of identities and categories comes only when we declare that our personal, national, religious, cultural, gender, and sexuality fictions are universal. Those who say fiction has a dangerous disregard for truth must understand that the danger comes not from believing lies, but from believing our own personal lies to be universally true. A trans person who feels that they are neither male nor female not only has every right to identify as genderqueer, or intersexed, or androgynous, but it is everyone's duty to create an identity for themselves as part and parcel of the care of one's personal care. And these imaginings will become true if we believe them and act in the world as if they were true. But no one should ever declare that gender is over; they should declare instead that "gender is over for me." Everyone has the right to challenge everyone else's fictional truth with their own fictional truth, but no one has the right to police the imaginaries of others with physical force and/or the rule of law. People's chosen fictional identities should not bear the burden of judgment in terms of practicalities; for they are imaginary. The only way we can decide what government benefits ought to be allowed to anyone, or what affirmative-action choices must be made concerning them, or what "special treatment" (as some call it!) we should give them, is by looking at the reality of their privilege or lack thereof, not the imaginary of their chosen identities. In an ideal world, we are all artists; and this is what art has to bring to "real" life. It is sad that philosophers like David Hawkes (and all those who criticize the postmodernists and Foucault for ignoring the real world) are so intent on forcing their notions of reality on the rest of us. The argument about whether trans identities—or any other identities—are "real" or "fake" will never be resolved; it is still the same old "essentialism vs. constructionism" dichotomy. If fiction could be respected for its enormous power; if people could only realize that we are creatures of fiction, creatures of art, and respect that, then the world would be a much more humane—and human—place.

In the YouTube webseries *Love with Leila*, Izad Etemadi plays the leading character, an Iranian immigrant from Tehran, who speaks with a heavy accent. Etemadi describes his character as a "bearded lady." Leila wears a prettily decorated yellow and brown hijab, carries a purse, and often sports a pair of large, colourful sunglasses—otherwise she has the facial features of a Middle Eastern male, replete with a very full beard (Leila forgoes Western-style feminine makeup). In episode two, the leading character perilously ventures into a coffee shop. (In Tehran Leila's parents did not allow her to drink coffee, believing it was a gateway drug to heroin.) After marvelling at the red hair of the coffee girl, declaring the colour is "like de debil!" she bonds with the pretty young self-described "ginger" behind the counter (Rebecca Perry). The two gossip about a cute boy employee trainee: "I order one of *him* 'to go'!" says Leila. The Red-Headed Coffee-Shop Girl has other ideas; but neither has a chance with the appealing barista in training, because after finishing work he kisses what appears to be his young male lover on the lips. Leila observes, somewhat wistfully, "This never happen in my countary [sic], at least in the public. You know—" at which point she makes a gesture for hanging. She and the Red-Headed Coffee-Shop Girl commiserate, with the latter musing that in Canada the only problem is that, sadly, all the cutest men are gay.

Love with Leila masquerades as a comedy webseries but is really much more than that. Although Izad plays the character of Leila with an innocent truth (right down to the accuracy of the accent), one might ask why the series lead is a bearded man in a hijab rather than a cisgender Iranian woman. Having a "bearded lady" as the central character of a comedy series neatly avoids accusations of colonialism—i.e., that it is making fun of Iranian fundamentalist Muslim culture. For *Love with Leila* does not simply critique the sexism of Muslim fundamentalism, but also points to the prejudice and barbarism that lie just behind the hypocritical Canadian liberal facade. We might say that Canadians are tolerant of Muslims. But if a *bearded* Iranian person—who may look to some like a man in a hijab—tried to flirt with men in a Toronto coffee shop, she would inevitably encounter fear and confusion. Indeed, she might very well engender hate and/or requisite violence due to the fact that we live in a sexist, homophobic, and transphobic culture.

Love with Leila is a recent example of a performance fiction that is also intricately connected with the creation of the author's own identity. In "real" life, Izad identifies both as a gay man and an Iranian immigrant. In real life he does not have an accent, and does not wear a hijab or carry a purse (although I have seen him wear colourful sunglasses!). To what degree is "Leila" a fiction, and to what degree is she a faithful rendering of Izad's experience of being a gay Iranian Canadian? One would have to ask Izad (and how effective is any artist at identifying their own motives?). But the piece offers a glimpse at how fictional identities may—in both real life and art—help us understand who we are.

How can fiction be true? It might be best to think—as Wilde does—on the minds of children. Of course it is still necessary to tell children that they mustn't touch a hot stove as they will be burned; these material facts need not be treated as fictions. But beauty, identity, morality, values, dreams, hopes, etc. must remain personal, fictional, and eternally controversial. I would argue that most of the time we consider all nominalisms to be quite true when they are not (does any of us know absolutely what "real" love is?), *so why not just imagine they are true*? I'm certain that Charles Kingsley would not have recommended anyone's children go and live underwater, and yet his advice to young readers of his children's tale "The Water-Babies," is relevant here: "But remember always, as I told you at first, that this is all a fairy tale, and only fun and pretence; and therefore, you are not to believe a word of it, even if it is true" (qtd. in Carpenter 41).

HOMESTEADING A NEW QUEER FRONTIER: QUEERING PERFORMANCE AND CULTIVATING COMMUNITY FROM OUTSIDE THE CENTRE

RICHIE WILCOX AND JAY WHITEHEAD

> *It's something of a miracle Theatre Outré exists at all: a vital queer theatre company, with a year-round facility, in the middle of the Albertan Badlands. They are more than a cultural space in Lethbridge; they are a paradigm shift.*
> —Jordan Tannahill

Lethbridge is a small city of around one hundred thousand residents nestled in the rolling coulees and prairie grasslands of Southern Alberta. It is the fourth largest city in the province and is known as much for its staunch religious and political conservatism as it is for its relentless prairie winds and warming winter chinooks. The city was founded in the late nineteenth century as a coal-mining community and remains to this day mostly blue collar, with a community working predominantly in agriculture, industry, and the public sector. Lethbridge sits in what is often considered the most unchangeably right-of-centre region of Canada but contains a hidden dichotomy. Just as it buries its unique and interesting past as the last city in North America to shutter its once popular red-light district (boasting thriving brothels open and active well into the mid-twentieth century), it hides a blooming counterculture grounded in the hard-working arts and academic communities. In the midst of the city's conservative core—comprised of many strict religious communities, including larger-than-average populations of Mormons, Hutterites, and Dutch Reform congregations, sits a liberal-arts university with areas of study including fine arts, sociology, women's studies, and other humanities. The university has infused the city with liberal pockets of thought, politics, and artistic practice that are only recently beginning to reach their full potential, creating an ever-evolving counterculture whose fervent need to be "counter" in this conservative stronghold is only augmented by the traditional reputation of the place in which it exists.

Also emerging from the shadows in the past several years is an increasingly visible queer community. Queers in Lethbridge, like in cities across the continent of similar size and demographics, are marching bravely into a new queer frontier full of potential and necessity. This is in contrast to queer residents of larger urban centres, who more and more see arts, culture, and events like Pride as corporate-sponsorship opportunities, or simply another weekend out in the "gaybourhood." Instead, these small-city queers, these "Fairies on the Prairies," are, like Laura Ingalls herself, proverbially prancing through Wild Rose country with their sisters in tow, celebrating Pride and diversity for important political and social reasons beyond an excuse to wear that new tank top. And at the forefront of this movement, in the small conservative community of Lethbridge, is our emerging queer theatre company, fully taking advantage of the fertile climate here for queerly homesteading new opportunities for change: Theatre Outré.

Only a few short years ago, the queer scene in Lethbridge was stuck in the past; a big-city dweller could be thrown back decades when confronted with the closeted characteristics encouraged, whether it be benignly or unknowingly, by the queer organizations and events of the day. GALA, the local gay organization, would produce, at that time, bimonthly dances, which certainly had the intention of bringing together the community; however, the location of these dances was a key factor in deterring the community from uniting and from feeling any sort of pride about their sexuality and themselves. The dances were located at a Croatian hall rented out cheaply for the occasion. The building itself was outside of city limits, down a long dirt road with no street lights. The mysterious and unknown night cloaked people in darkness and hid them from public view. This drive that placed everyone in a private and segregated world was not liberating or tantalizing—it was shaming. The location inherently communicated to people, "It is okay to be part of the queer community, but we need to be in the shadows to be safe." The entire function was catering to people who did not want to be out or seen as gay because of fear. Only a few years before people had to know a password in order to be allowed into the dance as a safety precaution. The city of Lethbridge did not have a consistent queer-positive space downtown and there were few to no signs of queer culture visible in the city. Information and communication were predominantly transmitted through online forums, social media, and smart phone applications such as Grindr and Scruff. The physical gathering of the queer community was almost non-existent, and when it did occur, it was behind closed doors. The Pride organization did not have a march or parade at this time, either. While the queer population was very present in Lethbridge in 2012, it was covert to the point of being invisible. Enter Theatre Outré.

Theatre Outré had its roots over fifteen years ago when, in 2005, as a politically motivated, if naive, undergraduate student in the theatre department at the University of Lethbridge, Jay Whitehead, set out to create a small queer performance event in town. He booked a small acting classroom for the event, rallied like-minded student performers and sold five-dollar tickets for a cabaret called *Pretty, Witty & GAY*. The show sold out and filled to capacity with a diverse student and community audience. This was the very first inkling that there was an audience for theatre that represented sexual minorities in a place as seemingly unlikely as Lethbridge, Alberta.

When Whitehead returned to Lethbridge years later, he was delighted to find that *Pretty, Witty & GAY* had become entrenched as an anticipated annual event in the cultural landscape of this small conservative city. He quickly jumped back on board and became involved in the event once again. In the years since, *Pretty, Witty & GAY* has now grown to become Theatre Outré's flagship event. What once was a terrified undergraduate queer's intended singular experiment in a community where he felt invisible has now become a week-long celebration of sexual diversity and hedonism that reliably sells out.

Pretty, Witty & GAY was operating on a small scale long before Theatre Outré as an official company and registered theatre society was first conceived. The formation of the company did not actually happen until January 2012, when theatre director Richie Wilcox and his husband, Aaron Collier, a sound designer and musician, moved to Southern Alberta. Wilcox, like Whitehead, had been hired to teach as a faculty member at the University of Lethbridge; soon after we met, it became very clear to us that we were artists whose personal and creative values aligned, and whose skill sets complemented each other. We were quick to recognize the potential of a queer theatre company in our new small-city prairie home, and we hit the ground running at full speed almost immediately. Theatre Outré was born.

Having lived and worked in bigger cities, it was evident to us both that rental space was incredibly cheap in a city like Lethbridge. Consequently, we rented a room on the third floor of an historic downtown building, above a pub and art gallery, for six-hundred dollars a month. The space was small and intimate, able to seat about thirty patrons. The impetus to operate our own space came from examples being set by theatre artists in larger centres, who were following DIY trends; this included the successful undertaking of Jordan Tannahill and William Ellis at their very experimental Toronto space, Videofag. The rented space in Lethbridge, which we named Bordello, was dilapidated and had no air conditioning; the toilets clogged, and when it rained the roof leaked. But people were excited about the space and about the work we were doing. A buzz about this mysterious new queer space was built primarily through word of mouth and social-media efforts.

The name Bordello emerged from the fact that the building the space occupied was rumoured to have been a brothel during Lethbridge's gold rush and mining years. With successful original productions such as *UNSEX'd*, which was co-written by Whitehead and Daniel Judes, and *The Drinking Game*, a co-production with Halifax's DaPoPo Theatre, as well as numerous musical and drag cabaret nights, Theatre Outré and our space, Bordello, quickly gained momentum in town. The small intended performance venue was evolving into a celebrated de facto "gay bar" for the community. As such, Theatre Outré rapidly outgrew its first venue.

We found our second and current space shortly after the onset of 2014. A previous dance studio in a well-appointed building, with a working thermostat, flushable toilets, and double the capacity, became available and, as a company, we decided the extra rent was worth the sacrifice for better, larger, and more accessible facilities; although more expensive than the first space, rent was still remarkably affordable at $1,500 a month. We invested a great deal of time, energy, money, and volunteer hours into the renovation of the new space and brought the name Bordello with us; however, we were no longer sharing the space with a pub and an art gallery. Our new neighbours were conservative business owners and it didn't take long for word to reach us, through our landlord, that these new neighbours were not at all happy to share a building with an organization called Bordello, a name they apparently took literally. Consequently, after a highly public and traumatic battle with everyone from our new neighbours to Lethbridge City Hall, we relented and changed the name of the new venue to Club Didi, named for Whitehead's popular local drag character, who frequently hosted events there.[1]

In the handful of years since founding the company and its accompanying venue, Theatre Outré has produced full seasons of theatre, including plays by celebrated queer Canadian playwrights (Sky Gilbert's *The Birth of Casper G. Schmidt* and Jordan Tannahill's *Late Company*), renowned international playwrights (Wallace Shawn's *A Thought in Three Parts*), and world-premiere productions of new plays by local and nationally recognized playwrights (Greg MacArthur's *White Gleaming Beach*, Liam Monaghan's *How To Leave*, and Whitehead, Wilcox, Collier, and Kathy Zaborsky's *Castrati: An Electro Drag Opera*). Theatre Outré has also toured their original work, including *UNSEX'd* and *Castrati*, to cities across Canada and abroad, proving that a city like Lethbridge can sustain theatre that is not only timely, but incredibly provocative in content and form. The company's location has also proven a remarkably fertile and inspirational laboratory to create experimental work

1 A multitude of articles on this battle for space can be found from various sources with various biases. See "Theatre Outré in Lethbridge" from *The Huffington Post* as a good starting point.

without the necessity of pleasing sponsors, the media, or reviewers, and with the financial freedom to take risks.

With cheap rent and a small space to fill, as well as a wealth of local talent constantly funnelling out of fine-arts programs at the local university, producing theatre in Lethbridge is remarkably less daunting than one might expect. Resources have proven readily available through donations from community members, sponsorships from local small businesses, and loaned theatre equipment—including lighting, set pieces, props, and costumes—from the university and other local theatre groups. In a small community like Lethbridge, where these resources already exist, they are more accessible and available than in cities that might be burdened by larger demand due to more crowded theatre communities and higher rental fees. Lethbridge also boasts a "small town" feel, wherein everyone knows everyone or is a friend of a friend at the very least, and finding materials and willing labour to produce professional-calibre theatre at affordable rates is relatively easy. There is, in a small city like this, less competition for advertising, sponsorship, and resources, and since the nearest large city is in excess of two-hundred kilometres from downtown Lethbridge, there is also a strong desire to see quality theatre produced for a community that feels underserved at home.

Additionally, the freedom to create theatre in Lethbridge that is provocative, out there, experimental, and daring, with content including extreme sexual situations, strong language, nudity, violence, and queer themes, is something that cannot be understated. The city of Lethbridge has very little entertainment journalism and its only local newspaper employs no arts or theatre reviewers. At a time when theatre companies in larger cities lament the loss of theatre critics and rely so heavily on that elusive four-star review to help sell tickets to pay for inflated downtown performance venues, Theatre Outré thrives artistically, and has for years, in an environment where our artistic output is rarely, if ever, held up for scrutiny by local media agents. There is tremendous freedom in such an environment to create theatre and art without judgment or fear of getting panned by analytical critiques.

The first major show produced by our company, and to be reviewed outside of our community, was *UNSEX'd*. The play tells the story of two boy players in a reimagined Shakespearean England duking it out to originate the role of Lady Macbeth in the Bard's new "Scottish Play." The writing and staging of the piece is inspired by unapologetically queer entertainment icons and historical practices, including the work of Sky Gilbert, drag performance, Shakespeare, *All About Eve*, and Charles Ludlum's Theatre of the Ridiculous. Creating the production in the non-cynical vacuum that is Lethbridge proved a testing ground for what was to come for Theatre Outré. Working in isolation from any geographic location that had ever seen queer theatre of this ilk—or even many of the show's inspirations—proved to be a rewarding artistic experience, and because of the necessity of selling no more than thirty tickets a night to fill the theatre there was little pressure to create a show that was a "safe bet" or easily marketable. With an entirely local company of actors, crew, and designers, the show opened to much celebration and praise in Lethbridge and sold remarkably well, bolstered by word of mouth alone. The show has since garnered interest from more established queer theatre companies across the country: it has been presented by Calgary's Third Street Theatre, Vancouver's **frank theatre company**, and Toronto's Buddies in Bad Times Theatre. It also played at the International Dublin Gay Theatre Festival. Our safe bubble, void of media scrutiny, however, was threatened on these sojourns out of our cozy little community. One perplexing review of *UNSEX'd* by Calgary critic Jessica Goldman, for instance, didn't understand the camp sensibility of the play or its crude humour, and she panned the production for what she wanted it to be rather than for what it was, saying that "obvious raunch and tiresome camp trampled what could have been a fun, smart play." Her tweets continued, going as far as to ask, "is there such a thing as a gay play? I think not." Her response indicates that she was unaware of the rich history in queer culture of using camp and raunch as artistic, social, and political tools.

Had *UNSEX'd* not already had a vibrant and rewarding run at home in Lethbridge, it's easy to imagine that a harsh review like this, from someone with the potential to deter audiences from attending, might have motivated us to alter the show to win public favour, or to abandon the project altogether for something more broadly accessible. Having been protected from such analysis at home, we were safe from any such distraction to our true artistic vision and were able to take the show as far as our imaginations and our respect of queer theatre history would take us. Since then, this gay, vulgar, camp fantasia that is *UNSEX'd*, created in the isolated bubble of small-city Lethbridge, where it was untouched by media scrutiny, has flourished on continued tours to cities and festivals from coast to coast and beyond. And it has garnered many positive reviews, which for us is flattering, but we see that as the icing on the cake that we've already enjoyed at home. Theatre Outré produces fast and produces often. Our space is a laboratory and we present our experiments frequently to live audiences hungry for representation in their own community with little to no financial or critical risk; and the resulting work, in terms of quality, as evidenced by interest from outside of Lethbridge, has not been affected negatively by working in these rare artistically fertile and freeing conditions.

It is fruitful to compare the Theatre Outré experience with Buddies in Bad Times Theatre's developing years, as it shows the similarities in philosophies that have popped up over thirty years later in our relatively rural setting. As stated on their website, founding artistic director Sky Gilbert brought forth a vision for Buddies "that was unapologetically political, fiercely pro-sexual and fundamentally anti-establishment" ("Our History"). A look at this trio of values in further detail is necessary to analyze Theatre Outré's status as *the* counterculture in Lethbridge.

The act of being "unapologetically political" in Alberta does not necessarily take much: a liberal thought can be looked at as an act of rebellion by some. As described and defined on the Facebook page for Theatre Outré, to be outré is "to violate convention or propriety; pass the bounds of what is usual; out of the common course or limits; bizarre; outlandish; extravagant; queer." Our mandate continues to proclaim our mission against the status quo as "we seek to provide an uncensored and uncompromising voice to those in our community who are often considered to exist beyond the fringes of social propriety, sexual norms and gendered expectations" (Theatre Outré). We present theatre content that is not only considered alternative in the theatre community, but is labelled alternative by society as a whole. Shows such as our original production of *Castrati: An Electro Drag Opera* feature a hybrid of theatre, media, ritual, and performance art that challenges the viewer aesthetically, but also challenges the audience with brutally open discussions and representations of sexuality, gender, nudity, and more.

Buddies in Bad Times was known, and is perhaps still known, for being fiercely pro-sexual. Their infamous dungeon parties allowed people to come to the venue to experiment with S/M. The company is likely one of the only major Canadian theatre companies whose former artistic directors would post nude and sexual pictures and videos of themselves on the Internet. Theatre Outré's work is embedded in sex and body positivity. The surrounding conservative environment most likely helps drive us to further extremes in that regard to counter the status quo. Our production of *A Thought in Three Parts*, for example, featured all nude performers simulating various sex acts on stage: on their own, in pairs, and in groups. We are continuing to delve into ideas revolving around sex and fetishism with our new play in development, *Tab & Landon*. The play is set in the 1970s and examines the relationship of twin brothers who perform in porn films together in the genre known as "twincest." In the same vein as Bruce LaBruce's canon, or films such as *Shortbus* and *Lie with Me*, this play will feature previously recorded scenes projected onto the stage showcasing the actors performing actual sexual acts. While laws forbid live sex shows, we are interested in pushing the boundaries of social propriety and questioning why such things are off limits in our time.

The space we run also serves as a gay bar, which is not unlike the Buddies model with their space, Tallulah's Cabaret. We hold many club events that celebrate body- and sex-positivity. We host a monthly dance called Panti Raid, where people can feel comfortable partying in their underwear. Another event similar to this is Strip Spelling Bee. The participants can be anyone and everyone. The support of bodies and the respect afforded bodies of all types within these two events alone make a big difference in the mentality and attitudes of our community.

The Junk Booth, an ongoing art exhibit in our space, likewise speaks succinctly and powerfully to our fiercely pro-sexual beliefs. Patrons of the space are invited at any time to go into the Junk Booth, a small partitioned space, to take an anonymous picture of their anatomy (whichever part they want) and drop it into a locked box. The pictures are later displayed proudly, pinned to bulletin boards that live by the bar, or, if they are so honoured, framed in one of the several collages of snapshots that adorn the space. For some people in our community, the act of taking these photos can be a big hurdle to jump, although the release and liberty of showing off your "junk" to others (even if it is anonymous) helps people accept themselves more fully and encourages them to love their bodies both mentally and physically.

The third foundational Buddies value stresses its "fundamentally anti-establishment" stance. This one is tougher to follow through for Theatre Outré. Thinking of establishment in a literal way, we started out buying one-off liquor licences, had no business licence, no occupancy load, no sponsorships, and no official lease. But just as Buddies ended up where it is today, we have definitely fallen into the bureaucracy of it all and jumped through the necessary hoops. We have always been a registered society as Theatre Outré, but because of the club part of the space we now have a business licence to run the private Club Didi. We have an official annual liquor licence that took months to obtain, and because of this licence we have to sell food (which we overprice so it won't actually sell). We have an occupancy load of sixty people in our space, a stipulation we tend to abide by strictly because it's not necessarily the area where we choose to push the envelope—we pick our battles. Technically, any nudity in our space is supposed to occur on stage with a legally determined number of metres between performers and audience, and no nudity is allowed amongst the patrons. Does all this make us part of the establishment? We do enough so we don't fear getting shut down at any moment by the fire department, liquor board, or local police, but we also don't take their rule books as gospel. In such a small city, we do not have the luxury of being as underground as Videofag, for example, where you can be mainstream in certain circles yet remain under the radar in a very big city. We don't wish to suggest that Videofag and spaces like it in larger centres don't face challenges of their own, but as stated previously, we are *the* counterculture in Lethbridge: all eyes are on us, whether they be friendly or not.

Comparing the Lethbridge queer culture of 2012 to the state of affairs within Lethbridge in 2017 can be shocking, inspiring, and heartening for even the bitterest of old queens. Club Didi, which is located smack in the middle of downtown Lethbridge, offers weekly club nights, week-long runs of queer theatre, improv nights, music tributes, and poetry jams. The rentable space also serves as a meeting and practice room for a local rope-fetish club. The queer social culture is thriving in a very public way, where the location encourages openness and inclusion of all. Patrons of Club Didi regularly hang out on the downtown street in front of the building for cigarette breaks. Patrons venture over for a beverage at other downtown clubs during the night, hand in hand with their loved ones. The visibility of queerness permeates downtown now, though there is still a ways to go in this seemingly homogenous community in fostering an audience that welcomes and includes queer POC and Two-Spirited communities. Club Didi hosts drag cabarets regularly and the number of drag queens that have been birthed in just over four years is astounding. Drag queens perform at the club but also venture to fine-dining lounges, dance clubs aimed at a straight demographic, and late-night pizza shops. The past two years have seen Casino Lethbridge hire Lethbridge Pride to organize a drag show for their venue. At the same time, the local HIV-outreach organization, ARCHES, produces the annually sold-out Condom Couture Fashion Show in a city where the radio station refuses to say the word *condom* to promote the event.

The visibility of transgender people in the community and the downtown core has also increased; for example, a local funky fashion retail store, Drunken Sailor, hires and promotes staff who are transitioning, and the fine-dining lounge Plum regularly hires a trans DJ. The queerness of Lethbridge is not in the shadows anymore but is part of its everyday downtown life. Lethbridge Pride now has a parade and in 2015 had its first-ever float, which was reserved for Theatre Outré and Club Didi to ride on. That momentous occasion served as a reminder that to be vocal and stand out as a community, especially in a city like Lethbridge, is a truly revolutionary act. This Pride parade is not a tourist attraction, but one that disrupted unknowing drivers in the downtown core and forced traffic to stop and be confronted with the visibility of a strong community of queer people who will not be denied their existence. Of course, as a theatre company we cannot take full credit for all of the changes within the past five years, but the space and the work that happens there has served, and continues to serve, as a catalyst for the visibility of the local queer community. As Brendan Healy, the former artistic director of Buddies in Bad Times puts it, Theatre Outré and Club Didi are "a beacon of queer expression and freedom in the most unexpected of places—a truly creative, risk-taking, boundary pushing theatre company that is MAKING community happen. An inspiration."

UNSETTLING THE FRONTIER FABLE

JEAN O'HARA

If history is not entirely a lie, it is no more trustworthy than a work of fiction.
—David Liss and Shirley J. Madill

A pervasive frontier fable developed alongside the invasion of Indigenous lands and the subsequent genocide of Indigenous people by Europeans in what are now called Canada and the United States. This fable constructed the idea (and image) of free open lands, rugged individualism of white heterosexual men, and the assimilation and elimination of the "savage" Indian (who later becomes the vanishing or Noble Indian). This fable was fuelled by the notion of manifest destiny in which a righteous god backs the plans of these invading Europeans in their fatalistic journey to create the Americas. Out of this fable came the iconic characters of the cowboy and the Indian. Michael Yellow Bird contends that cowboys and Indians are "part of the colonial canon asserting white supremacy and Indigenous inferiority" (34), to which Gerald McMaster adds, "the social Darwinian discourse of the nineteenth-century posited the weaker *Indian* disappearing in the face of *western* progress, as signified by the cowboy" (96–97; emphasis in original). Within this binary construct of the Indian/cowboy, the history of Two-Spirit[1] peoples was erased. The frontier

1 According to Qwo-Li Driskill, Daniel Heath Justice, Deborah Miranda, and Lisa Tatonetti,

> [T]wo-spirit is an umbrella term in English that (1) refers to the gender constructions and roles that occur historically in many Native gender systems that

fable was repeatedly constructed on stage, in nineteenth-century paintings, photographs, and later in television and film. This same fable is constructed and reconstructed in all forms of visual media to this day. In this essay, I will critically examine how Daniel David Moses's play, *The Indian Medicine Shows*, deconstructs the frontier fable, exposes the workings of the colonial imperialist project though a queer Indigenous lens, and situates gay and Two-Spirit subjects in history and on stage.

In 1996 Daniel David Moses created two pieces, *The Moon and Dead Indians* and *Angel of the Medicine Show*, and paired them for an evening of performances titled *The Indian Medicine Shows*. The pieces were developed individually and performed together at Theatre Passe Muraille, one of Toronto's original "alternative" theatres. *The Moon and Dead Indians* is set in a failing colonial town in late nineteenth-century New Mexico, where two cowboys contend with their mutual sexual desire and their murderous past. *Angel of the Medicine Show* is modelled on an Indian medicine show, breaking script to expose a love triangle, a murderous white mob, and an Indian who fights back. Keith Garebian argues that Moses "strive[s] to submit the clichéd underpinnings of the Old West to critical revisionism" and creates "a radical vision of re-interpreted frontier" (35–36). I will critically examine both pieces to consider how they subvert and queer the frontier fable, beginning with *The Moon and Dead Indians*.

Moses confronts the manifest destiny of Christian ideology through a cowboy's mother (Ma) in *The Moon and Dead Indians*. The piece opens with Ma holding a rifle in her hand singing "Jesus Loves Me." Ma clearly links Christianity to violence, genocide, and forced assimilation. Moses demonstrates the "schizophrenic" effect of manifest destiny through his choice to have Ma sing a song invoking love while simultaneously preparing to kill any

are outside of colonial gender binaries and (2) refers to contemporary Native people who are continuing and/or reclaiming these roles within their communities. It is also often used as an umbrella term with grassroots two-spirit societies . . . meant to be inclusive of not only those who identify as two-spirit or with tribally specific term, but also LGBTQ Native people more broadly (4).

Native people entering her "property" (Allen 21). Andrea Smith states that invading Europeans

> viewed the land and Indigenous peoples as something to be used for their own purposes; colonizers could not respect the integrity of either the land or Indigenous peoples . . . [W]ithin this colonial imaginary, the Native is an empty signifier that provides the occasion for Europe to remake its corrupt civilization. ("Queer Theory" 48)

In other words, Europeans employed years of war tactics with the intent to destroy Indigenous peoples and legitimize heteropatriarchal ownership.

Throughout *The Moon and Dead Indians* Ma invokes Christian deities and ideology: "Thank God, thank God Almighty" (49); "Jesus, Jonny, Jesus will provide" (50); "That's not how a Christian girl behaves" (60); "I pray to Jesus" (60); "I thank Jesus for you" (61); "Jesus in heaven"(65/67). Ma's repetition of Christian phrases seems to disallow any different spiritual belief systems and perhaps is used to distance herself from any Native peoples. In scene four, Ma tells Billy, "They kill Christians, don't they? They eat our hearts." (60). From her Christian manifest-destiny framework, she believes it is the Native people who should be feared because they are violent and savage. The "Indians" are viewed as uncivilized, brutal, and murderous, while the invading Europeans are considered victims and promoters of peace. Part of the colonial project is to invert history by rewriting its stories. Smith exposes a white history often omitted in history books, one that names the brutal violence conducted by colonizers, including:

> Andrew Jackson . . . supervised the mutilation of 800 or so Creek Indian corpses . . . he and his men massacred—cutting off their noses to count and preserve a record of the dead, slicing long strips of flesh from their bodies to tan and turn into bridle reins.
>
> One woman, big with child, rushed into the church, clasping the alter crying for mercy . . . the child was torn alive from the yet palpitating body of its mother, first plunged into the holy water to be

> baptized, and immediately its brains were dashed against the wall. ("Not an Indian Tradition" 75)

Instead of an honest portrayal of crimes against Native people or a depiction of Indigenous people as defending their homes and their communities, the colonial project fashions a history of Indigenous nations as warring tribes out to kill nice Christians or hard-working pioneers and cowboys. The denial of genocide has made fables into history, creating an "American amnesia" when it comes to the past (Allen 21). In scene two, Moses exemplifies this amnesia in a conversation between Ma and Jon:

> **MA:** The Indians got Joseph and Seth.
> **JON:** Them stupid Indians had no part in it.
> **MA:** And your father, Jonny. Think of him.
> **JON:** Stop it.
> **MA:** Apaches scalped your father, didn't they? The Mescalero Apaches? Are you going to answer me? Jonny?
> **JON:** Pa was drunk. He passed out and froze stiff coming home up the mountain.
> **MA:** No, Jonny—
> **JON:** And you know who got his scalp, Ma? Some coyote . . .
> **MA:** Don't say that.
> **JON:** I saw it, Ma.
> **MA:** He was your father, Jonny.
> **JON:** Let's just not talk about it, all right?
> **MA:** That's when I was sure it was Indians.
> **JON:** I'll go put the kettle on. (52)

Despite Jon's knowledge of the details of his father and brother's deaths, Ma holds onto the fable of Indians killing and scalping her family. As Indigenous Two-Spirit scholar Paula Gunn Allen retorts, "I suppose if I saw myself murdering, in one way or another, several million people and hundreds of cultures, I'd long to forget my past, too" (21).

The title of this first piece, *The Moon and Dead Indians*, foregrounds the multiple massacres of Indigenous peoples and nations in what is now called the United States. The editors of *Queer Indigenous Studies* argue that the first massacres began with the killing of Two-Spirit people and that it was through "the imposition of European gender relationships on Native communities that Europeans were able to colonize Native peoples in the first place" (Driskill, Finley, Gilley, and Morgensen 8–9). Moses does not create the noble or savage or drunk or vanished "Indians" of the colonial imaginings. In fact, his project in each of his pieces is to expose the tyrannous colonial war against Native people, which includes Two-Spirit people. By not allowing the "dead Indians" to vanish, Moses writes the torture and genocide of Indigenous people back into history. He creates Indigenous characters who "continually struggle to negotiate between absence and presence, being dead and being alive, in their desire to matter, *to be matter*" (Appleford, "Daniel David Moses" 158). Moses mirrors the work of Lynn Riggs and Tomson Highway by creating hauntings within his plays. He shares that his ghosts "exist to probe the white problem . . . to spook its metaphors" (qtd. in Helen Gilbert 689). All three characters in the piece—Ma, Jon, and Billy—are haunted by these "dead Indians" and the memories of the Indigenous peoples murdered by their communities and themselves.

In the first scene of *The Moon and Dead Indians*, Ma is being haunted by memories, or perhaps the actual spirits, of the Indigenous people who lived on the land she now "owns." Ric Knowles reads these Indigenous ghosts as "haunt[ing] the landscape and the repressed, collective unconscious of an already decadent capitalist 'civilization' " ("Look. Look Again" 196). Sitting on the porch with a rifle in her hand, Ma calls out to her son who is not there. When her son does arrive, she tells him, "I heard them, Jonny . . . Coming across the valley. You know the way the sound carries. They were down in the pine bush . . . I could hear the leather of their saddles creaking" (50–51). She shares that she can hear death coming and the Indians coming, to which Jon replies, "Then you're hearing ghosts" (51). We also learn in this dialogue that Ma is ill and is described by Moses as "pale in bedclothes as a ghost" (49). Ma is dying physically, mentally, and spiritually. If we examine Ma as representative of the "mother" of white people who committed genocide, we begin to see the effects of colonization on European peoples too. Moses inverts the image of the crazy Indian and exposes the craziness that colonization creates in the oppressor. Jon and Billy repeatedly call their mother crazy/loco, while Ma calls both men "crazies" (65). Moses exposes the dichotomous and dangerous Western split between spirit/flesh, mind/body, head/heart that allows one group to dehumanize, torture, and murder millions of people.

The haunting of "dead Indians" reappears in scene seven in a forced conversation between cowboys Jon and Billy. Billy has Jon pinned to the floor and asks Jon if he remembers the night they murdered (and tortured) the *Indios culiando* (the gay Indian). They recount how they enticed the Indian, "who acted pretty like a girl," got him drunk, knocked him out, and scalped him (74). According to Knowles, "The boy's crime was to attract the repressed homoerotic desire (for one another) of the play's two white men" (Introduction 46). Not satisfied with teaching the "*Indio culiando* a lesson" by just scalping him, Billy castrates the young man too (Moses 75). Garebian interprets this torture of the Native man as "a form of sadistic ecstasy for at least one of his white tormentors" (35). Moses haunts the audience with the historical heteropatriarchal hatred and fear of Two-Spirit men. Records as far back as 1513 cite the torture and murder of Indigenous "young men in women's apparel, smooth & effeminately decked," and those who engaged in anal sex, by Spanish conquistador Vasco Núñez de Balboa, who "ordered forty of these men to be fed alive to his dogs" (Justice, Rifkin, and Schneider 9). Moses links Billy to the conquistador not only in action but also in language. Just before their shared confession, Billy forces Jon to be sexual with him while he speaks in a combination of Spanish and English, telling Jon, "*Solo despues de muerto* (only after death) will you get away from me . . . *Tu eres mi chupa picos* (my cocksucker)" (73). Billy represents the continued regulatory power of heteronormativity by the torture and murder of Two-Spirit men, non-gender conforming men, men who show homoerotic desire, and indeed all Indigenous peoples.

Jon is haunted by his participation in the murder of the young man: "He looked at me, Billy . . . His dark eyes looked at me . . . He reached out his hand covered in blood . . . The blood looks so black in this light" (75). Moses mixes the past with the present: “looked at me” is written in the past tense and “black in this light” is written in the present tense. The playwright creates a presence for this young Two-Spirit man in the room/on stage. Knowles argues the ghosts “are the *not-seen*, who model a culturally repressed *what-really-is*, the repressed truth that must be revealed beneath and oppressive realism in order to release that *what-could-be*” (“Look. Look Again” 190; emphasis in original). This is made apparent when Ma quietly walks into the room, witnesses the entire sexually charged exchange and confession, quietly sings “Jesus Loves Me,” and then yells, “The Indians are here!” wildly shooting her gun and just missing her son Jon (76). Ma calls out to Jon, unable to see him or hear him, repeatedly saying “they're here,” and then kills herself (76). Within the framework of heteronormativity, Ma cannot comprehend or accept her son's desire for men and ends up committing suicide. Instead of an angel or a Christian god, Ma is met by Indigenous spirits. In this way, Moses refers to a belief, held by many Indigenous communities, that ancestral spirits inhabit the land to continue to guide others. According to Sealth, the spirits of Native people are all around: “At night when the streets of your cities and villages are silent and you think them deserted, they will throng with the returning hosts that once filled them and still love this beautiful land. The white man will never be alone” (qtd. in Allen 27). In the end, Moses gives presence and power to the supposed “vanishing Indians,” even after death.

The Moon and Dead Indians ultimately shows the failings of manifest destiny. In particular, Moses critiques the unsustainable concept of “rugged individualism”[2] (pulling yourself up by your bootstraps) “because community is what a human being must have to be human in any sense” (Appleford, “The Desire to Crunch Bone” 25). Corey Taber adds, “How you treat people around you and what you do to give back. That essentially defines you as a person . . . ” (qtd. in Driskill 104). We hear about the failing of manifest destiny in Jon's words when he speaks to his mom: “The minister left back in the summer . . . The

2 A phrase often used by President Herbert Hoover to justify the lack of government intervention during the Great Depression in the US, “rugged individualism” refers to individualism in social and economic affairs, and a belief not only in personal liberty and self-reliance but also in free competition.

town's dying. That little mine's all petered out. Everyone's going" (67). Later Ma shares with Billy, "It's not much of a town anymore" (59). Jon and Ma inhabit what is essentially a ghost town. An ideology based on individualism and "progress" destroys both community and the land. Allen speaks to the continued obliteration manifested by the colonial project: "The destruction wrought by *individual* initiative necessarily *haunts* us now, because everywhere we look we see death: past, present, future. And death is what America has fled for over five hundred years" (28; emphasis mine). We can hear Moses's voice resonate with Allen's when Jon asks Billy, "How the hell can you live with death all the time?" (71). The piece ends with Billy and Jon burying Ma while singing "Jesus Loves Me" and then going their separate ways.

In *Angel of the Medicine Show*, the second piece of *The Indian Medicine Shows*, Jon is joined by Angela. The piece opens with Angela longing for Billy while she sings, "Oh where have you been, Billy Boy, Billy Boy?" (79). We find out later, in a conversation between Jon and Angela, that death caught up with cowboy Billy, who was shot and killed. Like Ma, Angela has a gun handy and pulls it out when she hears groans under the wagon. Angela finds the severely wounded David and yells, "Chief! Chief, that you? Hey, stupid redskin, what are you doing here? How'd get away? . . . Hey, boy, what's wrong? Hey, I didn't hit you?" (80). We learn later that Angela did in fact "hit" him with a bullet from her gun. David is barely alive, bleeding from the gun wound, bruised and beaten with contusions on his neck from being hung by a mob of white people. Angela is emblematic of a homophobic and paternalistic ideology when she later calls David a "sissy" and a "baby" for hiding under the wagon. She is physically abusive, gruffly pulling David out from under the wagon and later hitting him on the head with a frying pan to make him "behave" (80–81). Angela blames David for the mob attack:

> **DAVID:** They wanted my blood.
>
> **ANGELA:** Can't says I blame them, Chief . . . That's what people do with wild animals. We all know that, even sober. That's what your people do.
>
> **DAVID:** No, Miss, no, not my people.

> **ANGELA:** So, there it is again! You're answering back. You're answering back!
> **DAVID:** My people are Christians, Miss.
> **ANGELA:** Don't! Don't answer back. That's not your number. Your number's all you got to do. Stick to your sheet . . . Say something or I'll put another hole in you.
> **DAVID:** Not never again, Miss. (85)

This short dialogue makes obvious the paternalistic overtones of settler discourse toward Indigenous peoples. It also reveals that Native people can never be accepted as citizens, even if they convert to Christianity and assimilate to other Western belief systems. According to Mark Rifkin, European American nationalism "serv[ed] as means of distinguishing those who were proper participants in the state from those who were simply the objects of its authority" (48). David is meant to submit and play the part of the colonial imaginings of the vanished Indian or be killed. His role in the medicine show is that of a ghost ("stick to your sheet") who sells "traditional Indian medicine." In fact, Angela only addresses David by his role, chief. He is a character and a commodity that helps put food on the table for her and Jon.

Two-Spirited David, along with all Indigenous people, is seen as a wild animal or savage through Angela's heteropatriarchal white-supremacist lens. Smith states, "The goal of colonialism is not just to kill colonized peoples, but to destroy their sense of being people" ("Queer Theory" 59). Two-Spirit peoples questioned and disturbed the heteropatriarchal notions of the gender binary and subsequently assigned sexualities that were deemed bestial. Part of the colonial project involves dehumanizing Indigenous people by making them seem less human and closer to wild animals who need to be tamed or shot. Aimé Césaire argues that the colonizer is in fact the animal: "Colonial activity, colonial enterprise, colonial conquest, which is based on contempt for the native and justified by the contempt, inevitably tends to change him who undertakes it; that the colonizer . . . tends objectively to transform himself into an animal" (81). Ultimately, the conquering colonizer does not want the Indigenous person or nations to answer back—to claim their sovereignty and traditional ways. The colonizer wants the frontier fable to supersede a more accurate history in which Europeans are exposed as brutal, savage, and at times acting like wild animals.

In *Angel of the Medicine Show*, Jon has transformed from the confused and remorseful cowboy in *The Moon and Dead Indians* into a controlling and later sadistic showman. When he returns to the campsite, he seems most concerned that all his belongings are there: his woman, his Indian, his horse, his stage, and his props. We learn that Angela is jealous of Jon's intimate and sexual relationship with David. Throughout the remainder of the piece she tries to convince Jon to get rid of David. Jon dismisses one of these requests: "Mister Smoke's the one true reason we've had a show out here. Them yokels love to see a wild Indian dance for his keep" (88). Moses breaks script with the colonial-constructed cowboy by queering him and exposing his sanctioned greed based in a capitalist framework. Jon understands that he profits from David's performance of the frontier fable's imaginary Indian and that without him the show would not continue. Moses demonstrates that Indian shows were created by and for white people. According to Donald Kaufman, "Early Indian drama was strictly a white man's show . . . [a] minstrel show as tragedy that befitted the doomed redskin . . . [D]ozens of Indian plays kept featuring doomed chieftains . . . " (116). Moses subverts the Indian minstrel by having defeated/ghost David break script and share actual Native beliefs, which confuses and angers the white audience, leading to his near death. Ultimately, Moses demonstrates the deep fear and ignorance of Indigenous people and exposes the commodification of Indigenous people by Europeans, which extends back to the first invasion and has continued until the present day.

In many ways Jon resembles the historical figure William F. Cody, a cowboy turned showman. Cody participated in the forced removal and subsequent deaths of many Indigenous peoples and would later employ (and greatly profit from) the surviving Native people, who then performed the imaginary Indian in his Wild West shows. Jon parallels Cody's actions by killing a Two-Spirit man and then later employing a Two-Spirit man. Perhaps, like Cody, Jon feels somewhat guilty for his choices. When Angela argues with Jon to get rid of David and claims they don't need him, Jon replies, "I need him to forgive me. For what we did to the Indians" (102). Jon represents a colonial guilt over genocide and the continued occupation of Indigenous lands. According to Moses, white guilt creates tragic, romanticized Indians, where it "seems that you don't want to heal, you want to keep the wound . . . you're dancing around the wound . . . it strikes me as really sick" (qtd. in Appleford, "The Desire to Crunch Bone" 22). The guilt constructs another divide between colonizers and Native peoples. Jon does not see David as a full human worthy of respect and understanding. Instead, David is a means for Jon to feel better about himself.

This becomes only more apparent after Jon finds out that Angela is pregnant with his baby. Jon's subsequent behaviour makes Angela's earlier cruelty seem moderately kind. He wants to rehearse the medicine show the same evening David has been shot, beaten, and hanged. Jon yells, "He's just lazy. Typical. *(He drains the bottle.)* He knows we need to get to work." To which Angela replies, "Jonny, he's weak. The blood he lost—" Jon interrupts her: "A scratch. He'll be fine. *(picks up his gun belt, straps it on)*" (104). Jon's abuse and labelling of David as lazy are representative of the victim-blaming of Indigenous people for their "predicament," which is interwoven into the colonial history/memory. Indigenous people are blamed for their poverty, for any drug abuse and violence within their communities. This perspective ignores the generational effects of genocide, relocation, forced assimilation, residential schools, sexual/physical/spiritual/emotional abuse, and continued loss of land and sovereign rights. Ultimately, Jon forces both David and Angela at gunpoint to practise their show. They both "co-operate" and even don their costumes. Jon responds, "That's my girl. And he's my Indian" (107). Moses's economic word choice carries immense historic weight. Rifkin argues that heteronormative reproductivity is used as a means of legitimizing foreign occupation and control over Indigenous lands through privatization, ownership, and generational inheritance (14). Angela carries the next generation of occupiers that supports the ideology that white men own and run "North America." Embedded within the heteropatriarchy is a white supremacist and Christian ideology of white men reigning over all people of colour, women, queers, animals, and the land. In short, God made everything for Adam.

Christianity, backed by capitalism (a.k.a. manifest destiny), promotes white male ownership in which all other people serve or are exploited for his gain/comfort. The phrase "my Indian" displays the colonial project to control and subsume Native bodies: to annihilate, to violate, and to regulate all Native peoples, including Two-Spirit people.

But the colonial project has not been entirely successful, as demonstrated in *Angel of the Medicine Show*. The Two-Spirit character, David, despite being seriously injured, fights back, while the white cowboy's failures are exposed through Moses's Indigenous gaze. When Jon and Angela stumble into the wagon, David has a gun pointed at Jon and tells him to "stay away" (96). He rightly accuses Jon of being a liar and confronts Jon for leaving him to hang:

> **JON:** Baby, please, listen to me.
> **DAVID:** Piss off. I saw my blood on their boots. My blood.
> **JON:** My poor little Indian.
> **DAVID:** Fuck you.
> **JON:** You feeling wild enough?
> **DAVID:** I'll kill you first.
> **JON:** You're just sick now, baby.
> **DAVID:** You make me sick. (97)

David tells Jon he is leaving and Jon immediately offers him alcohol. David doesn't fall for his offer and fires his gun at Jon. Jon calls him a "stupid redskin" and knocks David out with the bottle (97–98). Through the creation of a queer cowboy and an "Indian" who fights back, Moses subverts colonial Wild West images. Most Wild West movies leave Native people mute, while Moses's Native character says "fuck you" to the cowboy's racist and paternalistic remarks.

The playwright also exposes the colonial tool, alcohol, as another means to regulate/dominate Indigenous peoples. Alcohol and subsequent addiction was unheard of before the European invasions of what are now called the Americas. David's line, "You make me sick," also carries enormous historical weight. Besides the obvious deaths of millions of Indigenous people from European diseases, the effects of manifest destiny/"progress"/capitalism have created an incredible imbalance in the natural world. As such, David also responds to Jon's paternal coaxing, "Don't I take care of you?" with, "The Indian can take care of his self" (101). In this way Moses exposes the frontier fable and directly responds to the centuries of colonial paternalism toward Indigenous sovereign nations. Daniel Heath Justice, Mark Rifkin, and Bethany Schneider demonstrate how paternalism was promoted by US presidents who "began describing Indians as eternally childlike, playing around the knee of a colonizing state," and how the 1831 Supreme Court ruling made Native communities "domestic dependent nations," where the US government acts as guardian (16–17). Before that Indigenous nations had existed for thousands of years in sustainable communal clans. Allen agrees with Moses: "however benevolent America's patronage has been, it was always patronage; it is still patronage. Indians don't need patronage, they need respect" (30). Indigenous people can and will continue to take care of themselves, their communities, and their land.

David's final act of survivance[3] is to burn his ghost and war-bonnet costumes and leave Jon, Angela, and the faux medicine show far behind. The fire causes part of the medicine show stage to burn, acting as a distraction as David takes off into the night. After the initial shock, Angela tries to comfort Jon: "It's better this way, Jonny. Look at me. So, he's gone now. Look at me. Your Indian's finally done the goddamn vanishing act too . . . the goddamn vanishing act you been dreaming about" (109). This is not quite the vanishing act the colonial project had in mind: "As many Native scholars have argued, colonial logic holds that Indigenous people must disappear. In fact they must *always* be disappearing in order to allow non-Indigenous people's claim over this land" (Smith, "Queer Theory" 50). Two-Spirited David demonstrates that Indigenous people have and will continue to contest colonial occupation of their bodies and their land.

Ultimately, Moses creates two potent pieces that deconstruct the frontier fable while demonstrating Native survivance and Two-Spirit resistance. The

---

3 Survival and resistance, as defined by Gerald Vizenor; see his *Manifest Manners*.

cowboy is shown as ignorant, arrogant, fearful, abusive, and lost. The hauntings do not allow the characters, nor the audience, to dismiss Native people. Moses also shows the failings of manifest destiny in both the white and Native communities. The colonial imperialist project is equated with death—death in the past, present, and future, with no end in sight. He revisits and revises "how the West was won" by demonstrating the more complex story in which cowboys are sometimes cowardly killers, sometimes gay lovers—all of whom profit from the stealing of Indigenous lands. Moses's work ripples out beyond his play and "posits a memory that forever alters the bearer of that memory and imposes a responsibility to its remembrance and its reality" (Hill). Moses's stories also bring a queer Indigenous perspective to light, wherein Two-Spirit people fight against colonization and claim their rightful place in history. Through his work and artistry, the conqueror's history begins to crack, fade, and be exposed for its fallacies, while being replaced by a more complex Indigenous story/history.

QUEER YOUTH AND THE CULTURAL POLITICS OF FAILURE IN THE WORK OF JORDAN TANNAHILL

CORDULA QUINT

> *If at first you don't succeed, failure may be your style.*
> —Quentin Crisp, *An Evening with Quentin Crisp*[1]

> *At the risk of sounding ridiculous, let me say that the true revolutionary is moved by great feelings of love.*
> —Che Guevara[2]

In her introduction to *Queer Youth Cultures* (2008), Canadian sociologist and ethnographer Susan Driver argues that beginning in the late 1990s "queer youth have become innovative participants in do-it-yourself media projects, popular culture narratives, local drag performances, anti-oppression activism, online communities, and music subcultures" (1). And yet, as Driver continues,

> their cultural practices are not classifiable as either mainstream or marginal, they are neither inside nor outside dominant cultural institutions; rather, they criss-cross commercial mass media, grassroots

---

1 Gay icon Quentin Crisp here captures a transformational shift in queer subjects from an attitude and feeling of internalized shame, abjection, and socio-cultural banishment to resilient celebration of their subjectivity. See also Halberstam, *The Queer Art* 85; Stanley, "Failure Theatre" 16; and Tannahill, *Theatre of the Unimpressed* 122.

2 As quoted in quoted Rosemary Hennessy's *Profit and Pleasure*, page 204.

> subcultural production, and activist realms [and expand] public spaces, corporeal relations, and textual forms. (1)[3]

The artistic and activist agency of Canadian theatre and film artist Jordan Tannahill is a case in point, along with that of the fictional youth characters that populate his plays and productions. Yet, as Canadian sociologist and ethnographer Gloria Filax points out, sexual minority youth also continue to be "produced through their absence or as a special area of interest, as the abject Other; that is, as a deviant outsider within the realm of youth studies" (59). Arguably, then, queer youth also tend to be less visible in Canadian theatre, and theatre and cultural studies generally speaking.

Jordan Tannahill responds to this absence. His plays delve deeply into the psyche of queer youth and expose the socio-symbolic dynamics that come to define their emerging visibility. He examines the psychological pressures that attend queer individuation and foregrounds how queer adolescence continues to be marked disproportionally by shame and hiding, harassment, uncertainty, anxiety, confusion, ambivalence, fear, defiance, threats, humiliation, rebellion, rage, yearning, and, above all, intense vulnerability. Coming out remains, for most queer youth, a gruelling rite of psychosexual passage into the margins of a heteronormative socio-symbolic order. Tannahill's award-winning plays depict the social snares and pitfalls that accompany this fraught journey out of denial and secrecy, dispelling the truism that "we've come a long way" since Stonewall. Instead, his plays reveal deeply entrenched homophobic violence that persists despite the mainstreaming of queer visibility, while also portraying the complex process of queer *becoming*, political struggle, and resilience. My study will begin with a brief survey of the thematic concerns Tannahill investigates to situate his artistic voice generally. However, his portrait of a young queer Muslim performance artist in *rihannaboi95* (2013), as well as his aesthetic and critical "manifesto" *Theatre of the Unimpressed: In Search of*

3 The term "queer youth" encompasses those who identify as lesbian, gay, bisexual, transgender, transsexual, Two-Spirit, intersexual, queer, genderqueer, and/or questioning. See also Driver 3; and Hennessy, "Queer Visibility" 34.

Vital Drama (2015), are of more central interest here. Together, these works prove particularly relevant for a discussion of queer theatre in Canada today as they explore the nexus of social, cultural, aesthetic, and material influences that inform and impact contemporary queer culture-making.

In *Late Company* (2013), a "well-made play" strongly reminiscent of Yasmina Reza's commercially successful *God of Carnage* (2006), the dramatist investigates the profound emotions and sheer incomprehension that often underpin parent-child relations when queer teenagers begin to give voice to their experience as sexual- and gender-minority youth and take their first steps at articulating queer desire. Joel Shaun-Hasting was a creative and resourceful teen who had begun to produce positive queer self-representations and was consequently victimized for it. He is absent in the play's dramatic action due to his untimely suicide, which becomes the springboard for the other characters' investigation of the reasons underlying his death—that is, their own and the community's institutionalized homophobia.

By contrast, *Concord Floral* (2014) situates queer experience on the threshold of strip-mall consumerism and the Canadian wilderness and reveals hidden queer yearnings underneath the perfected veneer of affluent and successful bourgeois family lives. More disturbing are echoes of the Holocaust that lie deeply buried in the play's portrayal of the raw and merciless cruelties that its teenage characters discharge on their unwitting victims. More centrally focused on queer themes, the three solo plays collected in *Age of Minority* explore the lives of "sublime outcasts"—"three young people backed up against walls, metaphorically and literally, who risk everything for a chance to love and be loved" (*Age* iii). In *Get Yourself Home Skyler James* (2010), Tannahill makes a compelling argument for the right to asylum of queer refugees. Inspired by the shocking murder of Barry Winchell, an infantry soldier in the US military before "Don't Ask, Don't Tell" was repealed, the play portrays the gay-baiting and violence against a young working-class lesbian and throws into relief the callous indifference up and down the chain of command of army personnel who condone it.[4] Three years later, in *Peter Fechter: 59 Minutes* (2013), the dramatist creates

4 The film *Soldier's Girl* (2003) is based on Winchell's murder.

a memory play to explore the life of a young East German bricklayer who was among the first to attempt an escape from the German Democratic Republic in 1962. His death at the age of eighteen at the hands of border patrols has become an iconic representation of Cold War totalitarianism. Effectively blending history and fiction, the play's style elegantly evokes the character's memories and present experiences as he lies bleeding to death in the notorious "death strip" of the Berlin Wall. Focused on Fechter's childhood, and especially on his family life and friendship with Helmut Kulbeik, the play only vaguely implies its exploration of queer love. The third play in *Age of Minority*, *rihannaboi95*, lays bare the intercultural and intergenerational complexities that come into play when the ethnicity and culture of first-generation immigrants clash violently with the Canadian contemporaneity of their queer sons and daughters.

Without a doubt, Tannahill's dramatic portrayals reflect the research and political advocacy of André P. Grace, who points to the continuing hardships queer youth suffer and argues that the "current spate of gay-male youth suicides in Canada and the United States . . . indicates emphatically that life can become unbearable for some sexual and gender minority youth" (128). Yet, in *Queer Youth Cultures*, Driver cautions against inscribing queer youth "within tropes of victimization and risk" and defining them "reactively against dominant systems," since this approach denies them "the chance to exceed hegemonic discursive influences" (3; see also Gonick 137). Tannahill's works are a case in point. His characters learn to negotiate a troubling social duality, where official legal sanction continues to be met with grassroots homophobic resistance "in the streets." While he investigates the adversities that attend his characters' *queer becoming*, he also emphasizes their culture-making and their ability to overcome victimization.

Notable for my discussion here is *rihannaboi95*, one of the solo plays included in *Age of Minority*. The play is inspired by the playwright's experiences as a workshop facilitator in Toronto's youth shelters (see Tannahill, *Theatre* 105–09) and responds to "the overrepresentation of queer youth of colour in the shelter system" (qtd. in Thomas). According to Tannahill, " 'many of [these youth] were coming from first-generation families . . . [and] were very religious' " (qtd. in Thomas, "Jordan Tannahill"). His purpose in writing the play was to help represent "voices [which] were not being heard on our stages" (qtd. in Thomas, "Jordan Tannahill"). While Tannahill is clearly sensitive to the privileges he enjoys as a white male author, his assumption of the voice of a non-white subject arguably falls short of resolving the social inequities that attend questions of under-representation. Nevertheless, the play exhibits the hallmarks of *resonant theatre* as he defines it in *Theatre of the Unimpressed*, where he contends that "complexity, specificity and relevance" can "together . . . be described as a play's 'rigour of thinking'" (31). Indeed, *rihannaboi95* is of interest to my discussion here because it is marked by a detailed "awareness of context, both socio-politically and in relation to broader contemporary culture" (31).

Apart from the dramatist's exposure to homeless and disadvantaged youth of colour, the play was also inspired by an event curated by Jon Davie for Toronto's former cinema and performance lab Videofag.[5] The evening's program was entitled "Sissy Boy YouTube Night" and consisted of "a dozen videos shot by preteen and teenage boys dancing and lip-synching to the pop songs of female divas" (Tannahill, *Theatre* 106). For Tannahill, there "was something intensely familiar in these videos—as if the formerly private, formational rituals of [his] own preteen queer identity were being reflected back to [him], shamelessly and publicly for the world to dissect" (Tannahill, "The New Intimacy" 10). The mostly gay male audience "saw fragile moments from [their] own queer coming-of-ages reflected back to [them] and, in an act of profound communal catharsis were able to celebrate these sissy boys, laughing with them and at [themselves]" (10). What impressed the playwright the most were their "supremely uncensored and unselfconscious expressions of persona, gender and inner desire" (10).

Not surprisingly, then, *rihannaboi95* explores the circumstances that precede someone's "escape" into the shelter system and offers us the disheartening but ultimately uplifting portrayal of the coming-out process of a young queer Muslim. The play investigates the transition queer youth make into

5 Videofag was co-founded and run by Tannahill and William Ellis in a storefront venue in Kensington Market, Toronto, from October 2012 to June 2016.

young adulthood and highlights their continuing struggle with an at times overwhelming intensity of internalized homophobia, denial, and self-hatred. Moreover, despite recent legal victories and changes in cultural and educational policies that seek to eliminate systemic discrimination, the journey toward self-affirmation is still one that many queers must undertake on their own. The process often begins in silence and social isolation. However, the play's protagonist, Sunny, incrementally overcomes this marginalization. The character's nascent, still unconscious sexuality finds at first clandestine expression in a series of YouTube videos showing him dancing and lip-synching to a handful of Rihanna songs. This allows Tannahill to delve deeply into the psychosexual roots of camp sensibility, and to reveal how the performativity of "failed style" captures the complex inside/outside tensions of queer identity. The play reveals the contingencies of queer self-formation and highlights the parodic use of heteronormative intertexts to achieve intelligibility. More importantly, Sunny's videos lay bare the socio-cultural and material conditions of queer culture-making, and of queer aesthetics generally.

Sunny lives with his family in a small, cramped apartment in Lawrence Heights, one of Toronto's first large public-housing projects. Known colloquially as the "Jungle," it is an urban area marked by population density and pervasive income inequality. At first, his queer desire is unconsciously refracted through the romantic fantasies that are embedded in the song lyrics and the performances of his pop-culture idols. When he begins making videos of his own, his mimicry allows him to assume the female subject position in heteronormative narratives of romantic love and to embody his naive quest for an *idealized femininity*: "I was watching some Rihanna videos . . . God she's so sexy . . . I just want to watch her, learn her, be her" (41). Sunny's impersonations manifest initially as an innocent and non-political desire for (sexual) self-affirmation. Given his socio-economic milieu, Sunny's experience reflects the perspective of "many lesbians and gays who have not had the social resources or mobility to insulate themselves from heteronormativity's insistence that sex equals gender" (Hennessy, "Queer" 42). For them, as Rosemary Hennessy points out, "drag has been not so much playful subversion as a painful yearning for authenticity, occasionally with brutally violent results" ("Queer" 42). Indeed, as Judith Butler posits, Sunny's videos remind us that "hegemonies of oppression . . . operate" in a Gramscian vein,

> through *rearticulation* . . . where the accumulated force of a historically entrenched and entrenching rearticulation overwhelms the more fragile effort to build an alternative cultural configuration from or against that more powerful regime . . . The citing of the dominant norm does not, in this instance, displace that norm. (*Bodies* 132–33)

The homoeroticism of Sunny's desire is initially refracted through the lens of heteronormative popular culture and only becomes gradually apparent when he reveals his attraction to one of his teachers, Ben Bailey, who proves particularly supportive and encouraging of Sunny's creative projects:

> . . . we were driving down Allen Road when Rihanna started playing and he turned it up and I could hear him listening to me listen to the song and I was listening to him listening to me and suddenly I felt like I fucking was the only girl in the world, his only student, and this was the only car, and it didn't even feel like we were driving but that we were flying through apartments, over houses, or maybe we were on a road trip and would leave the city forever. (44)

Such identifications bespeak the innocent yearnings of queer youth. They manifest an unreflected nostalgia for the alignment of the external expression of gender identity with inner desire, for "authenticity" and "being" within a heteronormative socio-symbolic context, and are ultimately contained within and by the dominant culture (see Halberstam, *Queer Art* 100).

As Butler explains in her influential argument about gender and discursive power, such yearnings derive from an illusionary *metaphysics of substance*. In *Gender Trouble*, she posits that the

> notion that there might be a "truth" of sex . . . is produced precisely through the regulatory practices that generate coherent identities

> through the matrix of coherent gender norms. The heterosexualization of desire requires and institutes the production of discrete and asymmetrical oppositions between "feminine" and "masculine," where these are understood as expressive attributes of "male" and "female." The cultural matrix through which gender identity has become intelligible requires that certain kinds of "identities" cannot "exist"—that is, those in which gender does not follow from sex and those in which the practices of desire do not "follow" from either sex or gender. (17)

As a result of the illusory "metaphysics of substance" which underpin the heteronormative mainstream, cisgender subjects are privileged at the same time as homophobia ascribes to the queer subject a *failed*, *damaged*, *incomplete*, *lost*, *abject*, and/or *inauthentic* gender identity. Indeed, in *Bodies that Matter*, Butler highlights that homophobic terror is often a "terror over losing proper gender" (238; see also 235; and Halberstam, *Queer Art* 100).

In this sense, Sunny's pop-culture daydreams and his "learning" and "being" Rihanna in his early drag performances are at first clearly an attempt to remain intelligible to himself and his online YouTube followers. He seeks to accommodate his sexual desire within the dominant socio-symbolic context surrounding him. His idealizing re-embodiments of Rihanna thus manifest his non-political yearning to be at once supremely seductive and desired. Paradoxically, however, his rearticulation of a heteronormative ideal, as Butler explains, "becomes the means by which that dominant norm is most painfully reiterated *as the very desire and the performance of those it subjects*" (*Bodies* 133; emphasis mine). Not surprisingly then, Tannahill's protagonist exhibits the psychological volatility and contradictoriness of the coming-out process, veering at times violently from vulnerability, anxiety, shame, and denial (" 'I am not a queer' . . . I was so angry but I knew I shouldn't be . . . Like I knew I wasn't gay, or at least I didn't wanna be" [47–49]) to a slowly emerging sense of pride and self-esteem, when his performances receive public approval ("By the weekend 'Only Girl' had 321 views . . . I was worth watching" [49]).

Yet the homophobia entrenched in his social milieu and the depth of Sunny's residual shame prohibit a free and open acknowledgement of his identity and desire *offline*. Going anonymously public on YouTube, in contrast, enables Sunny:

> I started making the videos longer, better, more moves, pushing harder, but still making no noise, dancing in silence, my family always just on the other side of the door. The better I made them, the more y'all watched, till it was up to like a hundred and fifty a day. I was living a total double life, like a superhero—quiet Sunny in the hoodie at the back of the class during the day . . . and then rihannaboi95, a fierce booty-shaking force of nature with five thousand views . . . the whole time living a secret under everyone's noses. (51)

Sunny's self-perception as a "fierce booty-shaking force of nature" is here deliberately contrasted with his sense of "being a failure" *offline*. Adolescence is for him marked by acute sibling rivalry and by his older brother King's corrective humiliations: "Sunny, you're a girl-boy"; "Don't stand like that, don't talk like that, you embarrass us"; "Be a man" (39). When Sunny's "secret" videos are discovered by King and shown to his family, friends, and neighbours, profound emotions are mobilized and surface violently, emotions which normally stabilize the homosocial bonds and intercultural dynamics among the men of Lawrence Heights:

> [King] starts to tell me how his friends've been beating on him for it, calling him a fag, and to get them to stop he said he's gonna help them . . . put me in my place—"They're gonna come for you, man." . . . "You don't get it, Sunny: it's the block, Serb, Bengali, Somali, all these guys, we're brothers, it's how the other blocks see us, our family, and you can't go disgracing us like this, dancing like a faggot on YouTube. You don't think about our honour? . . . *Wallahi*, so stupid. (54–55)

Here, King's threats align themselves with Butler's observation that we live in a world where performing "one's gender wrong initiates a series of punishments both obvious and indirect, and performing it well provides the reassurance that there is an essentialism of gender identity after all" ("Performative Acts" 528). In fact, Sunny's story highlights the intense interactional and performative labour that is required to reaffirm and sustain men's individual masculinity along with their homosocial bonds. Sunny's presence in the neighbourhood unsettles and subverts the *illusionary* "metaphysics of substance," which must be relegitimized through punitive interventions to ensure collective intelligibility and social cohesion (see Butler, *Gender* 16–18; McInnes and Davies 107). Thus, the men of Lawrence Heights police the gender binary in the name of their collective ethnic honour, but this ultimately bolsters the underlying theoretical assumptions that legitimize and give meaning to their privileged identity as heterosexual males (see Halberstam, *Queer Art* 100). In this sense, homophobic violence erupts to ensure the survival of heteronormative idealizations as a *substantive* and *immutable* metaphysical foundation of the extant socio-symbolic, cultural, ethnic, and political order. Eve Kosofsky Sedgwick has identified these definitional barriers as sites of a "brutally anxious will to power over the interpretation of selfhood" (qtd. in Edelman, *Homographesis* 7). In other words, King protects and endorses the men's violence as a performative *self-fashioning*, which is called into question by his younger brother's unintended and uncomfortable *becoming known as queer* among them.

These developments, however, do not prevent Sunny from growing toward queer self-actualization. He eventually moves from an initially *naive* desire to attain and embody idealized femininity toward post-metaphysical self-awareness: "I looked at myself in the mirror, like this. *Sunny does the look.* Very movie-like, very dramatic" (47). He begins to apprehend in a Butlerian vein that gender is "theatrical," an imitative and contingent structure "tenuously constituted in time [and] instituted in an exterior space through a *stylized repetition of acts* . . . a performative accomplishment." (Butler, *Gender* 140–41; see also Garber 21 and 223).

It's important to note here that Tannahill subtly differentiates between two types of drag performance. *Naive* drag participates uncritically in the perpetual miming of heteronormative gender imperatives and thereby relegitimizes the dominant socio-symbolic framework. It reflects a hopeless quest for an unattainable "authenticity." *Ironic* drag, in contrast, reflects and highlights the performer's subtly *ironic knowing* and *camp* sensibility (see also Tannahill, "The New Intimacy" 11). It inserts a playful, critical distance into the performance, a self-reflexive "attitude" in a Brechtian sense (citational acting), and thereby interrogates, subverts, and displaces heteronormative imperatives at the same time as it foregrounds its performativity. Moreover, as Hennessy contends, the performance and reception of drag is contextually determined and involves the recognition that "signs are sites of social struggle" which "ultimately leads us to inquire into the social conditions that enable and perhaps even foster the slipping and sliding of signification" ("Queer" 44). The slippages promoted by *ironic drag* manifest a queer, post-metaphysical *un*grounding, a process that opens itself to the future and gestures toward "alternative cultural configurations" (Butler, *Bodies* 131–32).

In *rihannaboi95*, the playwright carefully maps a trajectory that starts with Sunny's clandestine yearning for an idealized femininity, for "authenticity" and *being*, as well as scopophilic approval—that is, for embodied and ontologically grounded heteronormative ideals. However, he progresses toward the discovery of their performativity and cultural contingency (see also Hennessy, "Queer" 59). The process then gives way to the counterdiscursive agency of irony and the political erotics of camp sensibility. Camp, as Peter Dickinson observes in *Here is Queer*, is a "tactically deployed, politically resistant self-styling" (63; see also Evans 41). However, the political efficacy of these subcultural tactics is also marked by the ambivalence that attends all ironic discourse. While ironic drag cites, twists, and queers heteronormative gender identities and brings them "into relief as heterosexual imperatives," these imperatives are not, as Judith Butler points out, "necessarily subverted in the process" (*Bodies* 237).

Despite these discursive limits, the psychological shifts that underpin Sunny's progression from naive re-enactment to performative *camp* are also accompanied by a transition from intense vulnerability to defiance and self-confidence. When five grade-twelve boys later harass Sunny at school and ridicule his videos, "dancing right up in [his] face, acting all gay and doing Rihanna moves in [his] face," he feels exposed, but responds with a tactic of defiant resilience: "Watch them all . . . three hundred of you gave me the thumbs up, you think I care what they think?" (51). Thus, Tannahill's queer youth gradually experiences a social, psychological, and political repositioning. In his Civics and Careers class, Sunny criticizes the abusive and misogynist behaviour of Chris Brown, Rihanna's partner, and challenges women to exercise feminist agency (40). This critical insight will later enable him to politicize his queer identity and cultural praxis, online as well as off.

Following King's declaration of allegiance with the neighbourhood men, Sunny becomes a genderqueer fugitive in his friend Keira's apartment (57). From here, he streams his last YouTube appearance, which the play's audience witnesses *live* like Internet voyeurs. However, shortly before Sunny's confession reaches its conclusion, a noisy commotion is heard outside the bedroom door, and the audience thus shares in the visceral experience of the threat homophobia poses for queer subjects. Despite his fears, however, Tannahill's protagonist now experiences a *cathartic transformation* and defies his tormentors. He responds to the attack through the lens of his identification with Rihanna as a victim of domestic violence, and yet he rewrites her enabling inertia in a feminist vein in his own defense:

> It's fucking Chris Brown; he's here for me but I ain't gonna let him touch me. I'm gonna be strong. I'm gonna live tonight. I'm gonna live. And one day I'm gonna go back to Replin Road and I'm gonna walk down the block with no shame, my head held high . . . and it'd be like a music video with fireworks and a sick beat, and the boys kicking ball against the wall will stop and they'll say, "Shit, look at Sunny." . . . And all the faces in all the apartments, they'll watch . . . I'll hit each move perfect, the music blasting, tight jeans, big hair, low-cut, own it, serve it . . . we're faggots, we're weapons cocked and fully loaded—we're alive, we're alive, rihannaboi95. (58)

Importantly, the play's resolution presents the protagonist's eventual socio-symbolic emancipation not as a social fact but as his scopophilic fantasy, a defiant and utopian daydream, if you will, which envisions nothing short of a queer future of *civic co-belonging*.[6] Tannahill clearly links Sunny's dancing and drag performances to an activist energy that will now reclaim and transform the communal spaces of his "ethnic" neighbourhood, Lawrence Heights. Sunny's decision to openly "own" and "serve" his performative identity in the streets of his community intersects at once with a wide range of other social affiliations, chief among them his ethnicity and Muslim religion and culture. The play thus ends with his open struggle for visibility and legitimacy within different social constellations—his family, his block, his neighbourhood, and the intercultural brotherhood of "Serb, Bengali, Somali" to which King refers (54). His imagined "flamboyant" display of an identity which has been debased and tainted by homophobic hatred effectively manifests what Cindy Patton refers to as "dissident vernaculars," a type of discourse that, as Dickinson explains, consists of "meanings created by and in communities that are upsetting to the dominant culture precisely because speaking in one's own fashion is a means of resistance, a strengthening of the subculture that has created new meaning" (Dickinson, *Here* 62 and 203; see also Patton 148n). In this vein, the ironic hyperbole of Sunny's imagined "Sissy Boy performance" in the street also resonates with Butler's reflections on the "theatricalization of political rage" and her observation that

> the subject who is "queered" into public discourse through homophobic interpellations of various kinds *takes up* and *cites* that very term as the discursive basis for an opposition. This kind of citation will emerge as *theatrical* to the extent that it *mimes and renders hyperbolic* the discursive convention that it also *reverses*. The hyperbolic gesture is crucial to the exposure of the homophobic "law" that can no longer control the terms of its own abjecting strategies. (*Bodies* 232–33; emphasis in original)

---

6 In fact, Tannahill consistently explores scopophilia throughout Sunny's self-development toward his eventual socio-symbolic and political emancipation. The process is largely constituted by *relations of looking* (see Tannahill, *Age* 37, 47–49, and 58).

Equally important is the fact that Tannahill's portrayal echoes the long history of gay and lesbian activism and its intersection with community celebrations and dances. Sunny's final transformation begins when the bedroom door "*behind him is flung open,*" and when he "*gets up from his desk, turns the lights back on . . . begins to blast a Rihanna song [and] dances to it brashly—he gives it his all . . . He pays no attention to the open door*" (58). Here the play boldly contrasts his earlier description of surreptitious dance rehearsals and lip-synching under the covers with an unabashed demonstration of queer resilience. In "Dance Liberation," David Román defines gay club dancing as "a kinesthetic ritual of knowingness that signals the subcultural codes of queer collectivity and belonging" (384). He also contends that perhaps

> the reason that so many accounts of gay club culture read [dancing] as utopian has something to do with the idea that dance . . . does not simply forecast a possible world; it puts into motion the material bodies of queers in public spaces that were created out of political and psychological necessity. Dance signaled not the promise of gay liberation but its practice. (381)

Likewise, *rihannaboi95* merges the protagonist's development toward political struggle with a fantasy of social celebration and a utopian vision of (self-) affirmation *within* and *by* his queer *and* ethnocultural community. The play's resolution also anticipates *the future* of Sunny's culture-making, which will arguably be deployed from now on as an intentional critique of heteronormative exclusions and, as such, be politicized. His fantasy of a flamboyant claiming of the neighbourhood streets echoes the political tactics of such historical activist groups as Queer Nation which, as Hennessy observes, are/were committed to "transforming the public spaces in which a (hetero)sexualized national imaginary is constructed in people's everyday lives—in shopping malls, bars, advertising, and the media" and seized them "as a zone of political pedagogy" (*Profit* 51). Moreover, his embodied, performative activism reflects Elspeth Probyn's theory of belonging, which "returns the concept first of all to the body, that reconfigures community relations in terms of desire and power, and that encapsulates the tensions between a mode of individual existence ('being') and a fantasy of social interaction ('longing')" (*Love* 64; qtd. in Dickinson, *Here* 104).

At the same time, the dramatist foregrounds how social stratification, race, religion, and ethnicity situate queer subjects differently in mainstream society, and reveals how a lower socio-economic milieu and migrant background in particular can prove a significant barrier for queer self-actualization. Although the race and ethnocultural origin of Sunny on the one hand and his high-school teacher and his husband on the other are left somewhat ambiguous, the play highlights their differences in education, class affiliation, and sexual politics. Ben and Paul represent a professional married couple who fully benefit from Canadian law reform, in particular, the Civil Marriage Act of 2005. They are also thoroughly assimilated as "successful" middle-class citizens within contemporary commodity capitalism. Living in their new house at 14 Maplegrove, on "a winding street in North York just a few blocks from the mall," they sport a comfortable, suburban lifestyle (49). Their preferences for classical music and reading *Walrus* magazine reflect their aesthetic tastes and higher education (56). These are contrasted to the cultural life of Lawrence Heights, which is marked by TV soccer, popular music and gaming videos, as well as by youth kicking balls against the walls of their neighbourhood sport courts (48).

In this sense, Tannahill's text reveals how the social dynamics of race, class, religion, and ethnocultural origin co-determine in complex ways the degree of assimilation or marginalization of queer subjects in mainstream Canadian society. In *rihannaboi95*, he throws the disparity between the victories of queer activism, as embodied by Ben and Paul, and the discrimination and harassment suffered by Sunny starkly into relief. These inequities reveal *the limits* of a queer-rights-oriented activism that is blind and indifferent to the ways diverse queer subjects are positioned differently in relation to the legal victories that have been achieved. In particular, the playwright's mapping of class differences thus strongly resonates with Lisa Duggan's concept of *homonormativity*. In *The Twilight of Equality* (2003), she explains how the advent of post-1990 neoliberalism was accompanied by the narrowly focused, conservative sexual politics of such US groups as the Log Cabin Republicans and the Independent Gay Forum, among others, defining these politics as one "that does not contest dominant heteronormative assumptions and institutions, but upholds and sustains them, while promising the possibility of a demobilized gay constituency and a privatized, depoliticized gay culture anchored in domesticity and consumption" (50). In Tannahill's portrayal, Mr. Bailey initially encourages Sunny to participate in the "Queer Youth Video Project" (47) and later lends his laptop to his student to assist in his productions. However, this emotional and material support is instantly withdrawn when the teacher finds out about Sunny's choice to "go public" on YouTube, and when he witnesses the harassment the youth suffers at the hands of his peers. He tells Sunny that he is making himself "into a target" and that his choices could also put him (Bailey) into an "extremely compromising position" (53). He asks Sunny to return the laptop, thereby curtailing his political agency and visibility. Sunny refuses: "What the hell's the point of making art if you can't even show it to anyone?" (53). Clearly, then, Bailey's preference for exchanging queer artistic expression "discretely" within the "privacy" of their one-on-one student-teacher relationship foregrounds the limits of his political positioning. In fact, Bailey's *homonormative* agency pressures Sunny to "demobilize" and shift toward "a privatized, depoliticized gay culture anchored in domesticity and consumption," as explained by Duggan (50).

At the same time, Tannahill interrogates other inequities, in particular the material conditions of queer culture-making generally, and those of queer youth in particular. Since Sunny's videos are available on YouTube, the dramatist situates embedded queer aesthetics first and foremost in relation to the dominant popular culture surrounding them:

> You have no idea how hard it was to make a video in my apartment, everyone living on top of each other . . . The only time my family left the apartment was Saturdays . . . I only had like two hours. I set the laptop up in front of the bathtub 'cause we have this shower curtain

> with all these flowers on it that look kinda like the ones from Rihanna's video and, like, if I leaned back on the curtain like this it looked like I was lying back on the flowers like she did. And I strung these blinking Christmas lights I got from Dollarama along the curtain rod to be the fireworks and wrapped our tablecloth around me and put on this headband . . . I pressed record, climbed into the tub, and began singing to it in my head and doing the moves, exactly like Rihanna did, like so specific, singing right to Mr. Bailey in his car. (45)

Sunny's "tactical deployment" of cheap and mundane "everyday objects" (shower curtains, Dollarama electronics, tablecloth) *cites, twists, and queers* the commodity glamour of Rihanna videos and thereby throws into relief both the heterosexual and capitalist imperatives embedded in them. While the "low production values" of Sunny's videos are determined mainly by the fact that he is a teenager and by the unavailability of resources within his socio-economic milieu, their reception—that is, their critical reach and/or lack thereof—is overdetermined as much by a male/masculinist and heteronormative economy of desire and cultural production as by the social imaginary of commodity capitalism generally and the flows and penetration of marketing and advertising in diverse social spheres. Arguably, however, these material conditions help to enhance *the ironic distance* of Sunny's camp sensibility, a distance that inevitably resists the reification of the embedded cultural values. On YouTube, one of the most widely used video-sharing websites worldwide, his "dissident vernaculars" thus have the potential to intercept the uncritical consumption of popular culture along with its socio-symbolic imaginary. While the protagonist exercises "merely" a *contingent* queer resistance in a Butlerian vein, his agency nevertheless defies and destabilizes his cultural marginalization with pride.

More potent yet are the social effects the potentially global reach of YouTube has for the visibility of queer culture. In "Preaching to the Converted," written in the mid-1990s, Tim Miller and David Román reflect on a history of trivialization of gay and lesbian theatre and performance by mainstream critics and gay and lesbian audiences alike. They highlight "many dismissive responses," among which "the accusation that [queer theatre and performance were] preaching to the converted [was] perhaps the most frequent . . . Work that [was] explicitly directed toward a queer audience and performed in a community-based or queer-friendly venue [was] underattended, undervalued, and mocked . . . for its alleged naivete or predictability" (172). In contrast, the accessibility of YouTube to amateur producers like Sunny effectively emancipates his *queered* parodies to the originals (Rihanna and Beyoncé), which exist side by side within the website's socio-symbolic "universe." The cultural politics of his "failed style" can thus unfold its full transformative potential.

Not surprisingly, then, Tannahill strongly endorses theatre that engages with the Internet (*Theatre* 106–113). For him, Sunny represents "the amateur as a self-determined and enfranchised participant. It is the amateur who will inherit the twenty-first century" (113). YouTube, along with its search engines, is a powerful antidote to the risks of social isolation and ghettoization, and it helps to emancipate queer performance by "levelling the playing field" in terms of accessibility.

Moreover, the *kitsch* or *camp* style that derives from the material conditions of Sunny's culture-making exemplifies the "aesthetics of failure" Tannahill champions in *Theatre of the Unimpressed*. Inspired by the ideas of Sarah Garton Stanley, the arguments of British theatre scholar Sara Jane Bailes, and the ruminations of Judith Halberstam in *The Queer Art of Failure*, Tannahill describes "failed aesthetics" as "nothing less than a renunciation of . . . a tyranny [of perfection] imposed not only upon theatre, but upon society at large by capitalist hegemony" (118). For the dramatist, YouTube has a "humanizing potential" because it "broadly disseminate[s] narratives and experiences, particularly those of otherness" (108–09). Sunny's "failed aesthetics" represent in this sense "a powerful form of pacifist resistance to capitalism where failure, as embodied by queerness, can exist outside the market and other hierarchical understandings of success" (122; see also Halberstam, *The Queer Art* 88–89).

In contrast to Sunny's queer parodies of popular culture, however, the dramaturgical form of *rihannaboi95* rehearses neither the experimental and avant-garde "aesthetics of failure" that has inspired Tannahill's theoretical reflections, nor does it take the aesthetic risks of some of his other works, such as *Concord Floral* and *Peter Fechter: 59 Minutes*. Nevertheless, the simplicity of form that marks the dramaturgy of *rihannboi95* is of interest here and is reminiscent of Spalding Gray's autobiographical monologues. The play is performed in a bedroom and *live-streamed* over the Internet, and in this sense its "talking head" format deliberately withholds the visual pleasures of "successful" theatre in a conventional sense. Instead, it cleverly teases the threshold of liveness and mediatization. Indeed, it provokes an intriguing conceptual hybridity and challenges the audience to rethink obsolete ontological distinctions, including the simplistic opposition of the "live" and "mediatized" that preceded the advent of *live streaming* in cyberspace (see Auslander 7; and Tannahill, *Theatre* 100). More importantly, for Tannahill, *live video* inherently gestures toward the future since the Internet itself "is a study in radical liveness . . . in a perpetual state of mutation"; it manifests "the essence of performance—events in constant flux, unmade the moment of their making," a "perpetually unfolding present." It has "immersed us in a paradigm of failure—the failure of coherence, of permanence and authority" (113).

However, this quasi-utopian potentiality is at the same time counterbalanced by the historical and economic context in which it unfolds. In "Queer Visibility in Commodity Culture," Hennessy reminds us that in a capitalist society "processes of commodification pervade all social structures" (33). Moreover, "the visibility of sexual identity is often a matter of commodification, a process that invariably depends on the lives and labor of invisible others" (31). Content producers such as Sunny/rihannaboi95 allow themselves to be commodified along with the advertisements that are increasingly part of YouTube's scopophilic culture and, in this sense, exemplify a familiar tension for queer visibility between political intervention and co-option. Nevertheless, Sunny's queering of music videos inserts "gay spectacle into the centers of straight consumption" and demonstrates, as Lauren Berlant and Elizabeth Freeman posit in "Queer Nationality," that "the commodity is a central means by which individuals tap into the collective experience of public desire." For Hennessy, Sunny thereby disrupts "the heterosexual presupposition on which that desire rests" (Berlant and Freeman 164; qtd. in

Hennessy, *Profit* 52). Sunny's Sissy Boy confessions on YouTube in this sense unsettle "the spectacular organization of everyday life in commodity culture" (Hennessy, "Queer" 56) and target a youth audience with their messages.

While Tannahill is clearly influenced by queer advocates of an angry "politics of negativity," in particular Lee Edelman and Judith Halberstam (see Edelman, *No Future*; Halberstam, *The Queer Art*; and Caserio et al.), his broader cultural perspective is deeply marked by utopian thinking (Tannahill, *Theatre* 122). Although the protagonist of *rihannaboi95* appears at first unprepared for the depth of homophobia his videos will unleash ("Why they gotta hate so much, it's not like anyone is forcing them to watch . . . " [54]), his emerging artistic voice remains inflected by an inspiring resilience and a *pro-social politics* based on love, human connection, and community:

> And I know there's a lot of haters out there, posting shit like, "Only thing better than a dancing fag is a dead fag," . . . but there's like a hundred people out there who give me the thumbs up . . . so I ain't got no time for haters. I make these videos for you—whoever you are—watching in your bedrooms with the volume low down, or on your headphones, under your covers. I love you. And I need you tonight. (38)

For Halberstam, a queer aesthetics is defined by a "particular ethos of resignation to failure, to lack of progress and a particular form of darkness, a negativity" (*The Queer Art* 96). Tannahill's artistic vision, in contrast, champions love, positivity, and optimism. As Hennessy elsewhere reminds us, "the fight for social justice is not just fired by rage and indignation but is also generated from this most complex of human capacities we call 'love' " (*Profit* 204). In fact, in *Theatre of the Unimpressed*, Tannahill posits that "only by understanding what theatre truly does best, by emphasizing, promoting and celebrating the very fact of its liveness—the full, messy experience of human connection—can theatre reclaim its relevance and vitality in our mediated age" (20).[7] For him, *rihannaboi95*

7 See also his discussion of Sarah Garton Stanley's "Failure Theatre: An Artist's Statement" (*Theatre* 17).

offers audiences "an intensely communal but private experience" (107), while its aesthetics of failure makes "a profoundly optimistic and human proposal, one that reconstitutes failure as hopeful iconoclasm" (123).

Tannahill's fascination with the regenerative promise of *failure* has a rich genealogy in Western culture. In *Performance Theatre and the Poetics of Failure*, Sara Jane Bailes maps this cultural legacy and contends that "failure opens up a fruitful, tragicomic ground where subversion and resistance can be tried out or rehearsed" (3). In the same vein, Tannahill's thinking about performance is premised on the *regenerative* power of failure (*Theatre* 118). For Tannahill, theatre ought to be "a radical space of togetherness, where we become other people to unpack the complexity of being ourselves, of being human" (62). In this sense, Sunny's YouTube confessions also epitomize what Jill Dolan refers to as *utopian performatives*—"small but profound moments in which performance calls the attention of the audience in a way that lifts everyone slightly above the present, into a hopeful feeling of what the world might be like if every moment of our lives were as emotionally voluminous, generous, aesthetically striking and intersubjectively intense" (5). Indeed, the spirit of Dolan's *utopian performative* infuses queer pride celebrations generally, and Sunny's fantasy of claiming Replin Road in particular—*we're alive, we're alive, rihannaboi95.*

QUEERING GENRE AND *TRAGIC COMMUNITAS* IN MINH LY'S *GA TING (FAMILY)*

EURY COLIN CHANG

Positioned to critique the finished products heteronormativity demands, queer/disabled perspectives can help to keep our attention on disruptive, inappropriate, composing bodies—bodies that invoke the future horizon beyond straight composition.
—Robert McGruer, "Composing Bodies"

Minh Ly's *Ga Ting (Family)*, developed by **the frank theatre company** in association with Vancouver Asian Canadian Theatre, revolves around three characters mourning the death of a man named Kevin and the critical dialogue and ensuing debate between them. Hong Lee and Mai Lee are Kevin's Asian Canadian parents who are living in Toronto. They struggle with the loss of their son, who was living in Vancouver at the time of his death. Over time Kevin's parents come to realize that they did not know him as well as they had wished. Early in the play, Hong and Mai meet Matthew, Kevin's Euro Canadian ex-boyfriend, who has come to Toronto for a complexity of reasons: partly to confront the Lees with the reality of their closeted son's sexuality, but also as a way to relieve his own guilty conscience.

The remounted 2016 production—it premiered at the Richmond Cultural Centre in March 2014—of *Ga Ting* at the Vancouver East Cultural Centre was well-attended and well publicized, signalling the show's relative success.[1]

1 I saw *Ga Ting* on the afternoon of 19 March 2016 at the Vancouver East Cultural Centre. All dialogue quoted in the paper comes from the recently published play text. While the full title of the show is *Ga Ting (Family)*, I refer to the show simply as *Ga Ting* as an abbreviated form.

Christopher David Gauthier's set design offered audiences a stereotypical yet acceptable "Asian-style" family home that included rosewood coffee tables and chairs, bamboo stalks, porcelain dining ware, and a functional kitchen area complete with rice cooker and cooking utensils placed within a cleverly conceived shelving unit. The mood-appropriate lighting design by Gerald King was enhanced by a carefully constructed blend of surtitles (English when Cantonese is spoken, and vice versa), with photography and videography by Ian Chan. The play's design, however, hinged on its ability to transport audiences from present to past, and back again. Although the audience never saw Kevin Lee in the actual flesh, his photographic likeness was projected on the back wall at various moments throughout the production. Constant references to Kevin's life ensured that the deceased son and boyfriend remained an omnipresent figure.

My reading of the play, inspired by the most recent production, deals with the two questions that have lingered with me long after seeing the work. First, to what extent does the play conform to the characteristics of a tragedy of passion, a genre with a long history and clearly definable features? And, second, what does a contemporary queer-themed Asian Canadian play such as *Ga Ting* offer to the constantly evolving genre of Western tragedy? My answer to both questions coalesces around Minh Ly's foregrounding of death as a catalyst for *tragic communitas*, a term I use to describe the bonding that results across real or perceived boundaries as family and friends confront their collective duty to the deceased and to each other. Further, I suggest that tragic communitas is an umbrella term that also acknowledges the complexity and circuitous nature of the grieving process: one which is quite often exacerbated as individuals struggle with grief, anger, shame, and blame. At the same time I honour the Latin roots of communitas, drawing attention to Victor Turner's influential prioritizing of the term in the discipline of performance studies. Turner has suggested that communitas is not a homogenizing concept: "Thus, in the workshop, village, office, lecture-room, theatre, almost anywhere people can be subverted from their duties and rights into an atmosphere of communitas . . . For me communitas preserves individual distinctiveness" (45–46).

In its content, the tragic communitas of *Ga Ting* differs somewhat from that found in classic tragedy.[2] In Ly's play, tragic communitas updates the sub-genre known as the tragedy of passion by showcasing the suffering of historically marginalized characters who wrestle with love, passion, and death within a decidedly gay or queer context. This innovation, I believe, is in turn important when considering *Ga Ting* alongside the larger canon of Western tragedy, which has almost always showcased love as a heteronormative phenomenon. The tragic communitas found in Ly's play invites audiences to empathize with the range of characters by forging a deeper understanding of shared grief across gender, sexuality, age, and cultural background. At the same time, the play features the patriarchal Hong's psychical difficulty in admitting his son's sexuality while allowing Matthew into his family's grieving process. By retaining some of the characteristics and familial structure of Western tragedy but instead placing characters within a decidedly queer and intercultural context, Ly exposes the limits with which classical tragedy, writ large, can be judged to represent universal human experience. No doubt, tragic communitas can also refer to relationships fostered amidst social disasters and mass death; however, this essay focuses more specifically on the dramatic representations found in Ly's portrait of a fictional family, knowing well that such representations have impacts on theatrical audiences and their understanding of people in the "real world."[3]

This essay unfolds in three parts. In the first section I begin my argument by drawing attention to overarching definitions of Western tragedy and how *Ga Ting* operates within this genre. In the second, I trace how the play's three principal characters experience intimately connected emotions such as grief, anger, and love. Finally, in the third section, I explore how shame

---

2 Classic, Western tragedy, whether Greek or Shakespearean, is noted for its focus on the lives of royalty, nobility, and/or the upper classes. Canonical works such as *King Lear*, *Antigone*, *Oedipus*, and *Romeo and Juliet* are a few examples in this genre where love relationships are decidedly heteronormative in nature.

3 Tragic communitas can also refer to the gathering and efforts of grieving people in the aftermath of events such as the mass shooting at the Pulse nightclub; Hurricane Harvey's storm and floods; and, closer to home, forest fires that ravaged parts of Western Canada.

impacts same-sex relations, a phenomenon that further complicates my belief in tragedy as a complex and evolving form. I conclude by exploring the efficacy and limitations of the *Ga Ting* play text and production, which unfolds by and large as a transformative vehicle for its diverse characters while working uneasily within the well-trodden narratives found in both tragedy and queer theatre. With this approach, the essay seeks to highlight *Ga Ting* as a progressive play that queers the Western tragedy of passion, updating it both structurally and thematically while drawing attention to an Asian Canadian family in stages of grief.

PART ONE: TRAGEDY OF PASSION

Ga Ting has been variously described as a family portrait and a gay drama that explores the politics of identity. In her review of the play, Erika Thorkelson questions the ways in which identity issues are brought into theatre: "Do you make a kind of surrealist pastiche of a Ted Talk and sketch comedy as in *The Gay Heritage Project*... Or do you put characters into a room and see what happens over dinner as in Ayad Akhtar's *Disgraced*?" Other reviewers used various adjectives to describe Ly's debut script. In his newspaper review, titled "Playwright Minh Ly Uses Family Portrait in *Ga Ting* to Reflect Realities of Being Gay and Asian," Colin Thomas draws attention to the play's nuanced complexity: "In *Ga Ting*, Ly explores homophobia within the Asian-Canadian community... *Ga Ting* also examines racism within the gay community... And, just by existing, *Ga Ting* challenges the pervasive whiteness of Canadian theatre." It remains important to note that *Ga Ting* is the Cantonese word for family; the play illuminates the aftermath of familial loss, demonstrating the tragic consequences of discrimination toward queer love, especially when denied or left unexamined.

At this point, it seems quite necessary to position the *Ga Ting* play text and production as part of a larger and more established sub-genre known as the tragedy of passion. Before delving into the play's characterizations, I want to first draw attention to the ways in which Western tragedy has been defined over time. In *Fools of Time*, Northrop Frye delineates tragedy into three categories, each involving themes of order, passion, and isolation respectively:

> There is, first, a social tragedy, with its roots in history, concerned with the fall of princes. There is, second, a tragedy that deals with the separation of lovers, the conflict of duty and passion, or the conflict of social and personal (sexual or family) interests. And there is, third, a tragedy in which the hero is removed from his social context, and is compelled to search for a purely individual identity. (16)

Elaborating further, Frye finds precedents for these categories in the Western theatrical tradition. He deftly observes, "In Greek drama, these tragic structures might be called the Agamemnon type, the Antigone type, and the Oedipus type" (16). Frye also connects the second Antigone-type tragedy with a subsequent Elizabethan counterpart, known as "the tragedy of the sacrifice of the son" (16). It seems as if these recurring elements—separation of lovers, conflicts of duty, the sacrifice of the son—are to be found in many renowned works of tragedy, both classic and contemporary. In Sophocles's play *Antigone*, the "tragedy of the sacrifice of the son" unfolds as Creon speaks of Oedipus's sons and his nephews:

> Eteocles fought for the city, and for it he died . . .
> As for his blood brother, Polyneices by name,
> He broke his exile, he came back hungry for our blood,
> He wanted to burn his fatherland and family gods . . .
>
> No one in Thebes may bury him or mourn for him.
> He must be left unburied. May birds and dogs
> Feed on his limbs, a spectacle of utter shame. (9)

While it remains beyond the scope of this paper to engage in a comparative analysis between Paul Woodruff's translation of *Antigone* (2001) and *Ga Ting*, it is worth noting that both plays embrace narratives that clearly manifest

Frye's definition of tragedy. In both plays there is a separation of lovers; a conflict of duty and passion; a conflict of social and personal, sexual and family interests; and a sacrifice of the son. In *Antigone* there is a separation between the title character and her fiancé, Haimon. Similarly, in *Ga Ting*, there is a physical and literal separation between the deceased character, Kevin, and his ex-boyfriend, Matthew. As such, it is interesting to consider *Ga Ting* as an "*Antigone*-type" tragedy of passion manifesting within the twenty-first century: reincarnated, as it were, as a resonant queer and inclusive model tragedy. While I am not suggesting that Minh Ly has consciously emulated the Western classic structure simply for effect, an examination of similarities and differences between *Ga Ting* and its predecessors reveals tragedy as a flexible and evolving genre.

Why should a contemporary play, often discussed as queer or Asian Canadian, be placed among more notable Western classics? In my critical reading and reception of *Ga Ting*, I reference *Antigone* alongside a textual and performance analysis strewn through theatre and scholarly theory to understand the play's intersectionality. Jacqueline Lo and Helen Gilbert believe that "the increasing significance of cross-cultural theatre both within the academy and the performing arts industries in the West demands that this practice be critically situated within a historicized and politicized configuration" (31). By positioning a queer-themed Canadian play within the dramatic continuum of Western tragedy, it is possible to challenge preconceived notions of genre. In her book *Antigone's Claim*, for example, Judith Butler draws a connection between modern kinship and Greek legacy: "This is a time in which kinship has become fragile, porous and expansive. It is also a time in which straight and gay families are sometimes blended . . . What will the legacy of Oedipus be for those who are formed in these situations?" (22–23). Addressing notions of modern kinship within Western idioms need not be limited to the concerns of strictly bourgeoisie and/or heteronormative protagonists. Playwrights like Ly are responding, however directly or indirectly, to Butler's astute queries by infusing cross-cultural conflict and queer identity into larger, idiomatic frameworks such as tragedy. As any overview of tragic genre reveals, such works are also marked by a common and recurring feature: the death of a family member or lover. This recurring feature anchors the sub-genre with a sense of familiarity and *gravitas*.[4] I return to this topic more specifically in the following sections as they pertain to Minh Ly's play.

Here, I take up the second question I have in response to *Ga Ting*: How does a contemporary queer-themed Asian Canadian play allow the genre of Western tragedy, more generally, to contemporize from within, evolving the form in new and unexpected ways? In setting up my response to this question, I recall Nicholas Birns's comments on how Butler "queers" classical Greek tragedy:

> There is nothing explicitly "queer" in Butler's reading of *Antigone* in that nothing in the play relates literally to same-sex relations. But Butler's questioning of what it means to be an individual and a society partakes of the destabilizing effect of queerness, of its creative ability to imagine new relations (and give fresh readings of texts). (269)

Whereas Butler uses contemporary queer theory to unpack fresh readings of an age-old, classic play, I instead look backward, referencing the lofty traits of Western tragedy to better contextualize *Ga Ting*, suggesting that preconceived notions of genre can be challenged and, ultimately, revised through new iterative love relationships. *Ga Ting* unfolds as a queer-themed family tragedy—premised on a shared grieving process and tragic communitas—in which differences in the characters' genders, ages, sexuality, and cultural backgrounds, far from being negated, are actively engaged and openly acknowledged as the plot unfolds. Ly's play effectively transforms the heteronormative frame of reference which has characterized the Western sub-genre of tragedies of passion for centuries.[5]

4 In Sophocles's Theban plays, the wives of both Oedipus and Creon commit suicide; similarly, both "lovers-to-be" Antigone and Haimon commit suicide. In *Ga Ting*, the lovers are also separated, and though it is not certain that Kevin has committed suicide, such a reading is possible as his death is shrouded in mystery and seemingly could have been avoided.

5 Many classic tragedies from Greek to Elizabethan theatre position love relationships as heteronormative, whether Oedipus and Jocasta, Antigone and Haimon, Macbeth and Lady Macbeth, or Romeo and Juliet.

PART TWO: GRIEF, ANGER, AND LOVE

In order to understand how tragic communitas operates within *Ga Ting*, it seems necessary to look to Kevin's death, observing the circuitous unfolding of grief in the play. Most, if not all, cultures around the world honour the deceased, whether that homage takes the form of cremation, funeral, memorial, and/or celebration of life. Though cultural practices differ from culture to culture, a common and undeniable feature of grief-stricken events is the presence of family and friends. Earlier, I proposed a concept of tragic communitas that alluded to the gathering of individuals during shared grief, despite differences in either opinion or world view. As such, the death of Kevin Lee in *Ga Ting* obviously becomes a catalyst for tragic communitas between Hong, Mai, Matthew, and the audience. The public display of emotion recurs within most Western tragedy and is also necessary for the Lee family: accepting Kevin's queerness is pertinent to the realities of the situation and to grieving over the person *he actually was*, not *how he should have been*. What is most troubling and perhaps tragic about the discussions that unfold between Hong, Mai, and Matthew is the fact that Kevin's sexuality is never fully acknowledged; as such, his parents grieve over an idealized, estranged son whose very identity they have not yet fully embraced. Hong's denial thwarts any reconciliation between him and Matthew, causing unexpected and unnecessary conflict. As Butler has stated:

> After all, if someone is lost, and that person is not someone, then what and where is the loss, and how does mourning take place . . . This last is surely a question that lesbian, gay, and bi-studies have asked in relation to violence against sexual minorities. (*Precarious Life* 32)[6]

---

6 Various kinds of violence are thrust upon sexual minorities. During the span of writing this paper, a number of violent events took place in the United States. On 12 June 2016 an armed gunman killed forty-nine individuals and injured fifty-eight more at a gay nightclub, Pulse, in Orlando, Florida. As part of his ongoing attempt to conquer and divide, President Trump tweeted the following message on 26 July 2017: "After consultation with

In *Ga Ting*, Minh Ly develops a situation whereby Kevin's funeral is described by Hong and Mai but audiences never get to see the gathering as it takes place before the play starts. We hear that Matt was not invited to the funeral despite the fact that it would have given him a space to mourn publicly: "Just because I'm not blood, doesn't mean I didn't love him. I called and called . . . left messages . . . sent you a letter about Kevin I wanted to share at the funeral. I tried to find out what was going on, but no one got back to me" (33). In this scene, the boyfriend pushes for an answer, expressing his own discontent over being excluded. He opens up to Kevin's parents, letting them know what he feels about the situation: "Kevin's funeral was my chance to say goodbye to him, and you couldn't give me that" (33). Soon thereafter, the father, Hong, responds with equal frustration: "You have no idea what we go through. You only think what you want. What you think is right. You give money for funeral? You organize everything? You raise Kevin from baby to big man? You know him two, three years. That is all" (34). The scene reveals the father's frustration, and his status and duty to his deceased son, which at first glance seems quite altruistic and *natural*. And yet this imperfect moment seeks to respond to Butler's question, *how does mourning take place*? The results of Matthew's exclusion are deeply felt and set the stage for another kind of grief in the play: that resulting from Hong's stark homophobia. Mai, in her own response, speaks alternately to her husband and then to her deceased son's boyfriend: "**We should have invited him.** *(Beat.)* Matthew, when Kevin died, it was all too much, we cannot handle. Too much family visit already. But tomorrow . . . if you want, we can take you to cemetery" (34).[7] In this moment the formation of a tragic communitas can be seen and felt as the mother offers this meaningful gesture to Matt, who responds, "I would like that" (34).

---

my Generals and military experts, please be advised that the United States Government will not accept or allow . . . Transgender individuals to serve in any capacity in the U.S. Military."

7 As indicated in *Ga Ting*'s published play text, any bold-lettered dialogue found in the script is spoken in Cantonese, with corresponding English surtitles projected on the back wall of the stage. To keep with this tradition, I retain the bold lettering to show readers when Cantonese text is spoken on stage.

The importance and opportunity for Matthew to mourn publicly, alongside Kevin's family, cannot be overstated; this applies not only to seeing real-life subjects mourn but can also be applied to seeing the dramatization or fictional representations of historically marginal subjects as they mourn publicly within the dominant heteronormative culture. In addition to Butler, theatre scholars have written specifically on the importance of recognition and mourning. In his article "Brothers' Keepers, or, The Performance of Mourning: Queer Rituals of Remembrance," Peter Dickinson addresses the complex issue of large-scale memorialization and how the public recognition of groups is often resourced differently depending on the deceased individual's sexual orientation, cultural background, class, or gender. While Dickinson's scope is much broader than the dramatic case studies presented here, I draw attention to his research to reveal a cognate argument and larger phenomenon: heteronormative society's seeming hesitance and ambivalence toward mourning or honouring the death of marginalized people. Within this group, a marginal status may be applied to particular members of the queer community, or those who die under suspect circumstances such as suicide. Recently, a growing body of literature has focused on queer-related grief, even though Butler acknowledged the gap as early as 1990 in *Gender Trouble*: " . . . there has been little effort to understand the melancholic denial/preservation of homosexuality in the production of gender within the heterosexual frame" (78).

As the mother character in *Ga Ting*, Mai is portrayed as honest and empathetic, acting carefully as a mediator between her husband—a dogmatic figure of patriarchy and heteronormative prejudice—and the son's ex-boyfriend, who seeks to release himself from his own guilt over being absent the night Kevin died. By contrast, Hong comes across as belligerent, claiming to speak on behalf of his family, despite his wife's noticeably different point of view. On the surface, the verbal conflict seems reminiscent of a game of machismo, one that keeps Hong and Matt warring and apart. However, Ly's characters eventually begin to change and evolve. By the play's end, Hong, Mai, and Matthew's collective grief becomes a shared endeavour, and despite their initial difference of opinion, all three begin asking each other what they could have done to prevent Kevin's death. As noted earlier, Turner's communitas is comprised of individuals, each with his or her distinct social role. As such, tragic communitas is sustained through an uneasy tension between individuals following a death, then realized over the desire for common ground. Mai, Hong, and Matthew gradually form a bond as they relive and seek to deeply understand the events leading up to the loss of their loved one.

In *Ga Ting* the funeral allows the family members to begin their process of mourning, and in the scenes that follow I cannot help but feel the heavy weight of the parents' loss. Ly's dialogue suggests that the parents deal with their son's loss with a sober tone, gesturing toward a familiar and quiet process that often accompanies grief. By contrast, Matt's grief seems exacerbated by a type of confusion and exclusion from the family funeral—this fact provokes me to think about the friends of the deceased man, who were also denied the dignity of participating in this important event. It seems important to note that Minh Ly has publicly identified himself as a queer playwright; as such, the representation of this awkward situation does not unfold in a stereotypical manner, but instead gestures toward a reality and the consequences of queer exclusion. As a character Matthew is seen as somewhat proactive, opinionated, and intent on expressing his respect and grief over his ex-boyfriend's passing. He does so by proposing to host a celebration of life back in Vancouver. Matthew has come from Vancouver to Toronto with the hope of securing a blessing from Kevin's parents, in turn, requesting a letter of comfort from Hong and Mai that could be read aloud for invited guests. Matthew suggests that such a gesture would prove meaningful for Kevin's close circle of friends, many of whom are part of the gay community. On the surface it may seem suspect for an ex-boyfriend to make such demands from Kevin's parents, but upon closer inspection the request carries significance for Matthew:

> **MATTHEW:** I'm planning to have a memorial for Kevin when I get back to Vancouver.
> **HONG:** A memorial?
> **MATTHEW:** We didn't really get a chance to say good-bye. It's an opportunity for everyone to say their farewells . . . have a bit of closure.

> **MAI:** Oh.
> **MATTHEW:** Nothing big, at a local art studio. Just a bunch of his friends. Everyone would love to hear a bit about Kevin from his parents. I was hoping you could write a few words for me to share. *Beat.*
> **MAI:** Yes.
> **HONG:** No. (59)

At this key moment, the father's deliberate "no" attempts to thwart Matt's event-planning, revealing a highly patriarchal viewpoint and the tragic consequences of homophobia. This conflict between Hong and Matt places Mai in an uncomfortable yet important mediatory position, testing and exacerbating the tragic communitas in the play. Matthew's desire to host a celebration of life for Kevin never falters, even while he is caught between Mai's "yes" and Hong's "no," revealing the playwright's interest in reconciliation and transformation.

Ly's focus on familial and social reconciliation can be understood as a portal into the characters' flawed but necessary grieving processes. When Hong denies Matthew and Kevin's friends the right to mourn publicly, I am reminded that tragedy is always populated by grief-stricken subjects, and by extension queer protagonists in contemporary tragedy are often characterized by violent and unnatural deaths. I return to the tension between tragedy's public grief and the politics of queer death and its reception at the end of the paper. Meanwhile, I draw attention to Butler's observation on where and whom grief is placed depending on one's positionality. In *Precarious Life*, she writes, "I am as much constituted by those I do grieve for as by those whose deaths I disavow, whose nameless and faceless deaths form the melancholic background for my social world, if not my First Worldism" (46). Hong and Mai Lee are portrayed as accented immigrants who have come to Canada, a First World nation, to build a life for their family. Ironically, Hong's disavowal of his son's queerness upholds a heteronormativity and the First World hierarchies that intensify the family's melancholic grieving process. I read Hong's "no" to Matthew's request as the result of indoctrination and social conditioning, whereby hard work, sacrifice, and marriage are necessary for a successful life. Matthew often finds a strong, willing ally in Kevin's mother, while the father remains tightly bound and at odds with his son's sexual orientation. Even when Mai has agreed to supply a statement that could be used at her son's forthcoming celebration of life, Hong refuses any involvement: "I want no part of this," he says, even going so far as to accuse Matthew of wrongdoing: "It is for you. You want my son to be someone not normal" (61).

This accusation, perhaps more than any other statement in the play, portrays the father as having an issue with his son. The equation of queerness with abnormalness and straightness with normality are reiterated by Hong's actions and words, to the dismay of the other characters. During one of the staged flashbacks Hong questions his son's creative impulses: "**Painting? How would you pay for rent and food? . . . You don't know how hard the real world is. You think not being afraid is enough? Huh? How will you raise a family?**" *(Beat)* (44). The father seems ignorant about his son's sexual orientation, assuming that Kevin would automatically take the role of a husband and father. Elsewhere, Hong expresses the view that his son's sexuality was correctable: "I would have help him . . . there are doctors . . . " (63). Hong's blatantly prejudiced beliefs harken back to the days when homosexuality was pathologized by individuals working in medicine and the legal professions.[8] To refute Matthew's desire to host a celebration of life, Hong conjures this historical pathologization of same-sex desire: "It is for you. You want my son to be someone not normal" (61). At times the parents seem overprotective at worst, and well-intentioned at best, but Hong's excessive, heteronormative beliefs create a friction with Matthew while negating Kevin's true sexuality. As mentioned earlier, Kevin wanted to become an artist, and according to Hong this was not an ideal choice, especially for someone expecting to raise a family. Together, Hong's disavowal of his son's creative pursuits (painting), mental health (bipolar disorder), and sexual orientation (queerness) are inextricably linked to the father's obsession with socially constructed notions of *normalcy*.

8 In his book, *Homosexual Desire*, Guy Hocquenghem explains how same-sex desire has been pathologized by institutional structures over time: " . . . psychiatry tends to replace legal repression with the internalisation of guilt. But the passage of anti-homosexual repression from the penal to the psychological stage has never actually brought about the disappearance of the penal aspect" (67).

As an augmentation to ideological differences between the parents and the boyfriend, the playwright offers a unique moment for Mai to show her internal grief and rage. The stage directions suggest that "Mai intentionally smashes the platter of mango pudding on the ground" (74). In the Vancouver production, the actor held the bowl of pudding high above her head before smashing it into pieces, at which point the audience gasped deeply in mutual shock and sorrow. The smashing sound echoed through the black-box theatre, punctuating the argument between Mai, Hong, and Matt with a poignant full stop. The very act of smashing the porcelain bowl offered a kinetic and aural metaphor to the common phrase *picking up the broken pieces*, one often used to describe individuals dealing with a great loss. As such, the production rendered the mother's grieving process literally and figuratively, offering audiences a palpable, physical metaphor that commented more broadly on the strained relationships between the three principal characters.

Displays of grief are common in Western tragedy, and placing *Ga Ting* within this evolving tradition, even briefly, becomes revealing. Once again, I return to two classic examples to show how the loss of a son, daughter, or spouse is historically linked to heightened emotional distress and tragic communitas. Not unlike Mai's grief over losing her son, the title character in Shakespeare's *King Lear*—obviously more regal and lofty than Mai, but also not coincidentally as dogmatic in his patriarchy as Hong—is seen in his most vulnerable state as his only loyal daughter remains lifeless in his arms: "And my poor fool is hanged: no, no, no life? / Why should a dog, a horse, a rat, have life / And thou no breath at all? / Thou'lt come no more, / Never, never, never, never, never" (86). Lear's grief intensifies the moment he realizes he has lost what is *most* important: not his kingly status, but his very own beloved kin. Similarly, in Sophocles's *Antigone*, the title character becomes remorseful over her broken family: "I've had no man, no wedding celebration, shared nothing with a husband, never raised a child. My friends and family have abandoned me in misery . . . What have I ever done against divine justice? How can I expect a god to help me in my misery?" (39). In all three plays—*Ga Ting*, *King Lear*, and *Antigone*—a loss of a family member provokes mourning and a sense of reflection. In both classic and contemporary examples mentioned previously, I cannot help but notice how each of the characters left standing also experience a complex mixture of nostalgia and remorse, whereby death becomes a catalyst for emotional release and personal and familial transformation. Taking these ideas into consideration, I see *Ga Ting* as a contemporary tragedy that maintains the key trait of the genre, which is arguably the staging of private grief, an otherwise secret family affair, and the opening of that process to the gaze of public consumption.

Reflection plays a big part in evoking empathy from the audience; in *Ga Ting*, the simple act of sharing a meal, especially in Kevin's absence, becomes profoundly ritualistic and haunting. After eating together and arguing over a number of differences, Matthew offers Mai and Hong one of Kevin's paintings, which he brought from Vancouver as a gift:

> Kevin wanted you to know how good he was. There was this abstract piece of Toronto and Vancouver he did a few months after we met. His *heart* really was in both cities. It was the first time I realized how talented he was. Kevin's *love* for his work was contagious . . . he inspired me to do more of what I *loved.* (48; emphasis mine)

In this passage the multiple references to "love" and "heart" reveal a vital relationship between memory, nostalgia, love, and grief. I believe the play is at its strongest when it makes this revelation. Such firm declarations of same-sex love and loss, intimately rendered in the privacy of a family home and nestled within the highly familiar structure of tragedy, offer a counterpoint to mass-mediated, heteronormative, or phallogocentric portrayals of love. It is also important to note that while Ly pushes against the boundaries of the genre, there is also an adherence to the Western mode of acting that invites a particular kind of reception, as least when it comes to reading emotions. In the US, for example, emotional realism is often portrayed through a brand of method acting, and while I would not characterize the Canadian actors in *Ga Ting* as strictly model "method actors," the portrayal of life unfolding behind a fourth wall is "method-like" with strikingly similarities to many family dramas found on stage. While Ly's characters are rendered differently, as queer and immigrant figures, they are also foregrounded in a manner that creates empathetic identification. This is important since "dramatic roles performed through the emotionality of method acting thus hold the potential to create connections that recognize differences and similarities in relation to a *wider racial matrix*" (Rogers 430; emphasis mine). In addition to classic tragedy, I argue that representations found in popular cinema are severely limited when it comes to portraying the emotionality of queer love or love not regularly affiliated with the dominant race, class, gender, or sexuality. This makes the immigrant parents' love for their son (despite Hong's learned patriarchy) alongside Matthew's same-sex love for Kevin increasingly important, as the juxtaposition gives focus to the *wider racial matrix* as well as a sexual diversity and intimacy not seen enough on stage.

Now might be a good time to comment on how *Ga Ting* speaks to local and national realities. The action of the play unfolds in Toronto and Vancouver, respectively, which is perhaps not surprising given the playwright's personal and professional connection to both cities.[9] Although the play has only had professional productions on the west coast, the reception was clearly framed by the demographic reality of both cities, which boast large numbers of Asian Canadians and robust, visible queer communities. Through its focus on private and public grieving, *Ga Ting* offers a unique perspective on death and family loss: one that expands the characterizations and content often found in tragedy. Ly's portrayal of an immigrant family and their son's queer boyfriend is refreshing and unique, forging an uneasy but plausible tragic communitas.

PART THREE: SHAMING AND BLAMING

As the patriarchal figure of an immigrant family, Hong expresses an ignorant, dogmatic belief mildly reminiscent of that often espoused by right-wing

9 Minh Ly was raised in Toronto but moved to Western Canada to study at the renowned Studio 58 Conservatory Actor Training Program at Langara College. The play was developed in Vancouver, through a number of dramaturgical programs and residencies, namely QWest & Clean Sheets (**frank theatre**) and MSG Lab (Vancouver Asian Canadian Theatre).

religious groups, one which connects homosexuality with sinful behaviour.[10] The presence of contrarian viewpoints addressed within a decidedly intercultural and same-sex context clearly differentiates *Ga Ting* from other forms of tragedy. But if familial grief is a primary characteristic of tragedy, I would argue that shame follows as a close, interrelated secondary characteristic. In particular, historically (and currently) marginalized communities often face shame as a legacy and consequence of their exclusion from social definitions of normalcy. In some regards, the presence of shame exacerbates the grieving process, adding yet another complication to the formation of tragic communitas. As mentioned earlier, Hong has attempted to deny Matthew the right to host a celebration of life, and soon afterward he subsequently blames his very own wife for their son's sexual orientation:

> **HONG:** Two men should not be together like that. *(to MAI)* **That song make him gay.**
> **MAI: What are you talking about?**
> **HONG: That rainbow song, that gay song you sing all the time is what made him gay.** (61)

Even though the bolded text is spoken in Cantonese during the live production, the presence of English surtitles projected on the back wall ensured the comedic moment was not lost. Audiences at the CULTCH's intimate black-box theatre, some from the local gay community, shared a collective laugh at the father's ignorance, but the moment was still discomforting and awkward to watch; "that gay song" was a reference to "Somewhere Over the Rainbow" (which Judy Garland made famous in her starring role as Dorothy in *The Wizard of Oz*). Hong's comment reveals how homophobia might unfold within an Asian Canadian family while poking fun at stereotypical gay men

---

10 Although not popular, religious groups such as the Westboro Baptist Church (WBC) have picketed or threatened to picket at the location of queer-themed shows such as *The Laramie Project*. Additionally, the WBC operates the website www.godhatesfags.com, which outlines their intended picketing schedule.

who *love* musical theatre. At times Hong treats Matthew in a similar fashion to how he treats his wife, blaming him for Kevin's sexual orientation:

> **HONG:** So, can you blame me to want to give my son an easier life?
> **MATTHEW:** No . . . but you can't make a gay man straight.
> **HONG:** You make my son gay.
> **MATTHEW:** How?
> **HONG:** How I know? I not gay.
> **MATTHEW:** This is ridiculous. I can't—wow. (63)

Mai tries to reconcile this moment by saying "Mr. Lee need time" (63).

Through Matthew's testimonial and flashbacks set within the play, the audience members manage to ascertain the kind of relationship Kevin had with his parents. In the scenes that follow, it becomes clear that Kevin died quite unexpectedly and that Mai needs to know exactly what happened the night of her son's death. The father, by contrast, keeps many of his feelings closer to the heart and decides that Matthew cannot tell the parents anything that they don't already know. Near the end of the play, Matthew and Hong are seen on the outdoor patio together, sharing a cigarette and moment of male bonding. In the production, the men stood close together, commiserating through their feelings. This scene is in contrast to the rest of the play, where the family is sitting around the kitchen table wrestling over their grief.

Matthew confronts Hong's denial over Kevin's sexuality, and, in doing so, reveals how the father's acceptance is linked to the larger resolution: "Pretending. When Kevin was alive you were pretending everything was fine. Him being bi-polar, your relationship with him, his sexuality. And now . . . with me, you're just trying to fake it to make Mai happy. Why can't you just talk to me?" (69).

My interpretation of this patio scene becomes clearer with Matthew's final, pressing question. In this moment Matthew becomes the voice of the gay community as well as his deceased boyfriend, begging for a better dialogue and communication between himself and the parents. The patio scene demonstrates how tragic communitas unfolds after death, especially as differences between grieving parties persist. For me, the most compelling aspect of Ly's play lies in the very personal and ordinary way that Mai, Hong, and Matthew wrestle over Kevin's loss and sexuality. I believe the playwright offers signposts to suggest that the mother's desire for reconciliation and dialogue, and Matt's final question to Hong, are alternative ways to overcome the distance and harm created by strict patriarchal beliefs expressed throughout most of the show.

The characters' ability to grieve, and their acceptance of Kevin's sexuality within a forced and shameful history of exclusion, influence the formation of tragic communitas, marking the latter as more processual than terminal. I look to theorists to better understand this phenomenon and Julia Kristeva's insights on disability can be readily applied to Kevin's family and boyfriend:

> [T]he disabled person opens a *narcissistic identity wound* in the person who is not disabled; he inflicts a threat of *physical* or *psychical death*, fear of collapse, and, beyond that, the anxiety of seeing the very *borders of the human species* explode. And so the disabled person is inevitably exposed to *a discrimination that cannot be shared.* (29; emphasis in original)

Ly's dialogue suggests that his parents have made sincere attempts to love and support their son's plight even though they seem misguided at times. However, more often than not, Mai and Hong also seem unaware of how Kevin's bipolar disorder and sexual orientation have impacted his relationship with them. Kristeva's definition has interpretive value for *Ga Ting* since the father's homophobic attitudes toward his queer, disabled, and artistic son represent a "narcissistic identity wound" which is constantly thrust back upon his wife and Matthew, who share a sense of guilt over Kevin's demise. At the same time, audiences never see Kevin in the flesh, and so I concur with Kristeva, concluding with the belief that the deceased character must have experienced a level of discrimination, grief, and shame that remains immeasurable, despite its dramatic palpability.

In an essay on the film *As Good As It Gets*, Robert McRuer suggests that "disabled, queer figures no longer embody absolute deviance but are still visually and narratively subordinated, and sometimes they are eliminated outright" ("*As Good*" 87). Indeed, the disabled, queer figure of *Ga Ting* was not only narratively subordinated but physically eliminated: his body and funeral were never seen on stage. Kevin's elimination was countered only moderately as the live production included multimedia imagery and photos of Kevin during some of the flashback scenes. McRuer's belief that queer characters no longer "embody absolute deviance" gestures toward an evolution in social attitudes, and yet, Kristeva's belief that the disabled person "inflicts a threat of *physical* or *psychical death*" on those around him or her retains its suggestive power. Kevin's presence is not only eliminated in *Ga Ting*, he is deceased before the actual play begins. After speaking with Ly after the show, I learned that the choice to remove Kevin as an onstage character was not his initial impulse, but the result of a suggestion that arose during the dramaturgical process. I believe that the very act of removing Kevin as a speaking character has both positive and questionable effects on the play's outcome. Kevin's absence means that his character is heard and mitigated through the lens of his parents and ex-boyfriend, and while it was fascinating to watch as Matthew, Hong, and Mai wrestle through their differences and shared loss, it becomes increasingly difficult to understand Kevin's plight in his physical absence. It could be said that I empathized with those that lost their beloved but remain ambivalent or unclear of the struggles of the deceased. Further, it would be too presumptuous to say that Kevin committed suicide or died under mysterious circumstances simply because he felt alienated from his family or society. While the general circumstances of his life are revealed, for the most part, Kevin's deep pain and struggles are left unseen. The nuances of his fraught personal journey remain a puzzle that only the mother seems intent on solving or unravelling.

I cannot help but notice that queer-themed plays (and films) seem to feed expectations for the predetermined death of their protagonists. In short, most queer protagonists, by some turn of events, are often killed off by the end of the story.[11] My minor criticism of *Ga Ting* revolves around its logic: I question why Matthew has broken up with Kevin before his death and further why Mai only thinks of him as a "friend" and not as Kevin's significant other. In the published play text there is no mention that Kevin and Matthew were common-law or committed for life, and while this does not justify Matthew's exclusion from Kevin's funeral, the stakes seem low. Given these facts, my empathy for Matthew (the only queer voice) often feels unwarranted and unstable and might have been strengthened had both men been living together at the time of Kevin's death, or if Matt had already met with Kevin's parents prior to his death. As a result, Matthew's exclusion from the funeral seems not only plausible but perhaps even expected—not only due to his queerness but because he was never part of the tight-knit circle of the Lee family. Matthew's desire to host a celebration of life seems to be his only saving grace, a metaphor for the rights of all people to grieve and honour the deceased. To be certain, I am uneasy with the prospect of suggesting alternative endings, though my background and training as a dramaturg-turned-scholar has me thinking about the successes and limitations of *Ga Ting* and its contribution to the genre of tragedy and queer family drama.

Kevin's death seems an uncanny equivalent to the "sacrifice of the son," as described by Northrop Frye. As the play progresses, audiences are told that Kevin has died in the ocean, yet it remains unclear whether he has committed suicide or accidentally drowned from a drug overdose. The cause of death is never discussed in detail and always remains a mystery. However, the sound of recurring waves and ghostly projections of Kevin's face during flashbacks in the production suggests that his death was possibly self-induced rather than a result of a violent or traumatic attack. At this point, I am compelled to ask why queer death in theatre (and film) is often portrayed within seemingly

11 Many US films, from *Philadelphia* to *Milk* to *Brokeback Mountain* feature gay protagonists who have had their life cut short, resulting from disease or murder. Mainstream queer theatre such as *The Laramie Project* (though based on the actual death of Matthew Shepard) and, more recently, *Late Company* by Jordan Tannahill (produced by Touchstone Theatre) also feature gay protagonists who are never seen live on stage because their deaths were premature.

narrow frameworks and paradigms. In my view, the evolution of contemporary tragedy is dependent upon the inclusion of protagonists and antagonists from various gendered, classed, and racial backgrounds. If death is a recurring feature in tragedy, then I would expect that queer protagonists have the *right to die* on stage, and their families also have the *right to mourn* and grieve. On one hand, the choice to begin the play after Kevin's death makes sense if seen and understood as intervention into tragedy, asking audiences to identify and wrestle with the loss of a queer, albeit imperfect, human figure. In this regard, *Ga Ting* reveals a tragic communitas that asks its audiences to empathize with Matthew, Mai, and Hong, the play's representative queer, mediatory, and patriarchal voices struggling to find common ground amidst death. And yet the play also feeds uneasily (and perhaps unintentionally) into the growing body of work where queer figures are portrayed as degenerates: ill, sick, victims of violent or self-induced death resulting from societal exclusion and discrimination. The question remains: If given a full life to lead, what would a queer tragic hero or protagonist expect to act, look, and sound like on stage?

CONCLUSION: A TRAGEDY FOR EVERYONE

Ga Ting transcends the heteronormative relations often characterized in classic tragedies of passion. While the relationship between the immigrant couple, Hong and Mai Lee, and their deceased son seems to represent the standard nuclear family, it also comes to represent a broader demographic of common folk not always represented on stage. Arthur Miller, whose *Death of a Salesman* is notable for its portrayal of a common protagonist, once stated, "I believe, for myself, that the lasting appeal of tragedy is due to our need to face the fact of death in order to strengthen ourselves for life, and that over and above this function of the tragic viewpoint there are and will be a great number of formal variations which no single definition will ever embrace" (109). Though Miller's belief in the tragedy of the common man can be readily applied to the plot and characters found in *Ga Ting*, his plays, like many Western tragedies, follow the heteronormative framing of relationships. While I am not suggesting that tragic protagonists need to be queer, Kevin's immigrant family members and his boyfriend offer a highly refreshing familial structure that pushes against stereotypical characterizations.

Gilles Deleuze and Félix Guattari write about the relationship between the Oedipal figure and familial structure, suggesting that "[t]he culturalists invoke other triangles—maternal uncle-aunt-nephew, for example; but the oedipalists have no difficulty in demonstrating that these are imaginary variations of one and the same structural constant, different figures of one and the same symbolic triangulation" (174). In the triangulation between parents and offspring, Matthew temporarily replaces Kevin by acting as his mediator. Since Kevin is unable to give voice to his concerns or wishes, the ex-boyfriend must fill the void, essentially queering the family triangulation and manifesting as husband–wife–son's ex-boyfriend (Hong, Mai, and Matthew), rather than husband–wife–son. As such, *Ga Ting* moves the tragedy of passion away from its heteronormative roots while maintaining its enduring features as enumerated by Frye: "the separation of lovers, the conflict of duty and passion, or the conflict of social and personal (sexual or family) interests" (16). Indeed, *Ga Ting* contains all three of the features described in Frye's definition. A separation of lovers becomes apparent as audiences learn that Matthew and Kevin had broken up soon before being fully separated through death. A conflict arises when Matthew desires to host a celebration of life, which triggers the parental sense of duty and desire to save face, and there is the additional conflict of ideology between Mai, Hong, and Matthew as they attempt to reconcile the loss of Kevin, a man who lived his life as meaningfully as he sought fit. And, finally, there is the physically absent Kevin, the sacrificed son, who is not only queer but artistic and bipolar. By the end of the play, the parents strive toward seeing Kevin differently, not only through the adjectives of such as queer or normal, but as someone to be mourned and loved unconditionally. I would say that Hong's homophobia unfolds not simply as representative of *hamartia* (character flaw) or Asian Canadian patriarchy, but as part of a larger social phenomenon—misguided, unbridled heteronormativity—that plagues the entire family and community.

In the final scene of the Vancouver production, a photo of Hong, Mai, Matthew, and Kevin was projected onto a screen located on the back wall. It was a beautiful and hopeful photo, gesturing toward the family that *could have been*. In the photo, however, Kevin's face was blurred, making his death simultaneously real and ghost-like. Mai's final words directed to Matthew were equally haunting: "Maybe we blame you, but not because you are gay. Not because you are in relationship with our son. But because you did not love him . . . enough" (84). Shortly afterward Matthew responded, "I know that! Do you think I don't feel any guilt? But you can't just blame me and move on. We're all at fault, including Kevin" (85). From this point onward, the characters seem intent on accepting responsibility, and the last scene intercuts between two different onstage temporalities. In one scene we see Matthew speaking to his deceased boyfriend at the cemetery; simultaneously, in another flashback scene, Mai and Hong are engaging in meaningful dialogue that revolves around Kevin's coming of age.

Ga Ting unfolds slowly but surely, as grief often does, laced with moments of healing, hope, and clarity. In doing so, Minh Ly reveals to audiences a queerly Canadian play founded upon tragic communitas. Although Hong, Mai, and Matthew may seem quite ordinary as characters, their grief and love are experienced on the deepest and highest levels; their presence on stage contributes significantly to notions of belonging, class, sexuality, and their relationship to tragedy as a complex field of study.

RE: FORM: (AN INFORMAL SET LIST OF CONSIDERATIONS)

EVALYN PARRY

1. The irony that I have been procrastinating writing this "statement" because I have been stressing out over what form it should take.

2. As a formal non-monogamist, polyformist, pan-curious, trans-sectional formal adventurer, I have spent my career straddling disciplines and audiences, methodologies and communities.

3. Short forms were my first gateway to queer performance. Songs, poems, comedic personal monologues: brief, condensed bullets of expressions through which I began to insert myself into performance spaces, began to articulate and assert my sexual/gender/identity/politics.

4. I obsess over my set lists. The order of the material, the narrative carved out by the chosen sequence. How one song, poem, or story ties to the next in theme, style, tempo, key. How songs together build a larger story when held up next to each other. How form is built from fragments.

5. I have discovered curating a theatre season is akin to building a set list.

6. In my own artistic and queer formation—which were and remain deeply intertwined—formal exploration was foundational. Form is content, content is form.

7. Some days for me queer just means contrary. I tend to resist whatever I'm told to do and look for the loophole to do something else instead.

8. Can something be "theatre" but not be "a play"?

9. Where are the lesbian playwrights, anyway? We've been asking for so long. Still, even now, where are they? Are lesbians just instinctively not really drawn to playwriting? Do we prefer cabarets, performance art, knitting, and rock bands to "theatre"? Is this in any way linked to sexual preference? Social preference? How come?

10. Back in the '90s I wore a button on my grey-and-black plaid flannel jacket that said "**Silence = Death**" emblazoned on a pink triangle. I loved that button. It was of course about HIV/AIDS, but it was also so much more.

11. Ironically when I look back at it, my formative experiences inside queer spaces were quite silencing. I let myself be silenced by the definitive, apparently fully, confidently formed identities in conversation; unschooled, unformed myself, I didn't yet feel "queer enough" to insert myself, my questions, my voice.

12. I started out making theatre that used poetry as primary text.

13. A poem is like a seed: a condensed form, full of potential.

14. It needs to meet another few mediums (say water and sunlight) to start to grow, to find its full form.

15. Does a queer seed necessarily grow a queer tree? As queer makers, is all our work necessarily queer by virtue of extension of the maker's identity? Even when it's not exploring an explicitly queer topic? Is it the "what" that makes the queer or the "who"? Or the "how"?

16. In the same way as I believe queer identity is not a fixed thing but rather a living, breathing, evolving, relational way of being, so theatre and theatrical form must be alive, responsive, shifting, in a constant state of redefinition.

Queer form/s must not and will never be singular, since queerness is relational, pluralistic, reactive, positional, intersectional, oppositional.

17. As a songwriter I built up a repertoire of material that reflected my evolving, shifting experience. As I would write new songs, older songs would get knocked off the set list, the material in a constant state of flow, a constant conversation between old and new expressions, flexible and malleable to suit my own evolution, intuitive assessments of each audience and performance situation.

18. As a collaborative playwright, a play often takes so long that you are a whole new person by the time it's finished.

19. I have often struggled with the separation of form, the separation of my creative worlds, my formal ambiguity, multiplicity. The feeling that I should choose, focus, become exclusive. The fear that my polyformal tendencies would diminish me.

20. But why should anyone ever feel they need to be only one thing? We are not one thing; we never will be one thing and it's fucking complicated to hold space for the amount of diversity that we call "queer community." This is what I see the function of a place like Buddies to be: a container that can give form, shape to a community of voices. A space that allows itself to be dismantled, rearranged, unformed, and reformed.

21. I made a show called *SPIN* as an experiment in long-form short form. I wanted to make a distinctive, thematically linked show out of short pieces, which, together, created a full-length show. I don't call the result a play, but for sure it's theatre. Why don't I call it a play?

22. What makes a play a play anymore, anyway?

23. Then again, why does it matter what we call a thing.

24. Then again, naming a thing is powerful.

25. Some days I think the reason that I love running this queer theatre is exactly because of all the forms that coexist inside it. The multiplicity that Buddies can hold. What I crave is always bigger and more than I can ever be. This place, this building, this institution has that capacity. I can stand inside of it and feel momentarily, vicariously filled.

26. Like fragments can actually add up to something real and substantial. Like every drop matters.

27. Sometimes you plant a seed and water it. Sometimes you sprout it. Sometimes you eat a pile of seeds in your salad.

28. Clearly there is no conclusion. Form is transitory. You have a body for a while, then you die and something else happens to your energy.

29. Endings are always the hardest part.

PROUDLY WELCOMING: IS DIVERSITY IN THE QUEER THEATRE COMMUNITY BY INVITATION ONLY?

LAINE ZISMAN NEWMAN

> *Diversity can take the form of a welcome. People of color in being welcomed are treated as guests, as temporary residents in someone else's home.*
> —Sara Ahmed, *On Being Included*

On 28 June 2016 Black Lives Matter Toronto (BLMTO) posted the following on their Facebook page to address the anti-Black racism they experienced when protesting the unveiling of a Police/LGBT mural in Toronto, Ontario:

> Out of all the actions & hate-filled people we have encountered, Our organizers, many of whom are LGBT-identified, have rate [sic] felt such vile hate, as we did when a bunch of white LGBT folks were shouting "all lives matter" at our protestors, and other chants with the intention of taunting and riling up our peeps. The artist of the Police/LGBT Mural was one of the people who started said chant and taunting. How fitting that he, who was tasked with creating a fantasy of good relations between the police and the LGBT community, showed his anti-black racism. ("Some Tidbits")

I begin by recounting this scenario to emphasize the presence of anti-Black racism in the queer community and the need to actively combat it. I could easily opt to begin this essay in celebration. It is clear that in the performance industry Queer, Trans, Intersex, Indigenous, Black, and People of Colour (QTIIBPOC) have had increased visibility and mainstream achievements.

There are incredible works by QTIIBPOC artists that need to be celebrated, promoted, and more widely produced. I could begin this essay by discussing the improved representation at the 2016 Dora Mavor Moore Awards and note the progress made by the Jessie Richardson Awards since their dismal display in 2015. I could write about the improved gender representation on Canadian stages in the last few years, with plays written by women up 3% in Canada (though still only comprising 26% of what is produced on stage) (Playwrights Guild of Canada). But instead I am starting by recalling this moment in Toronto. Because, as a white Ashkenazi settler queer woman writing to other white queer artists in Canada, I feel the need to say we should be ashamed. But instead of looking back at the sequence of events and saying:

> "I would never."
> "I am sorry."
> "That's not me."

We should be saying:

> "I am accountable."
> "What must I do?"
> "How do I address this kind of oppressive anti-Black racist response within my community?"

In this essay I reflexively consider the role white privilege plays in programming and artistic scholarship in the dominant (read: white) Canadian queer theatre community. It is clear that Toronto's queer and LGBT communities have acquired general visibility and specific rights since the 1960s. However, accepted homonormative activities are only viewed as acceptable when they conform to particular ideological expectations. In the context of performance and theatre communities, while white cisgender gay men's works may have increased visibility and popularity on Canadian stages, the under-representation and lack of acknowledgement of marginalized queer artists in Canada complicates the vision of acceptance and inclusivity the country purports to possess. Indeed, as recent statistics collected by Equity in Theatre (EIT) demonstrate, Canada is far from achieving equity on its professional stages. Women artists, Indigenous artists, artists of colour, trans artists, artists with diverse abilities and disabilities, and those who inhabit multiple positions of marginalization are consistently under-represented in key creative positions in theatre and performance. As lead researcher Michelle MacArthur explains, little has improved for women and marginalized artists in Canadian performance since Rebecca Burton's 2006 national study (4). MacArthur writes, "The situation is worse for racialized, immigrant, aboriginal, and disabled women, who have limited access to artistic opportunities despite Canada's celebration of diversity as a cornerstone of its identity" (29). The 2014 Kelly Hill study also indicates that Indigenous artists, as well as visible minorities and immigrant artists, all earn less than artists outside of these categories (40). Though the queer community is still a marginalized group whose works may also be under-represented in mainstream programming, works by historically and currently minoritized groups and performers, particularly disabled artists, Indigenous artists, and women and transgender people of colour, remain under-researched in queer theatre (Halferty 6). With these statistics and studies in mind, we must unpack how the false notion of a monolithic "queer theatre" community erases the privileges many queer artists possess due to their race, class, ability, gender, or settler identity.

Throughout this discussion I hold myself and other white academics and practitioners accountable and consider how queer theatre is implicated in the erasure of multiple identities and experiences through the universalization and neutralization of patriarchy, whiteness, and settler colonialism. My objective in this essay is threefold: to interrogate how whiteness is strategically unnamed and positioned as neutral; to examine how the universal queer subject is often used as a means of both "diversifying" work and representing queer history, resulting in a lack of recognition and further erasure of more marginalized queer artists' contributions in performance; and to recognize and confront the necessity for new forms of leadership in order to establish long-lasting systemic change.

When I began writing this essay, I struggled with the notion that a focus on difference has the capacity to perpetuate inequitable categories of identities that I am seeking to denaturalize and confront. How does a spotlight on difference assume unified identitarian experiences and binaries, which universalize "the Other" as a singular entity? How does a focus on difference maintain and propagate categorical and systemic oppression? The very impetus to focus on identity through difference might reinstate the hierarchical systems of power and oppression that many performance scholars and creators attempt to problematize and contest. Madhavi Menon provides one response to this rhetoric in *Indifference to Difference*:

> Identity is the demand made by power—tell us who you are so we can tell you what you can do. And by complying with that demand, by parsing endlessly the particulars that make our identity different from one another's, we are slotting into a power structure, not dismantling it . . . Critiquing identity politics, then, is not a dismissal of lived reality, but, rather, a response to the oppressive demands that identity itself makes under the guise of progressive politics. (2–3)

The simple notion of "diversity" establishes a binary between white (as an invisible and neutral norm) and "diverse" (a universalized and violently unified category of Other). Using an intersectional approach might seemingly compel us to move beyond an essentialized view of binaried difference; yet intersectionality still necessitates categorization and emphasis of difference, which, as Lynne Huffer notes, "runs the risk of perpetuating precisely the problems intersectionality had hoped to alleviate" (18). These obstacles present challenges in confronting the complexities of identities and the multiple ways individuals experience privilege and oppression. However, even while constructed identity politics have the capacity to essentialize difference, the realities and oppressions that result from the lived experiences of these differences are undeniable. To refuse difference, in practice, might be to ignore the intersections of social locations and positionalities—the very real ways in which we experience and struggle through daily life. Therefore, I opt to use an intersectional approach to theatre equity here in order to critically analyze and explode the limitations of boundaries while persistently considering the disparate and messy oppressions and privileges queer artists experience simultaneously.

I begin this analysis with a discussion on the vocabulary utilized to describe productions and the ways in which they are marketed. I argue that the language used (or avoided) in the marketing and promotion of performance demonstrates universalizing and normalizing tactics, which erase whiteness and situate marginalized bodies as distinct and Other. What does it mean to remain unnamed and outside of the expectations of classification? Difference necessitates a label, but with privilege comes the assumption of a universal and the avoidance of classification. As a white theatre academic and practitioner, I am rarely expected to identify my race and my work is rarely seen as representative of my race. In this sense I have the privilege to remain unspecialized and invisible. I can remain neutrally "queer" without the need to fit my work into more specific categories of difference. Therefore, following Valerie Sing Turner and legal scholar Constance Backhouse, I note the need to declare whiteness and label white practitioners as white. As Backhouse asserts, "The transparency of 'whiteness' is misleading and contributes to an erasure of the privileges that attach to membership in the dominant race" (qtd. in Sing Turner 25).

The erasure of whiteness becomes apparent in the words used to describe people of colour, diversely abled people, and gender-variant folks on stage. Whereas reviewers and audiences will often refer to "cross-gender" or "colour blind" casting when a director casts a body deemed racialized or gender-variant in a predominant role, such verbalization is seldom used to refer to the *choice* to cast a white or perceived gender-normative actor. As Carrie Sandahl explains:

> Rarely is an actor of color, a woman, or a disabled person cast against type to play a character from a more dominant social position. Actors from marginalized groups must battle on two fronts, then: to be cast in roles that resemble their own identities and to be cast in roles that do not. (236)

The language used to express particular artists' inclusion (or exclusion) in a performance functions to normalize and universalize white and privileged identities. It is not seen as necessary to name privileged bodies in performance, because whiteness, able-bodiedness, and hetero/homonormativity become the standard expectation to which all else is compared. It is only when someone opts to introduce a racialized, dis/differently abled, or gender-variant body that it is deemed a choice at all. As Meera Sethi further explains:

> The visual production of women artists of colour in Canada is received within a hegemonic framework that takes as its starting place the centrality of white male artists, thus building onto that a discourse that situates women artists of colour outside its normalizing boundaries. (3)

By universalizing whiteness, able-bodiedness, and straightness as the absence of artistic choices, the racialized, crip, and Indigenous body is perpetuated as the visitor or outsider in a queer space. In this way, queer women of colour and those who are diversely Othered may be welcomed onto conventional or queer stages, but it is rarely as insiders to the experience. Their presence on stage is through extended invitation, not equitable inclusion. The absence of a label and refusal to name white work as white work illustrates Sara Ahmed's notion of welcoming an "Other," wherein marginalized groups are invited as temporary outsiders and guests in the privileged practitioners' home (*Willful Subjects* 148). In this dynamic a paradox of visibility emerges. Rinaldo Walcott articulates that "blackness in Canada is situated on a continuum that runs from the invisible to the hyper-visible" (44). Black bodies are *seen* in predominantly white spaces when they are *seen* as Other. However, in these instances of invitation, the privilege, resources, and rights that result from everyday white visibility are nonetheless denied to Black artists. The refusal to name whiteness and the presumed need to name marginalized groups leaves Black, Indigenous, and POC artists in a state of simultaneous invisibility and hypersurveilled visibility.

It is clear that this issue is not one limited to queer theatre, but I intentionally highlight it in relation to queer performance practice because of the capacity for marginalized theatre companies to create radical change. Queer theatres can lead the charge in denaturalizing whiteness by naming it as such. In making this claim I do not intend to devalue or trivialize the accomplishments of marginalized theatre practitioners, nor do I intend to erase their achievements. We should indeed be celebrating and supporting this work. However, considering mainstream and commercial theatre programming, we might note the ways in which works and practitioners are Othered in the very ways in which they are included.

As Paul Halferty notes, while there are many works that explore and exist at the intersections of gender, sexuality, and race, limited research in Canada focuses on this work: "The performance histories of queers of colour, an area that has generated some of the most vital interventions in queer performance studies in the US, are meager in the Canadian scholarly context" (6). The scholarly investment in charting and analyzing these works would have the capacity to change not only our current conceptions of the theatrical landscape, but also what is remembered, archived, and historicized. Moving beyond scholarship and academic theorizations, we can consider the way that queer and LGBT histories are enacted in performance on stage—what is valued as historically relevant? What is brought to Canadian stages as integral to the construction of communities, legacies, and cultures?

We explicitly saw the transparency of whiteness on stage in queer theatre with the titles of two collective creations produced at Buddies in Bad Times Theatre: *The Gay Heritage Project* (collectively created by three white men) and *Black Boys* (created with a collective of three Black men). The universalization of whiteness is clear based on the assumption that *The Gay Heritage Project* need not name the particular heritage and race of the performers. Where *The Gay Heritage Project* perpetuates a monolithic image of gay histories, the production of *Black Boys* successfully demonstrates the diversity within Black gay communities. The title of this production makes no assumptions about a singular experience of Blackness or queerness. The experiences and perspectives staged in *Black Boys* are expressed as three unique voices that often differ and diverge. Unlike *The Gay Heritage Project*, whose title alludes to an overwhelming singularity, *Black Boys* invites the audience to think through the multiplicity of experiences in Canada's Black gay communities.

The Gay Heritage Project, created by and starring Paul Dunn, Andrew Kushnir, and Damien Atkins, delivers personal narratives from the three creator-performers. It begins from their own personal familial narratives and works toward answering the question "Is there such a thing as a gay heritage?" ("The Gay Heritage Project"). The use of the article "the" in the title of the production insinuates a singular heritage, which all gay individuals presumably share. Those who do not have access to *the* gay heritage are therefore not included within its history—outsiders to the historical experience of being authentically gay. All three of the creators involved in the production are white. The recognition of whiteness and white privilege occurs in the production when the characters verbally reference their own white male privilege. However, such a disclaimer does not excuse one from critically addressing and practically dismantling privilege. Though the characters may suggest that there is no gay monolithic identity, the performance of their identities as "the" project of seeking gay heritage nonetheless contributes to a myth of a white monolith. As Hiram Pérez notes in *A Taste For Brown Bodies*, though queer theory (and I expand this to queer theatre communities) works to develop vocabularies and understandings of the relationship between desire, erotics, and power, it simultaneously "has participated at times in securing the transparency of whiteness, jettisoning questions of race as retrograde and provincial" (10). That is not to argue that the white male gay subject does not experience oppression. However, as Pérez further explains, "[W]e need to complicate the margins" (11). We must note the ways in which queer theory and queer theatre can work in the service of a normalized heteropatriarchal mainstream through the naturalization of whiteness and patriarchy (Pérez 10). While *The Gay Heritage Project* acknowledges the performers' whiteness as part of the production, it continues to memorialize and glorify a singular, universalized gay narrative.

The representation of gay heritage in this production does not simply disseminate white gay Canadian history; it actively participates in *whitening* history, excluding (and thereby erasing) the multiple queer people of colour's histories and narratives from "gay heritage." I borrow, here, from Huffer's discussion of feminism and apply it to queer theory. Huffer argues that "liberal feminist successes have been achieved at the expense of other, less privileged women. [. . .] [T]his deeper admission puts forward the challenging claim that increasing inequality between women is a result of the gains of liberal feminism" (147). We can similarly note the ways that white gay men's experiences come at the expense of significantly more vulnerable and oppressed queer peoples. The assumption that a space or theatre season is more equitable because of the inclusion of white gay theatre practitioners elides the ways in which gay spaces are organized and allocated. Pérez points to the all-too-common resistance to thinking through and theorizing about race critically in queer theory (98). He emphasizes that this "defensive posture helps entrench institutionally the transparent white subject characteristic of so much queer theorizing. Queer theorists who can invoke that transparent subject, and choose to do so, reap the dividends of whiteness" (98). With this transparent white subject in mind, we may ask how the erasure of particular histories and the continual propagation of dominant white narratives continues to benefit the white queer men's community in Canada. By naming privilege and being accountable to the ways it allows particular bodies to be seen, we refuse its transparency and can begin to address the ways that it shapes queer creative practice.

In addition to audience reception and historicization, we may consider the funding and economic gains associated with productions like *The Gay Heritage Project*. Who is reaping the benefits of this single story of queer history and whose stories are not being told? With development and production support from Buddies in Bad Times and BMO Financial Group ("The Gay Heritage Project"), allocated resources and funding are streamlined into already privileged sectors of queer communities. Following a very successful run and remount, *The Gay Heritage Project* toured across the country. According to the production's page on Buddies in Bad Times's website, the play aims to "discover [the performers'] connections to queer people and events in the past" ("The Gay Heritage Project"). Here, we see the ways in which funding and capital allow particular histories to travel both temporally and spatially in order to disseminate specific narratives of the past. These historical retellings work to perpetuate monopolies and privileges in the present through increased visibility, publicity, and resources. Ultimately, this affects what can be imagined in the future.

Though, arguably, there is increasing acknowledgement of white privilege in the performing arts, and perhaps more so in arts communities that cater to marginalized and racialized artists and audiences, the issues around inclusion and representation are still evident in valuations of artistic excellence through awards and programming. Although artists of colour created incredibly strong work in Canada in the 2014/2015 season, the Jessie Richardson Awards, which celebrate professional theatre artists in Vancouver, BC, were, as Sing Turner aptly notes in her article "The Danger of a Single Story," dominated by white artists' work. She explains that this outcome is anything but surprising because "there wasn't a single person of colour on the ten-person Small Theatre jury. There was also zero representation on the six-member Original Script jury" (22). Only three of twelve members of the Large Theatre Jury were artists of colour (22). While women were well represented on the juries, and white queer practitioners were nominated for awards, their works have the capacity to perpetuate white supremacy by erasing the need to consider equitable representation for more marginalized and oppressed theatre creators.

Similarly, on 26 January 2016, Canadian Stage in Toronto announced their upcoming season. For the thirteen shows programmed, all of the directors, choreographers, and playwrights were white. Despite this glaring and oppressive exclusion of marginalized artists of colour, prior to the season announcement Artistic and Managing Director Matthew Jocelyn announced "the diversity" of the season's casting (Nestruck). The question is not simply how an artistic director in Toronto can make such a gravely inaccurate (and ultimately oppressive) statement, but also what he believes "passes" under the umbrella term "diverse." Though roles may have been cast with minoritized or racialized performers, white theatre practitioners occupy all of the major production roles. "Diversity" is used strategically here to produce a particular kind of artistic image and reception. Ahmed suggests that the term "diversity" is a means of "accruing value," a hollow placeholder, aesthetic, or speech convention wherein "what is named as diverse becomes less significant than the name 'diversity'" (*On Being Included* 58). Perhaps, for Jocelyn, it is the white gay men in the season who are assumed to diversify the season's programming choices. Indeed, artists such as Daniel MacIvor and Jordan Tannahill were among those produced that season at the theatre. In this instance, the universalized white gay man may come to represent inclusion, radical progress, and diversity in these programs. The impact of nominations and programming extends beyond the productions in a single season of artistic creation. It sets and maintains a precedent that white men produce the most esteemed works, which limits queer artists of colour to the margins. In this manner, racial privilege that comes alongside whiteness is further neutralized and naturalized and the absence of artists of colour is invisibilized. When white queer theatre stands in for diversity, we fail to recognize the very ways in which works by queer artists of colour are devalued and excluded from programming and evaluations of artistic excellence.

The problem of "invitation" and "diversity" is deeply rooted in the distribution of power and control. Though major queer theatres in the country have programmed multiple works by and with people of colour, much of the time the artistic directors and those doing the programming for the season are white. As Sethi argues, the "mainstreaming of dissent" enables major artistic institutions to actively construct categories of racialized outsiders, employing discursive practices that establish and solidify a white Canadian sense of belonging through the categorization and isolation of "culturally diverse" artists (6; 7). As Sethi further explains, though Canadian cultural institutions appear to provide support and visibility to communities of colour, they refuse to provide decision-making power to these communities (5). Thus, while Canada claims to produce multicultural work, it is primarily the white theatre spaces that manage and regulate such productions. Ensuring such supervision and restriction is a means of maintaining a consistent power relation, in which primarily white male artistic directors and institutions control and program spaces for predominately white audiences. According to Sethi, these institutions position marginalized women of colour artists as "both the beneficiaries and burden of the state" (2–3). A lack of operational funding also ensures that these companies, festivals, and projects are financially unable to secure ongoing spaces and thus are dependent on theatre owners, predominantly white men, to approve and program their projects (Burton 40).

Companies that do cater to "culturally specific" communities are also often ghettoized or tokenized. With a designated company in place to program a particular culture's works, mainstream theatres can evade accountability for programming diverse works—a "queer" theatre can remain "queer," with a monolithic and universal queer subject as the centre of the programming. As Deborah Leslie and John Paul Catungal argue, rather than being portrayed as members of the city, "Immigrant and First Nations artists frequently find their work ghettoized in ethnic-based artistic communities, and subject to Orientalist representations that construct it as 'exotic' and 'other'" (117). Over the last ten years, the city of Toronto has seemingly emphasized and promoted a reputation of inclusivity and diversity in their approach and priorities through support of ethnic and queer festivals and cultural productions, such as Caribana and Pride (Leslie and Catungal 113). Theoretically, such an investment is seen as a potential source of economic growth through tourism; yet according to Leslie and Catungal, such improvement ultimately caters to and benefits only an elite creative class (114). The works produced are valuable and provide opportunities for many creative practitioners to showcase their productions, but at the same time they solidify difference and may limit the funding available to projects planned and implemented by folks who are part of the communities represented.

Queer artists of colour are creating notable and significant works in Canada. Often these productions are staged through festivals and one-off events, without access to funds for long-term development. Nonetheless, these works productively alter the landscape of queer performance in Canada through increasing visibility and demanding space for QTIIBPOC works on stage. The revival of *Strange Sisters* (later renamed *Insatiable Sisters*), curated by Kim Katrin Milan and Gein Wong in 2013/2014 and 2014/2015, emphasized the inclusion of marginalized and racialized performers; later, in 2016, Wong curated and produced *Helix* during Pride festivities at Buddies in Bad Times; Jotika Chaudhary, Jahanzeb Kazi, Dora Ng, Anoushka Ratnarajah, and Johnny Wu collectively created *The Pink Line*, a project facilitated by Fay Nass and C. E. Gatchalian at **the frank theatre**; d'bi.young anitafrika's *The Orisha Trilogy* was performed in three venues in Toronto; Stephen Jackman-Torkoff, Tawiah Ben M'Carthy, and Thomas Olajide collectively created and performed the aforementioned production of *Black Boys* at Buddies in Bad Times Theatre in November 2016; Native Earth Performing Arts presented the inaugural *2-Spirit Cabaret* in the same month; lee williams boudakian, Anoushka Ratnarajah, and Kamee Abrahamian's *Setting Bones* was awarded winner of the 2017 Fringe New Play Prize in Vancouver; and *UnSettled*, a Two-Spirit programmed exhibition curated by Adrian Stimson (Blackfoot) as part of the Queer Arts Festival (QAF), launched in June 2017 in Vancouver. Finally, while not explicitly queer, several organizations are compiling databases and lists of works by marginalized and equity-seeking communities, which include many works by QTIIBPOC artists (see, for example, Ad Hoc Assembly's "Catalogue of Works"; Indigenous Performing Arts Alliance's "Indigenous Body of Work"; and "The 49," an initiative from Fu-Gen Theatre Company). While this kind of survey and list has yet to be compiled exclusively for QTIIBPOC theatre works in Canadian theatre and performance, the current lists are a valuable starting point and resource for those programming queer artistic seasons.

These QTIIBPOC creators are not creating work in response to white supremacy, but independent from it. Their success should not be analyzed in relation to white-dominated theatre; to do so would continue to centralize white queer theatre as a standard against which all must be evaluated in order to gain credibility. As d'bi.young anitafrika, Artistic Director of Watah Theatre, explains, "Even while responding to the insidious unfairness of racism, it is imperative that we do not place whiteness at the centre of the art we create. Blackness does not exist in opposition to whiteness" (27). White supremacy, patriarchy, and colonization influence queer theatre communities; however, resistance against these forces should not be contextualized through a lens of victimhood, but rather artistic expressions of self, space, culture, and communities. Black, Indigenous, and POC performers are storytellers, not in relation to whiteness, but on their own terms as creators. In continuing to produce these works, Black, Indigenous, and POC queer creators "[insist] on [their] presence" and resist and reposition those in power through performance (Walcott 85).

In early July 2016, Toronto celebrated Pride through marches and parades with honoured group Black Lives Matter Toronto. When they performed in the parade, Black queer leaders took up space and insisted their rights and voices be more than a tokenized image of Toronto's "diversity" by making demands of Pride Toronto that would create a more inclusive and safe environment for those not currently represented.[1] Many of these demands directly relate to visibility and accessibility on Pride stages and at the performance

---

1 The demands, as articulated on BLMTO's Facebook page were as follows: Demands include:

> 1. Commit to BQY's (Black Queer Youth) continued space (including stage/tents), funding, and logistical support.
>
> 2. Self-determination for all community spaces, allowing community full control over hiring, content, and structure of their stages.
>
> 3. Full and adequate funding for community stages, including logistical, technical, and personnel support.
>
> 4. Double funding for Blockorama + ASL interpretation & headliner funding.
>
> 5. Reinstate and make a commitment to increase community stages/spaces (including the reinstatement of the South Asian stage).
>
> 6. A commitment to increase representation amongst Pride Toronto staffing/hiring, prioritizing Black trans women, Black queer people, Indigenous folk, and others from vulnerable communities.
>
> 7. A commitment to more Black deaf & hearing ASL interpreters for the Festival.
>
> 8. Removal of police floats/booths in the Pride marches/parades/community spaces.
>
> 9. A public townhall, organized in conjunction with groups from marginalized communities, including, but not limited to, Black Lives Matter Toronto, Blackness Yes, and BQY to be held six months from today. Pride Toronto will

spaces created during the festival. The halting of the parade was a performance in and of itself and was a performative gesture. Stopping the parade enabled the group to take up space in the queer community for just a little bit longer: to insist on a lasting presence both through their demands and through their refusal to move. However, in this instance, many members of the queer white community demonstrated, once again, that anti-Black racism is still prevalent in Canadian queer culture. Where there could have been support, there was disdain and defensiveness and attacks using rhetoric of "threat" and "hostage taking." Clearly, we are still far from equity. BLMTO received hate mail and threats for interrupting the Pride parade. Comments online in articles and social media posts demonstrated a clear rupture in response.

Although BLMTO's original non-violent action was met with racism, hostility, and oppression, six months later, in January 2017, members at Pride Toronto's annual general meeting endorsed all of Black Lives Matter Toronto's demands. This is an incredible outcome, and a direct result of the significant work BLMTO has undertaken. However, their accomplishment should not be seen as progress for the queer community at large. It is clear that the underlying problem with racism in the queer community is not a QTIIBPOC problem; this is a problem in queer white communities, which needs to be addressed by white queer people. And while the vote to endorse the demands makes some movement toward more equitable queer communities, much work still needs to be done for real systemic change. For white folks like myself, patting ourselves on the back and congratulating the queer community for advancing toward inclusion is in itself an act of erasure, which ignores the ways we are still perpetuating anti-Black racism and settler colonialism through our language, leadership, and curation processes.

BLMTO chose to participate but refused to register for the 2017 Pride parade in Toronto. They walked through the parade holding signs that read "May we never again have to remind you that WE built this." A refusal to register in 2017 is a refusal to allow Pride Toronto and the City of Toronto to

---

present an update and action plan on the aforementioned demands. ("Rain drop")

regulate and allocate queer space; instead, BLMTO is choosing to take space back as a political act of resistance. One of the group's organizers, Rodney Diverlus explained that BLMTO is not reclaiming or appropriating the event, "Pride is actually ours [. . .] Queer and trans people of colour actually started this" (qtd. in Shawn Ahmed). The assumption that BLMTO is "taking over" is an implicit assertion that Black queer people remain outside of the political resistance, despite the historically fundamental role Black transgender, lesbian, and gay activists have played in combating homophobia and transphobia. Both the refusal to register in the 2017 parade and the halting of the 2016 parade worked to demand recognition through a disruption of spatial organization. The acts not only draw attention to who is seen as belonging to particular spaces and who is given rights to them but also resist the mechanisms that whiten and depoliticize historical events.

Throughout this essay I have worked to identify some of the ways in which privilege functions and to hold white theatre practitioners and scholars accountable in queer communities. Moreover, I have begun to consider how queer "diversity" and equity are presented on mainstream and commercialized stages and asked if such productions are, as Sara Ahmed aptly notes, by invitation only. I do so in order to dismantle a monolithic queer-theatre industry and demonstrate the ways in which certain privilege is afforded to white theatre practitioners who inhabit or identify with queerness. I end by asking how we might complicate the very umbrella term "queer theatre." In a 2016 blog post, Jack Halberstam questioned who "we" are after Orlando. Halberstam writes, "It might be time to break up the fantasy of the LGBT monolith [. . .]" ("Who Are 'We' "). Even within the performance industry, there is a need to recognize that different practitioners experience identity, labour, and performance differently, with vastly different access to funding, resources, support, and leadership roles. In no way is this call an attempt to ignore or erase the performance achievements of many queer communities throughout the country or the strides made by theatre companies in the last few years. On the contrary, these radical works and theatres are integral to the country's changing performance culture and aesthetic. Yet we are still far from equity. Recognizing the ways in which the very term "queer theatre" assumes a unified theatrical experience, I assert here the need to expose the naturalization of whiteness and combat the active and violent whitening of queer histories and stages by naming white work as white work.

Who comes to represent "queer theatre" is a direct result of who is most visible on theatre stages, in classrooms, and in publications. The queer conferences, anthologies, research, and theatrical seasons planned need to prioritize and not tokenize those that have historically been erased from queer-identified theatre stages and publications. If it is only publications and seasons that focus explicitly on "diversity" that are held accountable to achieving this level of inclusion and equitable practice, then we will continue to implicitly contribute to a neutralization and universalization of whiteness as that which does not need to be named. It is time for white theatre and performance practitioners and scholars to step back, learn how to be better allies, and support the changes needed in the theatre and performance industry.

2-SPIRIT OR NOT TO SPIRIT? . . . IT'S NOT EVEN A QUESTION

RYAN CUNNINGHAM

ACKNOWLEDGEMENT: 23 JULY 2016

Tansi . . . My name is Ryan Cunningham. I am Non-Status, Plains Cree from Central Alberta, and I am the current artistic director of Native Earth Performing Arts in Toronto, Canada. I would like to acknowledge that we have gathered on unceded Coast Salish territory and I would like to pay my respects to the original people of this land. This includes the territories of the Musqueam, Skwxwú7mesh, Stó:lō, and Tsleil-Waututh nations, and I pay my respects to their Elders past and present.

I would like to share with you some reasons why I believe it is important to offer these land acknowledgements. I also think you will find that these reasons provide context for my position in the paper to follow.

I was recently in Australia for an international performing arts market and conference. Only in the past five years or so have land acknowledgements been given in public gatherings, conferences, and events there. Without fail, among the many speakers throughout the week, all from Australia began with an acknowledgement of the original Aboriginal people of that territory. This took maybe ten seconds each time and we probably heard four to six of them each day. On the last day I overheard a senior member in the arts community say, "Why do we have to hear this before every panel? Yes, yes, we know, we've heard it all week." I could not offer a response because I myself had not fully understood why it was so important to make these acknowledgements in our public gatherings.

I kept asking myself, why is this so important? If you look at it from the dominant culture's position, from a European gaze, once you hear one acknowledgement at the beginning of the conference that should be enough. Only in the past five to ten years in Australia has there been any Aboriginal presence at these major international arts conferences. Nor were there any Aboriginal artists represented on their stages, panels, or programs until recently: in short, no cultural presence or inclusion of the original people or their protocols.

In Canada, as in Australia, there is very little presence of Indigenous people or their culture in our public spaces. We rarely have positive representation in our social media, news, television series, movies, etc. This is a tactic of colonization: to disappear the original people; to forget they were even here (and still are) and/or position their culture only in the past, from an archaeological perspective.

This is why I believe it is important to acknowledge the original people of the land we gather upon. To pay our respects and to make space and give a presence to the vibrant culture of people who still live here, people who live their contemporary lives while still practising their traditions and ceremonies. I have also begun to incorporate a sentence from our brothers and sisters in Australia: "to pay our respects to their Elders past and present." This acknowledges the people, culture, art, and world view that have always been here; it asserts that the people, cultural knowledge, and teachings are still alive with our Elders and knowledge keepers.

POSITION PAPER

"Queer" and the identity categories of LGBTQ are European, Western constructs and concepts based on sexual preference and gender identity. I am 2-spirited. This is an Aboriginal concept tens of thousands of years old based on spiritual knowledge within an Indigenous universal framework. I am also Cree, a culture that has seven genders (or six, depending on the interpretation). Therefore, I am confused about how to speak about the term "Queer" and its use over the past two decades.

I also don't understand the term "Queer Theatre." Does that mean theatre created by "Queer" artists? Theatre about being "Queer"? Or theatre about being "Queer" by "Queer" artists?

Do I speak about the 2-spirited theatre artists that are only creating "Queer" stories? Or do I discuss the 2-spirited artists just doing theatre?

The distinction must be made that 2-spirited people should be contextualized within an Aboriginal framework. To put 2-spirited people within an LGBTQ framework is trying to fit a traditional Aboriginal concept within a Christianized, European framework based on sexual preference and gender identity. Being 2-spirited has nothing to do with sexual preference or gender identity, even though some of us do identify as being "Queer."

When one puts the 2S at the end of LGBTQ (which the mayor of Toronto has now made official for all City Hall communications) without providing the traditional Indigenous framework from which it exists, does it just become another form of tokenism? Does this in turn become another tool for the dominant culture to colonize Indigenous teachings? I believe the reframing of 2S within a European-based perspective is indeed another form of contemporary colonization.

To have 2S included in LGBTQ also has negative impacts in our communities. Homophobia in our communities is rampant because of Christianization and colonization and the forced patriarchal structure imposed on us. When homophobic people in our communities see 2S in the LGBTQ acronym they can say, "Oh, they are the other. They are part of the LGBTQ movement and therefore are not Native, since LGBTQ is a European construct and therefore must be part of the colonizing society."

And in the Indigenous way, I would like to tell you a story so that you may interpret these ideas in your own way.

In 2010 I was the artistic director of Alberta Aboriginal Performing Arts in Edmonton, Alberta, which I co-founded with the amazing Christine Sokaymoh Frederick. I was in Toronto and had just seen the remount of *Agokwe* by Waawaate Fobister, originally produced by Buddies in Bad Times Theatre. Winner of six Dora Mavor Moore Awards the year before (for Outstanding Production, New Play, Lighting, Performance, Direction, and

Costumes), this play affected me in such a deep and layered way. Yes, it was a fantastic piece of theatre, but the traditional teachings and lessons in the script (lessons that I had not heard of our traditional communities) were what affected me most. It was an incredible combination of great theatre and traditional teachings. So I approached the creators, Fobister (actor, playwright) and Ed Roy (director, dramaturg), and asked how I could bring this production to Edmonton.

After an award-winning premiere, remount, and national tour, Buddies in Bad Times Theatre agreed to hand over the production rights to the creators. The National Arts Centre of Canada (co-producer on the national tour) offered to give us the touring set, and thus the Agokwe Collective was co-founded by Fobister, Roy, and myself to continue to bring this play to communities across Canada. I would like to thank Peter Hinton and Nancy Webster, in particular, who also offered to store the touring set at the NAC warehouse for that first year while the collective applied for our first grants.

A year or so later we embarked on our first independent Canadian tour and travelled to six cities over eight weeks: Edmonton, Whitehorse, Calgary, Toronto, Saskatoon, and Vancouver. The first stop was Edmonton, where the play was presented by Alberta Aboriginal Performing Arts. The city's main theatre critic, who is usually very kind in her reviews, wasn't as kind in her review of *Agokwe*. I have to apologize that I paraphrase her review, because when I went online to find it this morning I discovered that it has been removed entirely from the Internet. When scrolling through the history of her reviews it is no longer there either. This brings to mind a quote that was just shown on one of the earlier panels that I would like to repeat: "The removal of evidence of something is evidence of something" (Sara Ahmed, "Evidence").

To paraphrase the review, "The production was quite beautiful, the performance was fantastic. But we've seen this all before. It's really just another story of one young man's journey of coming out of the closet."

And you know what? When I put myself in the reviewer's position I can understand her comment. As a middle-class white woman who has spent the past few decades reviewing theatre in Edmonton, she probably has seen her share of "coming-out" stories on stage. If I was seeing the world through the gaze of a white, privileged critic of contemporary European and Western-based theatre, I would probably have the same reaction: a story told really well but ultimately something that we've seen before and nothing really groundbreaking.

But seeing the reactions of Aboriginal people in the audience was amazing. At the end of the play there were people crying and jumping up to give standing ovations. In their faces I saw the reflection of what I felt when I first saw the show. People couldn't believe that these teachings were lost, that because of Christianization and colonization our Nations had forgotten the important and respected place that 2-spirited people had in our communities. To take a line from the play, "We didn't waste our people." In Q & As following the show Aboriginal people talked of their experience growing up with gay cousins or siblings and how there was no one to talk to and no one ever talked about it. And how difficult it was for them to live in our communities as 2-spirited people.

During the run in Edmonton we had a Cultural Elder come who was known to have homophobic views. After the show ended he was in tears and literally did a complete one-eighty. He began learning of the traditional place 2-spiritness had in our culture. He began teaching the historical importance of 2-spirited people on his reserve and taught the honour and respect they have had in our communities.

This Elder invited the play to come to his reserve the next year and asked if he could say some words before the show. Again, he spoke to the traditional teachings in the story and called on his community to remember the honoured place these people have in our community and to give them respect.

This play has deep meaning for Native people and is very powerful in what it brings to our communities. However, without the Indigenous framework or the Indigenous spiritual context from which it originated, then it is seen as "just another coming-out story." It loses its original meaning. The Indigenous is taken out of it.

Therefore, to speak of 2S or to add it to LGBTQ without the Indigenous context or framework removes it from our traditional teachings and cultural importance.

To come back to the question that I must assume is behind the intent of me being here: Who are the Native 2-spirited, queer-identified theatre creators who are creating work about being "Queer"?

I would like to repeat Harlan Pruden's comment from his paper on Tomson Highway: "Tomson is a Cree playwright and his stories are Cree." That's why there are always 2-spirited people in his plays: because there have always been 2-spirited people in our communities. No need to explain or justify anything. We are part of the community. Therefore, we will always be in our stories.

If I were to try and list the 2-spirited playwrights writing from a "Queer" perspective in Canada who are being produced or published, I can only think of three. There may be more, and I qualify this based on my limited awareness of the entire community. I also must acknowledge the growing numbers of 2-spirited theatre, opera, and dance artists working professionally in Canada, as well as the 2-spirited theatre artists creating exciting new work in festivals and Fringes across the country. But professionally produced, published theatre about being Aboriginal and Queer?

TOMSON HIGHWAY, WAAWAATE FOBISTER, AND BRAD FRASER

Before I close, I would also like to speak to something I have noticed while listening to these panel discussions all week. In so many of the statements, answers, and comments one could have replaced the word "Queer" with "Aboriginal" and it would have been completely accurate of both experiences. I have also noticed that many responses have felt like they come from an experience of great trauma. If you compare our cultural timelines there is a very recent experience of great trauma and loss in both cultures. The AIDS crisis "ended" in the late '90s just as the last residential school closed its doors. This ended a cycle of genocide in two communities that took so many of our people and robbed us of our Elders and their teachings—teachings that would have provided support, mentorship; teachings that should be passed to the next generation of Queer and Indigenous youth.

But there is hope! We now have the first generation of young people—Indigenous and Queer—growing up with support, pride, and, most importantly, information of who their community is and where they come from. And that information is now accessible from anywhere in the world. They have access to their culture and heritage and are self-determined about how they choose to engage with the broader community. And that gives me a lot of hope.

E'kosi.

DIVISIONS WITHIN: STAGING INTERNECINE CONFLICTS BETWEEN GAY SUBCULTURES

T. BERTO

Numerous writers, when commenting on twentieth-century queer theatre, have referred to the need for a political presence on the stage to promote the fight for equality for queer persons. John M. Clum refers to this aspect of queer theatre as characters moving from "domination by an oppressive voice to liberation through the finding of their own gay voice" (*Staging* xiii). Persons use such theatre to "fight to maintain the toe-hold (they) have gained in American and British society" (*Staging* xiv). Don Shewey reflects this notion in a different way, stating that "gay plays serve the primitive function of . . . acting as a corrective to neglect or abuse by a culture at large" (xi). Alan Sinfield echoes these ideas, claiming "the task is . . . to build on the diverse strengths of our constituency, to enlarge it, and to politicize it" (347). All the aforementioned ideas reflect the standpoint of an oppressed minority battling for acceptance and rights amidst a hostile majority. Yet in contemporary Canada, a country where we now have same-sex marriage, child-custody rights, and legal equality on most (but not all) fronts, many of the political battles formerly explored on our stages have been won. Thus, a question arises: In this current climate, what issues do (or should) our contemporary queer theatre bring us?

This essay considers a direction for such theatre. By looking to *Small Axe* by Andrew Kushnir, *Tom at the Farm* by Michel Marc Bouchard, and *PIG* by Tim Luscombe, I examine how these three recent gay plays look to a number of contemporary gay subculture(s) and find nuance, conflict, and disparity therein. I explore how some factions within gay subculture face marginalisation and contend for expression and recognition amongst each other. By looking at divides rooted in national origin, sexual practice, and a rural-urban binary, this essay brings to light new political arenas wherein certain kinds of gayness or queerness are seen as contending for presence among more centric identities. These centric identities can be considered as *homonormative* models of queer living. Lisa Duggan, in her book *The Twilight of Equality?*, was one of the first to use the expression homonormativity: "It is a politics that does not contest dominant heteronormative assumptions and institutions, but upholds and sustains them, while promising the possibility of a demobilized gay constituency and a privatized, depoliticized gay culture anchored in domesticity and consumption" (50). The explorations made in these plays battle against and reveal problems in the predominance of homonormative identity models, and ultimately challenge them as ideals for contemporary gay community.

SMALL AXE

In January 2015 Andrew Kushnir's *Small Axe* opened at the Theatre Centre in Toronto. A work of verbatim theatre, the play examines homophobia felt by Jamaican Canadians by recounting experiences of that community. It opens with Kushnir—a gay Ukrainian Canadian—playing himself on a bare stage in front of a scrim. He tells of a conversation from his past where he and a Jamaican Canadian actor recall encounters with homophobia. Kushnir states that "we have the same story," but his fellow actor strongly disagrees (*Small Axe*). The vignette thus presents an interrogative premise for the play as a whole, as Kushnir attempts to explore how and what these differences could be. Tearing down the scrim, he reveals five actors on scaffolding, facing upstage. Facing the audience, Kushnir takes a seat surrounded by the scaffolding. Each actor then, in turn, rotates to face the audience; playing various Jamaican Canadians, they recount their experiences with homophobia in Canada, their lines drawn from interviews with queer Jamaican Canadians.

The scene's design reflects ideas that Kushnir's investigation ultimately exposes. The staging mimics the idea that the characters' experiences exist but are mostly invisible to the audience until privileged attention—that is, a white person's concern—reveals them. Furthermore, the set design makes these experiences seem distanced from the audience. In a way, the audience becomes an accomplice to the production's framing of the Jamaican Canadians' experience as marginalised. We seemingly represent the mainstream and the placing of the actors atop scaffolding makes them seem as display cases, or like exhibits in a museum: objects that can be reflected upon as separate, isolated narratives, rather than as the experiences of a part of Canadian society. The placement of Kushnir's chair, central and close to us, allies him with the audience as he conducts the proceedings. Of interest is how Kushnir's initial discussion and presentation of his own homosexuality becomes de-emphasised as he positions himself as the investigator into his subjects' sexuality. Kushnir's distance from their narratives is further emphasised as their characters only turn to speak, to Kushnir and the audience, after he reassures them of their anonymity. His assurance seems an expected protocol for gathering verbatim material (in order to protect the play's sources); however, when combined with the proxemics between Kushnir, the audience, and his subjects, the power dynamics of a kind of subject-clinician relationship emerges, and this further highlights the gap between Kushnir's perspective and the experiences of his subjects. Thus the distance and, moreover, disconnection between the experiences of Kushnir's mainstream and those of the queer Jamaican Canadians is made plain. Kushnir is a good sport in this regard and sets up his stage portrayal of himself to seem as almost willfully blinkered at worst, and insensitive at best, to underscore his point.

The underlying roots of homophobia in the Jamaican community are revealed as increasingly complex and become further alien to the "same story" Kushnir had initially proposed. Slavery, racism, colonialism, class exploitation, fundamentalist Christian televangelism, and dance-hall music misogyny all frame the particular experiences of the "subjects" and offer partial histories to the particular anti-gay enmity that they feel. A broad intersectionality between these facets of Jamaica's history and their relation to contemporary homophobia reveals other power relations at play. As the character Anthony states, "[T]here is hardly any context in which I as a black man am free to stand up, either theatrical[ly] or publicly" and express condemnation about the various injustices amidst the African diaspora, referring to his diminished ability to fight such injustices due to his position and lack of agency as a Black man. After this revelation, he and the other actors then begin to break from the containment of their platforms, descend the scaffolding, and move about the stage, eventually crossing to and joining the audience. These actions serve to dislocate Kushnir from his position of control, and moreover from his centrality in the inquiry. His representation of the audience as the mainstream is broken as the other actors, playing Jamaican Canadian characters, become constituents of it. Kushnir finally appears to become aware of his failure to take into account his own positionality or privilege. He then begins to tear down the scaffolding, seemingly cancelling the play's project. He calls into question the ownership of the play's undertaking and his subjectivity changes as *he* then becomes the focus, alone on stage, for both us and the "subjects" of his inquiry.

Kushnir's portrayal of himself embodies the privilege that separates him from and obscures the experiences of Black Jamaican Canadians. It shifts him from a position of marginality as a gay man (as might occur in a heteronormative milieu) to one of centrality, not only as the narrator and presumed controller of the play's dramaturgy, but also as a white, cisgender male. As Kushnir, the character, finally realises this, the "project" of the play fails; however, at this point different understandings emerge. While the initial premise of the play had him believing the burden of homophobia that he bears was somehow comparable to that of his Jamaican friend, it is his difficulty in comprehending that he can be *both* a victim of homophobia and in a position of entitlement that makes up his journey. This exposes and lays bare the privilege of his position as a white, entitled gay man.

While the word is never spoken, it is Kushnir's expectation of a homonormative privilege in his friend that sets off his initial inquiry. He opens the play as a thirtyish, white, cisgender, out theatre creator. It seems (and this is likely the character of Kushnir exaggerated for effect rather than the playwright himself) that he may honestly not expect his fellow gay Canadians to live much differently than him. Yet his subjects, all Black, seem from all walks of life in terms of income, age, outness, and gender. As the legacies of colonialism, racism, and slavery are discussed, by play's end we find Kushnir's initial presumption of a similar experience between himself and his fellow actors begins to seem ridiculous.

We are finally left with the play's failed project and Kushnir's realisation, as he says, that he needs to "work on his own shit first" before digging into others'. One could argue that this presents a problem dramaturgically. The play sets out to look at Jamaican Canadians' experiences of homophobia. When the play instead becomes more an illustration of Kushnir's homonormative expectations, it allows for an interesting primer on this idea. Nevertheless, it remains a play where subjects shared their experiences with the playwright, likely with an expectation that these be used to tell *their* stories and perhaps reveal insights from them. The play further includes five African Canadian actors. One might expect that the work also reflect some understandings of the homophobia that *these* Canadians endure. However, one wonders whether these ideas can all be effectively explored in the same project. The play may not be able to tackle these ideas as thoroughly as some audiences may want, and thus may be considered under-resolved.

PIG

The Urban Dictionary defines the term "pig play" as: "commonly used in the gay male community to describe the act of having dirty sex. A man engaging in pig play may perform acts of watersports, urine colonics, defecation, tag-team sex, bareback, breeding, fisting, and cum swapping" ("pig play"). On 13 September 2013, Buddies in Bad Times Theatre opened *PIG*. As one might surmise, *PIG* explores a world that, further to the above, also includes BDSM, corporal punishment, bug chasing, P&P/addiction, and snuff fantasy. However, while the work's themes of sexual play are perhaps the most polemical ideas in *PIG*, the exploration of its characters' lifestyles reveals a troubling disaffection with a centric, homonormative model of contemporary gay living.

The lifestyles presented in *PIG* appear to range from that of homonormative privilege to situations where drugged prostitutes are violently gang-raped with the intention of seroconversion. We encounter these ways of living through three actors who play a number of related characters. In the conceit of the play's construction, these characters appear to straddle a continuum of reality, or realities. This continuum is comprised of somewhat normative, perhaps "real" characters, and their related, perhaps fantasy selves, which include: seemingly autobiographical characters from their "real" characters' literary works (each actor plays a writer at some point on the continuum), their online avatars in the sex trade, and role-play characters they use in their sexual recreation. All their lives form multiple narratives that relate to each other as various fantasy threads work in and out of their own and others' supposed realities. The structure can be slightly confusing, although the audience is helped in performance by the actors' various class-identified accents.

Luscombe's narrative structure and its metatheatricality are aligned to the premise and protocols of the role-play that takes place in sexual-fantasy recreation. Thus, heard throughout the piece at all levels is the repeated inquiry of "for real?" as various characters reaffirm the parameters of their fantasy realm of the moment (Luscombe 4 and passim). This query reflects the permissions and safe-word codes that often accompany fantasy/role-play. Such words indicate limits within which one may maintain illusion as effectively as possible while still creating a safe arena for sexual play. The dramatic tactic of emulating these protocols also has a profound effect on the audience. It allows us to move through the narratives with the same tentative investment that its characters must follow. We presume ourselves to be in the moment of the scene until a theatrical "safe-word"—so to speak—of narrative moves us from that particular world. Or doesn't. It is the not knowing whether our partner in the mimesis happening on stage is going to give us that word and thus move us to the next reality that keeps us paying attention and involved in the game. And while *PIG* moves easily throughout these worlds, it is when its characters move away from fantasy that trouble occurs.

PIG features, in their least radical representations, three writers. There is mid-twenties Joe, who used to be with, or at least have sex with, the much older Harry. Now, however, Joe is settling down with middle-aged Stevie. They plan to marry and dispense with various elements from their earlier lives that they may have lived through, or role-played, or perhaps have brought to life through semi-autobiographical writings through which they gain renown. These elements include, among them, drug addiction, prostitution, and hard-core BDSM. They now plan to embrace a homonormative model. They intend to be sober, successful, and presumably monogamous. Stevie says: "No more baths. Or clubs or toilets or tricks or trade. We're gonna help each other stay clean. We're creating a clean world" (Luscombe 21).

His declaration is problematic. It equates cleanliness with the homonormative arrangement they intend, both in the idea of being free of drugs, but also eschewing some kinds of non-monogamous, and traditionally gay, sexual behaviour. Stevie's statement thus conflates their previous sexual lifestyle and associations with the unclean. His declaration recalls homophobic AIDS rhetoric of the 1980s, where the places, the frequency, and the kinds of persons one had sex with, rather than actual sexual practices, were marked as dangerous. Joe and Stevie will now opt for a "cleanliness" that emulates traditional, monogamous, heterosexual marriage, dispensing with their previous ways of meeting and engaging with sexual partners. It makes clear that a homonormative marriage displaces their previous, non-monogamous sexual behaviours while, more importantly, also suggesting—through its "cleanliness" jargon—that it is somehow AIDS-averse. This notion is underscored by Stevie's assertion about their new lifestyle; he claims, "at least it's safe" (21). However, there is no discussion about considering safer sex, or accommodating changes in their actual sexual *behaviours* in regard to their marriage bed. Their "clean" model is made even more problematic when one considers that Stevie, at least in some of the realities that circulate around him, is portrayed as HIV-positive while Joe is negative. Thus, their terms conflate their expected homonormative life with a notion of being protected from infection, when unmentioned and undiscussed safer sex practices are necessary for Joe to remain seronegative. These sets of understandings, presented as a reflection of heteronormative marriage, make for poor health strategies. They create impressions where locations and participants are associated as the nexus of disease and addiction in place of actual sexual practices. Simultaneously, they presume homonormative living to be disassociated from those same perils, regardless of the habits of those involved. In this presentation, Stevie's and Joe's embrace of the homonormative comes across as problematised from its outset.

Harry objects to other aspects of the couple's proposed change in lifestyle. He calls their plans "regressing to old testament conformity" (21). Furthermore, he asserts that the sexual extremes he and the nuptial couple used to prefer are rooted in declaring and enacting sexual agency. He claims that he uses his denied legality, denied equal rights, and denied ability to adopt as a kind of redirected oppression, to allow himself sexual licence: "I got good at absorbing the oppression. Nurtured it, redirected it, and bestowed on myself the right to fuck limitlessly about" (21). Harry extends this idea further, presenting his sexual licence as almost a kind of threat to the mainstream that so denied him rights: "Isn't that the point of being queer? In the face of hetero rage, you make it your life's mission to inseminate, without constraint or concern—" (21). The unspoken continuation of the unfinished sentence might be that one inseminates threat or disease as an attack to counter that same hetero rage.

Harry's perception of his sexual practice has some resonances with writings on anti-relational sexuality by Lee Edelman and, earlier, by Leo Bersani. Edelman, in his *No Future: Queer Theory and the Death Drive*, ultimately offers a framing of non-bioproductive, anti-relational gay sex that frees its practitioners from the heteronormative pressure of reproductive futurity. However, Harry doesn't contextualise his non-bioproductive behaviours in this way. He sees his sex as an assault (with one of the only weapons he has that the mainstream fears), as revenge for their denying him the liberties they enjoy. Harry's tactic seems to operate on the idea that a heteronormative public might still fear his "death-drive" behaviours as threatening. As such, he plays tit for tat with those strictures that he sees—as put in place by the heteronormative mainstream—are meant to contain him. In this regard his behaviour recalls even more the work of Bersani. In Bersani's essay "Is the Rectum a Grave?" from the 1980s, he posits a number of connections between homophobia and oppression and the jouissance of unrestricted gay sex. Harry seems to reflexively use his sexuality to attack the oppression of societally imposed homophobia. Ultimately, both authors allude to such sexuality as a way to reform the thinking around the sexual politics and identities that surround them. Harry's sexuality may be read in a similar way. In the passage above he announces and performs his presence as a gay man fucking as he chooses to, without the containment of "hetero rage." His sexuality, performed as such, counters the behaviours that the couple intends to model in their new arrangement. In other words, he instantiates himself as a queer man uncontained by heteronormative pressures, and, by the very act of doing so, creates a threat.

The play illustrates other moments that critique homonormative living. Harry feels that the ways of living that gay inclusion has brought with it have become far too similar to a heteronormative malaise, and that these problems go unquestioned. At Stevie and Joe's wedding, he laments:

> Because we didn't do battle through the 60s, 70s, and 80s—against ignorance, hatred and violence—in order now to ape everything that's unworkable in breederland. One in three unions ends in divorce. Lawyers and accountants clean up. What part of that do we want? (31)

He further complains that homonormativity kills gay inspiration. He finds that living in the light of an accepting society dulls the difference that he used as an impetus to create art: "queer culture is dead—The queers are free of the ghetto—gone mainstream—so gay novels are redundant. It's called irony, little one" (52). The fear that queer culture is dead presumes that it has been replaced by the homonormativity that Joe and Stevie are to embrace.

Balancing the play's complaints about the homonormative, *PIG* offers the extremes of pig culture in ways that are no more appealing. As the play progresses, the characters seek more extreme experiences and need progressively more realness. Snuff fantasies appear to be planned as fantasies no longer. Bandages and hospital visits are called for as the limits of extreme physical engagement are shifted to make the sex play more real, or realise fewer safe words. And like the play's critique of homonormativity, Luscombe shows how, at the other end of the continuum, pig culture is also seen as lacking in an authenticity that its participants appear to ache for. Here as well they progressively call for more of the "real." This lack of authenticity appears founded in the norms that socially determine these ways of being. At both ends of the spectrum there appear to be controlling rules as to how to be the gay men they want to be. The lack of choice and control at both poles leaves the characters unsatisfied. Their dissatisfaction, in turn, makes their place in each subculture tentative. And this, in turn, reflects the play's structure as they continually shift out of realities. Their dissatisfaction is revealing. What they appear to need is the ability to control and declare their own wants and their own identities. In Act Two, Stevie's autobiographical character Knife states that his embrace of risky sex and drugs gives him such a semblance of control. His personal control over his encounters with drugs, sex, and death frees him and Pig (Joe's similar character) from an expected normalness—a place where they have no control. He says by not fearing but embracing sex, drugs, and death they are freed. He claims life as a prostitute gives him freedom from the roles he is expected to take on as a gay man, a freedom to define himself: "There's no rules for us. We can be anything we want. We don't have to be the fucked-up, self-hating queens our fathers and grandfathers were. Stay with me—we'll discover who we really are" (64). He further explains that the fear of death and the way it limits him and Pig is too confining. His perspective explains his immersion in pig culture: "I say we're gonna fuck death. We ain't gonna let it make the choices. *We're* making them. We'll choose where we die and we'll choose when we die and we choose who with. And I choose here and I choose now and I choose you. Stay here forever and die with me" (65). His statement sums up one of the play's prominent points. It advocates moving outside the conformity of the various identities that have been seemingly foisted on the Western, gay male population, hand in hand, as it gained rights and emerged from the shadows. As conformity looms, the characters need to define themselves against it.

While themes of pig culture are rarely seen in contemporary gay theatre, *PIG* shows a desire for ways of living that are not controlled or defined by expectations of socially determined hegemonies. The trouble that characters have with both homonormative and pig culture come out as needing a "real"-ness that neither (sub)culture appears able to provide. As such, *PIG* offers dystopic views of both the new gay-centric world, and of a rarely seen gay-marginal world. However, one might ask why this marginal world is so rarely staged. Gay life appears to have always intersected with the pursuits that *PIG* offers, whether they have been openly celebrated or not. Any venture into the shops of Church Street in Toronto, or into Internet porn, will underscore this notion.

TOM AT THE FARM

Tom at the Farm, by Michel Marc Bouchard, opened in its English-translation premiere at Buddies in Bad Times on 11 April 2015.The play deals with Tom, a young, urban, gay man who works in advertising in Montréal. The play begins as Tom arrives for his partner's funeral—located at the family's farm in eastern Ontario—where Tom learns that his partner never told his mother that he was gay, nor of the existence of Tom at all. What Tom also encounters at the farm is a familial culture that so completely closets homosexuality that it initially appears to be like travelling back in time. However, as Tom stays after the funeral he finds a place where heteronormative understandings of masculinity are exaggerated into primal cartoons of violence, and where life is rife with homoeroticism. As he adapts to this strange environment, his masculinity changes through violent engagement with his departed partner's brother Francis (the partner is never named; hereafter, he is referred to as departed). Throughout the play, as he becomes more injured by Francis, a central query emerges: why does Tom stay? While the answer is never explicitly given, the play appears to suggest that there is something about the life at the farm that Tom likes: the kind of masculinity he takes on, the violence and nature of his homoerotic engagement with Francis, and perhaps even the heavy policing against overt, contemporary, normalised expressions of homosexuality. His immersion into the farm's retrogressive culture presents a portrait of rural queerness that, while exaggerated and distorted by the play's dreamlike construct, reflects ways of living in contemporary Canada that exist outside of the homonormative.

As Tom travels further from Montréal he appears to be travelling back in time. The play codes this sensation in several ways. When Tom first arrives at the farm, his place in the moment seems unclear. He tries to imagine another time and place, and in the opening monologue he utters, "Imagine when you were little," asking that his consciousness regress to an earlier time (Bouchard 1). Other suggestions appear. Tom's GPS in his car fails, saying "Recalculating! Recalculating!" as if his location is not a part of the temporal now (1). Tom's speech appears as mere train of thought, as only ideas of his own thinking and not necessarily meant for others to hear. His words seem unheard by those around him, or at least unacknowledged. And while Bouchard's design in this regard also allows for Tom's assertion of his own outness to appear inaudible and thus closeting him, it also creates a strange positionality for Tom in the play. Rather than seeming in the moment, there is an aspect of reminiscence to his role—as if he is reliving each moment from memory and not really able to affect the here and now. This notion is supported by Bouchard's naming of sections of the play not as scenes but rather as tableaux. While the term *tableau* recalls the word *painting* in French, its use as a theatrical form popular in the nineteenth century, where actors pose still in order to create a living but motionless narrative, adds to this sense of recollection. Naming them tableaux further helps to frame the moments of the play—at least to a reader of the script—as unchanging flashes recalled from memory, rather than active, moving narratives of the present.

As Tom becomes immersed in the life on the farm, he becomes aware of how alien he is to his surroundings. Tom is initially presented as a successful, sophisticated man in the advertising business. However, at the farm, various aspects of this identity are seen and identified as strange and unseemly. Moreover, these appear to be coded as effeminate or neutered. Early after his arrival, while trying to comprehend his surroundings, he asserts he is "too delicate" to deal with the protocols of death at his age (2). Later he recalls how his departed partner described Tom to a salesperson: "His scent is Absence, absence of testosterone," suggesting he lacks in some hormonally induced aspects of maleness (9). Francis later claims that he knew some homosexual connection to his brother, one associated with art and poetry, would "show up someday"—creating a connection between Tom's sexuality and aesthetic pursuits (14). Tom is further seen to be associated with qualities of submission and weakness, even within his relationship to his departed. When recalling their lovemaking, he uses metaphors of being restrained and lacking agency: "... arms that held me prisoner ... then sentenced me again and again ... " (19). Even Tom's choice of clothing is seen as fragile. His "fancy-boy clothes" can't be functioned in, as they are like "tissue paper" (22, 30). These associations all recall the Wildean model of homosexuals; that is, Tom's appearance recalls how the publicity surrounding Oscar Wilde's trial created an identity construction of the "homosexual" marked by Wilde's physical and social traits. These included effeteness, effeminacy, idleness and weakness, opulent clothing, and an obsession with aesthetics, among others (Sinfield 32). Such associations are likely familiar to most audiences; however, to many in contemporary Canada they may now seem anachronistic.

While Tom initially appears effeminate, he changes at the farm. Early in the play Tom is assumed to help contribute to farm work (Bouchard 21). In the process Francis teaches him to milk cows after dressing him in the departed's oversized work clothes. Tom sees the clothes as awkward, yet finds intrigue in the synthesis of their rural utility and his own aesthetics. He comments that the clothes are "[t]oo recent to be vintage, too old to be Paul Smith," and while adding a rope for a belt, comments that he may "start a new trend" (22). At this point there appears a synthesis of his urbane aesthetics and a utilitarian function. This begins a process where he appears to be "masculinised" not only through farm work but also through absurd displays of violence and endurance. In Tom's first moment with Francis, the latter strangles him and threatens Tom's life if he reveals to anyone the nature of his relationship with the departed. He is to pretend he is only a heterosexual co-worker of the departed (10). Terrified, Tom does as Francis demands. However, as the play progresses, Tom slowly stands up to Francis and expresses his own agency. He declares, "You're not going to hit me" shortly after the funeral (13). However, Francis's brute strength leads to a litany of injuries for Tom. He is prevented from driving by wounds to his wrists attained after being dragged by a rope, hog-tied, through the fields (33). However, rather than seeing the experience as a series of assaults, the incidents become framed as a masculine form of play. And Tom further responds in kind. After he kicks Francis in the ribs, stage directions indicate Francis considers the blow as "*painful, but pleasant*," indicating he likes the engagement (33). When Francis's mother, Agatha, catches them fighting, she doesn't chide them for their brutality, but rather orders "[n]ot in the kitchen!" as if their behaviour is normal and expected horseplay (33).

As time passes Tom further embraces farm life, and revels in the experiences. Tableau Six shows him with his clothes now altered to fit, and with few traces left of his previous urbane manner. A certain absurd expression of masculinity is presented as he appears covered in blood from delivering a calf—an experience he describes as "Ecstasy! Pure ecstasy!" (42). Hand in hand with Tom's integration into farm life is the escalation of his violent interactions with Francis. Strangulation, injuries, and a bizarre kind of bondage—where Tom is strung upside down and swung over a pit of animal carcasses—all come into play. What also becomes apparent, as their violence increases, is a homoerotic undercurrent running between them. Early in the play this is expressed through vague comments, such as when Francis says, "I was starting to get attached to you" (26). However, as their violent interactions increase, the comments become more pointed: "[t]here, caught my man" and "[l]ook how handsome he is when he is mad" (32). Their attraction progresses to various intimate acts: Francis washing blood off Tom's naked torso, the two of them ballroom dancing together in the barn, and the two of them kissing. However, after they kiss Francis is compelled to strangle Tom once again (47). Strangling is "*calm and pleasurable*" for Francis, and he creates limits for Tom like those found in *PIG*: "You tell me when to stop. You decide. Give me a signal and I'll stop. It's up to you man. More? You're tough man, you're tough" (47).

The nature of the relationship is fascinating. It is well studied that rural environments in contemporary Canada tend to be difficult places in which to express non-heteronormative sexualities, especially for youth (Poon and

Saewyc). It seems that while Francis is strongly attracted to Tom, his rural culture is so self-policing against overt expressions of homosexuality that when their attraction becomes physicalised it must also be masculinised through excessive expressions of violence. While the violence between them originates in Francis forcing Tom to closet his relationship with the departed, the violence evolves to become part of their daily routine. What their behaviours create is an absurd rendition of a rural, queer relationship—one that, while it is strongly guarded from any Wildean aspects of queer expression, celebrates exaggerated flourishes of extreme masculinity. Of interest is how Tom takes it on. While he is clearly charmed by the farm animals—he is gentle with them and pets them—there is obviously a stronger attraction that keeps him there, even when he becomes "*so battered*" by Francis's violence that his bruised appearance raises alarm (22, 60). It appears that he at least partially enjoys the appropriated masculinity that comes with rural life. He obviously is drawn to Francis, who is seen as physically "identical" to his departed brother (57). However, Francis's country ways, with their overt expressions of masculinity, differ from the departed's more urbane and aesthetic concerns. Furthermore, we learn that the departed was consistently unfaithful to Tom, while Francis seems to care only for his mother, the farm, and, at times, Tom (66). Somehow, these aspects of life at the farm become more appealing to Tom than did his seeming homonormative life in Montréal.

Tom at the Farm might be considered a critique of the homonormative life that we presume Tom and the departed enjoyed in Montréal, if only for the fact that Tom seems to find something there that keeps him at the farm long after he ought to have left. However, it might equally be seen to comment on queer life in rural Canada. The reminiscing style of Tom's dialogue, complemented in its Buddies production by a spartan but effective set, further gives the play a sense of nostalgia. It presents as a counter to metropolitan, homonormative living the simplicity of a perhaps longed-for, pastoral, unaesthetic existence from a simpler time. In such a place traditional masculinities are pronounced and physical labour is celebrated—notions not commonly associated with homonormative models. While Bouchard presents this site as only a dream, a reminiscence, one where the realities underneath—such as a discomfort with non-heteronormative sexualities—bubble up in distorted and violent ways, some aspects of it nevertheless have a strong appeal.

CONCLUSION

All three of these plays rely on the differences between the experiences of gay men across a range of circumstances for their dramatic substance. While Jamaican Canadians and perhaps those involved in pig play can be considered subcultures of a queer mosaic, Bouchard's depictions of rural queer life in eastern Ontario may not be, as rural and urban distinctions are harder to quantify. Nevertheless, all these plays find dramatic fodder in how they explore persons in reaction to the centrality of the homonormative. While the word homonormative is a fairly recent coinage, the ideas it denotes have been expressed for a number of years. Mattilda Bernstein Sycamore has long written of how a culture of commodification and a tentative acceptance of queerness have led to an assimilation of queer culture within a dominant, white, male hegemony. This "assimilation robs queer identity of anything meaningful, relevant, or challenging" and instead "presents a sanitized, straight friendly version of gay identity" (Bernstein Sycamore 3). She believes that assimilation carries with it the "violence of cultural erasure" (5) and sees contemporary queer culture, in its embracing of same-sex marriage and other rites, promoting queers to behave in ways patterned after the heteronormative, consumer family, even though this ideal is usually only available to queer white males of means. She further claims that assimilation into a white, heteronormative "queer" ideal is violence against those living outside "a ravenous gay mainstream," which "seeks control, of not only our bodies and minds but . . . the very ways we represent our own identities" (5).

The interplay between the assimilationist and/or cultural-identity tendencies of an evolving gay culture can be troubling. While many celebrate the fact that we can regularly have gay theatre across Canada, attained with similar funding and theatrical practices as other mainstream and alternative works, is such acceptance within mainstream theatrical practice something that may bring with it its own problems or perils? Might the success, or no-longer-in the-shadows aspect, of contemporary gay theatre in Canada be helping, or at least ignoring, the erasure of other queer cultures? When one looks to *Small Axe* this may seem especially poignant. It is hard enough to see theatre about the Jamaican Canadian experience without imagining where one might find theatre about gay Jamaican Canadians. *Small Axe* begins to share some of these experiences but eventually folds back to the problem of its own premise. In 2016 its creator had three pieces mounted in three different theatres in a span of less than eighteen months. One might presume that he brought his considerable cultural capital to the project and thus assisted in it getting produced. However, it ultimately turns out to be a story about his character's hubris in trying to tell others' stories. The fact that these were told, and an audience was given insight into their lives, is nevertheless important. However, had the project been led by a Jamaican Canadian, one wonders if we'd have been able to see it.

Since Duggan wrote of homonormativity as "a politics that does not contest dominant heteronormative assumptions and institutions, but upholds and sustains them," her idea has been expanded upon (50). Some contemporary definitions offer more generalised understandings: usually as a practice in which heteronormative ideals and constructs are embraced by gay culture and assimilated into individual identity, often at the expense of particular or marginal aspects of subcultural identity construction. The characters in *PIG* seem at times torn between the homonormative marriage they see as a kind of haven and the marginalised sexual desires, practices, and culture that they like. These appear as the poles they have to exist between. These definitions of homonormativity promote the question: Must the culture a person likes be imperiled by the one that person feels safe in?

As inclusion expands across the globe, one might consider whether *all* aspects of gay and queer cultures, and their sexual subcultures, should fall within its orbit. Surely some gay men's subcultural sexual practices evolved out of the repressive heteronormative policing that formerly surrounded gay men—i.e., cottaging, etc. But does their provenance in a repressive environment make them any less legitimate as gay culture? Does gay inclusion, slowly happening now in a number of non-Western societies, mean that Duggan's kind of homonormativity is the end point of equality for gays there? And at what cost might this shift be to these subcultures and their ways of being as they exist now? A question needs to be asked: By what rubric, or on whose terms, do aspects of gay culture become acceptable or come under the totality of homonormativity? Are the aspects of what is, or becomes, homonormative determined by the patterns of its looming hegemon—heteronormativity—as Duggan seems to suggest? Will governing ideals of homonormativity pose degrees and limits on the kind of sexual/gender drift from heteronormativity that our society will allow and celebrate in terms of its sense of inclusion, while BDSM, tea-room trading, or other queernesses are rigorously policed against? And when Buddies shows a play full of pig culture, or cottaging, or any behaviours outside of the homonormative, is this an act of defiance, of inclusion, or perhaps of chastisement? Buddies in Bad Times might be perceived as a proudly alternative arts nest, but it is also patronised by a number of wealthy, male, white benefactors. These donors appear in many regards as—other than their presumed sexuality—conservatives and members of the one percent. What pressures might they bring to the presentations of queerness presented there? Does fiscal conservatism bring with it a sexual "conservatism"?

So what then should we see on our stages? Are homonormative narratives already too symptomatic of, and assimilated into, an elite system that is part and parcel of a neoliberal hegemony? Even if so, are they also likely to make queer theatre more palatable to the mainstream and/or conservative audiences at the apex of the theatre industry? Are such representations, if they go unchallenged, healthy for our stages? Do they belong there? Or must queer or gay theatre show the plight of the marginalised? That is, must it continue to do the work, as Shewey said, of "acting as a corrective to neglect or abuse by a culture at large" (xi)? Will it make a difference how assimilated, "gender-appropriate," and mainstream the characters we watch are? What are the effects of watching the homonormative as opposed to the marginalised?

Such questions cannot be answered easily or glibly. One might wish that all staged representations of queerness reflect the broad experiences of our audiences and communities. However, this is unlikely; anyone who is aware of Canadian queer theatre over the last thirty years will notice there are massive differences in its visibility, and, accordingly, in the grant monies disbursed to, say, lesbian theatre as opposed to gay men's theatre. An even wider chasm of opportunity and availability arises when one looks at theatre about trans persons. How might homonormative conventions and presences on our stages affect the ability for trans persons to see their experiences staged? Is there a homonormative identity construction available for trans persons? Marginalisation *within* queer communities is a fact, and a failure to analyse or at least recognise the meanings created by our theatre, and *how* it may mean to differently marginalised queer persons, could easily leave our theatre dominated by stories about white, cis-gender, English-speaking, married folks, as it was in the 1960s. Such a theatre would surely be as marginalising and problematic as was the theatre then. The only difference is that it would happen to be about gay people as well.

PRODUCTIVE CONTRARY: COUNTERPERFORMATIVE RESISTANCE OF THE QUEERED-QUEER, THE OTHERED-OTHER

SPY DÉNOMMÉ-WELCH

> *Silence is not a banal process; rather it is full of stripping, tearing, gouging, and* pain.
> —Shantel Martinez, " 'For Our Words Usually Land on Deaf Ears Until We Scream': Writing as a Liberatory Practice."
>
> *Testimony may involve discovering the words behind certain kinds of inarticulations but crucially also entails finding alternate strategies of tracing and presence-ing the very contours or shapes of our silences.*
> —Proma Tagore, *Shapes of Silence: Writing by Women of Colour and the Politics of Testimony*

PREAMBLE

Sitting here, gazing at my screen, I contemplate what exactly it means to think, write, and speak about Indigenous identity (specifically ways of being, seeing, and living), and how it relates to queer theatre and performance in Canada. How are these particular identities, entities, and spaces connected, or are they at odds given their unique, and perhaps contradictory, histories? These contradictions exist at the root of historical and ongoing exclusions of Indigenous (queer) bodies, obstructing their capacity to participate more broadly within "mainstream" theatre and queer performance spaces, thereby perpetuating similar structures of colonial dominance, and ultimately reinforcing "the erasure of indigenous knowledge, and the downplay of native traditions, turning the ones that survived into mere 'curiosities' " (Arboleda-Ríos 192).

There has been a plethora of work written on discursive topics of queer theory, identity, and performance. Many scholars, thinkers, activists, and artists alike have already examined and challenged the status quo and deep-rooted ideas and issues concerning heterosexism, heteronormativity, and heteromasculinity, and their impacts on the spaces and everyday lives of queer bodies. The term itself—"queer"—carries many historical, political, and emotional subjectivities, and has been scrutinized through post-colonial discourses and decolonizing critiques which examine, for example, the implications for Indigenous and non-Indigenous allyship and decolonization (Hunt and Holmes), decolonizing racial bias, gender binaries, and Indigenous invisibility in civil-rights issues (Morgensen), and decolonizing gendered knowledge and Indigenous queer performance (Arboleda-Ríos). While terms such as decolonization and Indigenization are loaded and have evolved into hot-button, go-to language, it remains to be seen how these will affect predominantly non-Indigenous spaces and queer theatre and, more specifically, heteronormativity (internalized or not) within performance spaces—particularly ones which remain silent and unresponsive to the cultural realities and experiences of queered-Queer Indigenous presence.

RUMINATIONS ON THE EFFECTS OF THE QUEERED-QUEER, OTHERED-OTHER

Notwithstanding the occasional tokenistic gestures masquerading as acts of kindness and inclusion (i.e., one-off Indigenous performance events or "traditional" opening ceremonies tacked on to festivals), there is an enduring struggle to create real Indigenous visibility among the sacred spaces of the theatre that is predominated by colonial ideologies. Given that many theatre spaces are lacking in terms of representations of Indigenous voices and expressions, let alone Indigenous queer (re)presentations, the challenge is with how to create real decolonization in performance spaces and structures within the theatre industry. I can appreciate the various ways that Indigenous (queer or queered) performativity is resurging within atypical spaces of performativity, such as healing ceremonies and community-based activism—spaces that may be more befitting and in alignment with authentic forms of decolonization. However, in the theatre I find myself averse to the unavoidable implications of prescribing definitions or categories, such as queer or Indigenous theatre, as these communities bear their own struggles and *pain*.

To define or construct one's own identity or the identities of others is certainly performative, but it is also a political act. In her work on queer performance and notions of resistance, Elizabeth Whitney argues, "Like all radical community endeavours, queer politics have been shaped through resistance to restrictive ideologies. There is always risk involved: a bit of danger" (250). While defining or constructing gendered and sexuality identities may create a sense of cultural or social visibility, they alone do not redress or even address the ongoing colonial violence faced by people with Indigenous identities, which occurs within and beyond the Canadian theatre. Merely adding terms like Two-Spirit, 2-Spirited, 2S, or similar language among the list of acronyms contained in a company's mission statement or vision is not enough to counter the persistent acts of exclusion aimed at Indigenous people. Rather, it takes a real ideological overhaul to create spaces that challenge the daily operations and "business as usual" forms of oppression and exclusion of the othered-Other.

So what then does queerness mean exactly in relation to descriptions, definitions, and categories of Indigenous theatre and performance in Canada? Furthermore, do these categories reinforce or challenge the continual erasure of (queer) Indigenous North America? Under no certain terms does this even come close to acknowledging or confronting the distinct isolation or pain that can be felt in the real, lived, day-to-day experiences of queer Indigeneity that exists beyond the vacuum of identity politics. Rather it exposes deep contradictions about the lack of Indigenous presence within largely non-Indigenous queer spaces, which is perpetuated by and through systematic colonialism, willful blindness, and the subjugation of Indigenous (queered) bodies that beget non-visible status. Therefore, the idea of presenting or presence-ing

Indigenous queer identity brings into focus the contradictory sites from which to perform decolonization and acts of resistance that counter hegemonic notions and imaginings of Indigenous identity and performance. Might these intersections and contradictions help illuminate or inhibit Indigenous theatre when Indigenous visibility itself has been queered as an art form while enduring ongoing oppression? In other words, while articulations of Indigenous theatre are already frequently queered by the very nature of it being Othered through marginalization, the visible and even non-visible dissident queer Indigenous is by default a whole other queered-Queer that threatens such establishments and is thus cast as the othered-Other.

Considering the real or contrived meanings of colonization and its consequences, I ruminate on some of the theoretical and methodological underpinnings of queer aesthetics and decolonizing performance, drawing on José Esteban Muñoz's idiom of disidentification as a means to consider how these may or may not be (re)enacted in my own work and collaborative creations. To synthesize parts of Muñoz's theories of disidentification, Brittany Chávez explains that "[d]isidentification breaks with binary models of resistance, which tend to fall back into the logics they purport to oppose" (151). The irony of a binary existence is that while it is simple to identify and subsequently disidentify with any form of dichotomy, is it necessarily a productive resistance? Muñoz argues:

> Disidentification is the third mode of dealing with dominant ideology, one that neither opts to assimilate within such a structure nor strictly opposes it; rather, disidentification is a strategy that works on and against dominant ideology. Instead of buckling under the pressures of dominant ideology (identification, assimilation) or attempting to break free of its inescapable sphere (counteridentification, utopianism), this "working on and against" is a strategy that tries to transform a cultural logic from within, always laboring to enact permanent structural change while at the same time valuing the importance of local or everyday struggles of resistance. (11–12)

Arguably, being Indigenous and queer presenting, or at the very least queered by way of one's work and, furthermore, resistant to the embrace of colonial imaginings, presents a form of disidentification or by design a way of "confronting audiences with the sometimes dangerous truths about queer life" (Whitney 246). Needless to say, confronting or challenging such sensitivities does come at the risk of suffering from "stripping, tearing, gouging, and *pain*" (Martinez 7), and requires some amount of social, political, and economic ambidexterity to navigate a system built on the dialogical patterns and algorithms of oppression. This point is not made lightly, nor does it attempt humour or metaphor, although both are necessary to survive in the hostile and relentless landscape of colonialism. Rather it is necessary to contend with the reality that our collective history has engendered much violence toward Indigenous queer people, and, regardless of our will to wish it all away, it is as with anything else acutely woven into the pathology and psyche of our theatre system. But to which end, and to whose will, do we even begin to untangle this?

A TOKEN FOR THE SHOW: DISLODGING THE COLONIAL CLUTCHES THROUGH COUNTERPERFORMATIVITY

Is it necessary to subscribe to specific definitions of "queer" when and if one's work is already queered by virtue of it being othered? What potential contradictions or dangers could emerge as a consequence of assuming or subscribing to rigid categories and definitions? As Muñoz suggests, might there indeed be a different space, structure, or way to examine these imposed definitions of queerness and Indigeneity within theatre without as a result becoming didactic, or othering, or implicated in a paradigm of oppression? It is difficult to know if any of the answers to such questions exist, given the longitudinal range and far-reaching expanse of colonialism. Basically, it is a big problem without simple answers, and it is easy to dwell in the hopelessness of the idea that there will never be change. Change is always happening, occurring at exceedingly rapid speeds, but it does not mean that all change is productive or useful. The relics of change as a result of some form of impact can take up a lot of unproductive space, just like anything else. For instance, while theories of the big bang or expanding universes suggest impact and expansion, they exist in relation to a form of opposition and even nothingness. In fact, at any given time we can stagnate while being in motion (something as simple as sitting on a moving train) or exist without living (contemplating the meaning of life while living in fear of death) or know without being aware (being given an answer to something that takes you fifty years to comprehend).

The continuum upon which resistance and impact coexist is conceivably fixed while being constantly in flux (again, a contradiction), producing some of the most profound histories of silence within moments of performativity. But in order to consider ideas of a so-called Indigenous queer theatre, one must take into account, and contend with, the temporal duration and performative characteristics of violence. However, it does not quantify or qualify the extent to which acts of violence toward Indigenous people (in particular the queered-Queer, othered-Other) have been occurring ever since contact, playing out before citizens and passersby (the audience) who are complicit in the theatre of colonial violence—the theatre of the othered-Other.

It is difficult to process the lingering, well-implemented, and compounded organism of colonialism while still existing within the very clutches of its shadow. So what is it to have a queer or Indigenous queer theatre in Canada? Is it that queer, let alone Indigenous queer, theatre simply exists on the basis of there being a theatre house, a company, a collective, an anthology, or a production? Or, is it that all Indigenous theatre is a form of queered theatre? Whereas the queered Indigenous queer—the queered-Queer, othered-Other—is a further permutation and display of an even more radical queered theatre, one deeply affected by the fissures of colonial violence that functions no differently than the oppressive systems that underscore our nation? In other words, do our theatres, like our nation (the producer), merely reproduce the traces of colonialism (the production, season by season) that permeates all structures and preserves expressions of oppression across our commonwealth (including theatres of government, politics, law, policing, etc.)?

Given the extent to which the queered-Queer and othered-Other Indigenous body has been colonized, it will take some deep decolonization, a type of critical performative pedagogy, to dislodge, unlearn, and purge itself of this. When considering the body and its relation to critical performative pedagogy in education and the performative role of the educator, Dominique Hill explains how it is "an educational intervention used by educators who believe that we, as educators, are responsible for critiquing, identifying possibilities of what could be, and bringing to action potential visions" (166). Similarly, to activate any formulae of Indigenous resistance using critical modes of queerness requires rigorous yet self-compassionate decolonizing strategies that are mindful to "the performing body" (Dominique Hill 167). Being mindful and compassionate to the body means having to counterperform the role of the colonizer/colonized, which we have come to rehearse and perform to near total perfection. To produce counterperformativity through queerness and Indigeneity is a striking form of decolonial intervention that disrupts heteronormativity and the "isms" of colonialism, which together live and breathe profusely within and beyond our theatre walls, through twisted public and private spectacle, and what has become the scripting of the queered-Queer, the othered-Other, into obscurity.

The notion of politicizing art is not exactly a new thing, but in Indigenous theatre it is precipitated by the fallout of colonialism, and is used as a tool for survival, necessitated by the need to create a radical presence that disrupts colonial heteronormativity and subjectivity, which would otherwise continue to suppress the othered-Other—the Indigenous queer. The use of satire and decolonization, which I have used in my own work and will discuss in the final section of this essay, could present a modality for disidentificatory forms of counterperformativity (Muñoz, *Disidentifications*). Muñoz illuminates, "Disidentificatory performances sometimes mimic and remake those performances with a critical worldmaking difference, but such performances are some among many" (*Disidentifications* 199). Arguably, without recognizing the way things are and have been, or having a vision for what could be otherwise, we are fated to perpetually fail at disengaging and dislodging the body of its tepid colonial veneer, and that begs the question, what is the purpose of our theatres, music halls, or galleries, if only to reproduce the same old circus?

VICTORIAN SECRETS AND DECOLONIZATION AS COUNTERPERFORMATIVITY

In 2014 I began work on a three-part music/theatrical work, entitled *Victorian Secrets*, with my collaborator, Catherine Magowan. This would be our third theatrical/music work, which is written for three actors with accompanying piano. Prior to this creation we had also developed and co-produced with Native Earth Performing Arts our first full-length opera, entitled *Giiwedin*, which was written for nine voices. Between and since these two projects we have also co-composed chamber works drawing on different instrumentations, themes, and subject matter.

While each of our collaborative works has to some degree been presented as a form of disidentifactory performance, what I will discuss here for the sake of this essay are some of the components through which *Victorian Secrets* has served as a form of counterperformativity. As with virtually all other aspects of our work, we have constantly needed to challenge notions of collective theatre and opera creation, queered Indigenous sexuality and gendered norms, and colonial constructs of heteronormativity. Further, our process of collaboration, particularly in areas of music, requires challenging dominant ideas and discourses of composer voice and single authorship, as there exist so few examples of co-composer works in the fields of music and opera. As a consequence, when creating new works, our collaborative process has required an ongoing decolonizing process, whereby each project undergoes its own (re)visioning to work through the dynamics of co-composition and creation. Although I take on the role of playwright/librettist, having written the text for *Giiwedin* and *Victorian Secrets*, Magowan and I share the role of co-composers, which is where much of the decolonial work occurs in rich and textured ways.

Victorian Secrets[1] came about through reenvisioning ways of disrupting colonial narratives and restrictive ideologies about sexuality and gender through theatre, music, and performance. By applying a critical lens to Victorian sexuality norms and gendered boundaries, the work combines a script for three actors with accompanying piano. Using Victorian-era images, the work is comprised of three ten-minute scenes (vignettes) that explore the constructs of sexuality and sexual repression, juxtaposed against contemporary language and technologies, and uses satire to examine historical and present-day forms of oppression through human relationships. It is presented as a surreal, minimalist cabaret, bringing to the fore humour and satire to draw critical observations and parallels about gendered and racialized forms of colonization in North America.

The work applies a queering lens, beginning with titles for each scene that borrow from Victorian-era slang and expressions: the first vignette is titled "Tallywags" (slang for testicles) the second "Kettle Drums" (slang for breasts), and the third "Storm of Heaves" (slang for getting it on). The scenes can be performed by actors of various gender identities, specifically "Tallywags," which is written for two male characters (Man 1 and Man 2); "Kettle Drums," for a female character (Woman) and non-gender/sex descript human computer (Doctor Internet); and "Storm of Heaves," written for two female characters (Woman 1 and Woman 2). The piano accompaniment, which establishes the tone at the top of each scene, also underscores the dialogue and action that takes place on stage. The composition draws on different musical styles and aesthetics, used to accentuate the elements of queerness that build throughout the piece. Here I look at two specific vignettes, "Tallywags" and "Kettle Drums," to elaborate on some of their decolonial approaches around performativity and queerness, which counter dominant ideologies of colonization as it is (re)enacted through expressions of heteronormativity and masculinity.

The work was first presented in 2014 at Native Earth Performing Arts's Weesageechak Begins to Dance festival; it featured actors Nicole Joy-Fraser,

1 *Victorian Secrets*, co-composed by Spy Dénommé-Welch and Catherine Magowan, with text written by Spy Dénommé-Welch.

Michaela Washburn, and Keith Barker, Cecilia Lee on piano, and was directed by Moynan King. The work was presented a second time in June 2015 in association with Toronto Pride as part of Free Jane, hosted by Sky Gilbert at Buddies in Bad Times Theatre. The second performance featured a slightly different cast, including Michaela Washburn, Falen Johnson, Craig Lauzon, and Cecilia Lee on piano, and again was directed by Moynan King. Seeing the work presented in two different spaces, with two different sets of audiences, was an excellent opportunity to see the ways in which the satire and political aspects of the work transgressed and translated to different groups of people.

"TALLYWAGS" AND "KETTLE DRUMS"

Some years ago, as I was rummaging through an antique booth, I came upon a bunch of old, faded, discarded photos and cabinet cards. Many of the images stood out to me, including one with two men standing right next to each other in a park looking directly at the camera. Much like any other discarded thing or object, I could not determine exactly where or of whom this image was taken, except to say that it dated back to approximately the Victorian era. The image itself did not unlock any secrets about Victorian culture and society, but instead offered a pallet of shapes and traces of sepia past that was ripe with colonial subjectivity. It also provided a springboard to consider a different way to imagine a counterperformative approach to storytelling and decolonizing performance. While contemplating these shapes, I began to imagine a different story, one premised around two Indigenous male characters (Man 1 and Man 2), dressed in attire reminiscent of Victorian fashion, working as peddlers in a park trying to push their products.

At the very top of the scene, Man 1 is already standing in the park, working his usual turf, gesturing to his regular clients and other passersby, looking to make a quick sale (unbeknownst to the audience he is stocked with risqué merchandise tucked under his jacket). Soon after, Man 2 enters and moves in on Man 1's space. At first Man 1 assumes Man 2 has come to purchase some product, only to learn that in fact Man 2 is there to sell his own line of merchandise. What follows is a battle of words between Man 1 and Man 2 over turf, dirty business, markets, and profits, bringing to the fore a satirical examination of the effects of colonization on Indigenous people, land, goods, and trades. In writing this scene I was examining the parallels between the colonization of land, consumerism, and capitalism next to queerness, sexuality, and Indigenous identity. This intermixing of themes presents a decolonizing portrait of colonial life and its aftershocks, thus in turn presenting colonialism as the perverse. The following excerpt from "Tallywags" happens early in the scene, illustrating some of this interplay between Man 1 and Man 2:

> **MAN 1:** Are you here for product?
> **MAN 2:** Well, actually,
> I'm here to sell it.
> Not buy.
> **MAN 1:** On my turf?!
> You've got nerve!
> **MAN 2:** I'd like to see this more
> As a company merge.
> Or I'd like to entertain the possibility.
> **MAN 1:** Whatcha got to sell
> I don't already have?
> **MAN 2:** Beads. (Pause)
> Feathers. (Pause)
> Paddles. (Pause)
> **MAN 1:** What are you looking for?
> **MAN 2:** Some turf . . .
> Some of this fine, fine, fine SPACE!
> Would you look at this space?!
> Who needs ALL this space
> For themselves?
> **MAN 1:** Beads . . . feathers . . . paddles, eh?
> **MAN 2:** Yup!

MAN 1: Sounds kinda cheap.
Think I'd fall for that one?!
That might've worked
For the guys stealing Toronto and New York . . .
But here? Ha! (5–6)

This short excerpt utilizes double entendres and queer undercurrents to challenge dominant notions of sexuality and gender, punctuating and subverting heteronormativity with decolonizing subtext and affect. These two seemingly generic characters, performed by Indigenous actors, disrupt the colonial gaze by playing on archetypes and tropes. For instance, the specific reference to beads, feathers, and paddles suggests sex toys on the one hand, while on the other it conjures up the stereotypical, romanticized images too often associated with Indigenous people (e.g., the feather-and-bead wearing Indigenous person in a canoe), and furthermore acknowledges the histories of unfair trade, theft, and pillaging of Indigenous land. This interaction and sexualized wordplay becomes a site of rupture, with undertones that turn the colonial gaze and heterosexist imagination on their heads.

Victorian Secrets is a work that literally and figuratively takes up heavy and loaded histories but gives these topics a satirical treatment—a theatrical device aimed at rupturing static notions of Indigeneity and queerness. In particular, the second vignette, "Kettle Drums," examines the pathologization of Indigenous bodies, minds, and spirituality that has been long subjected to clinical dissection. From the top of the scene, Woman expresses concerns about her health, and Doctor Internet proceeds to question her mental and physical state in a way that becomes increasingly invasive, ridiculous, and offensive, which in turn breeds anxiety. The following excerpt from that scene illustrates how invasions of privacy are (re)enacted through forms of medical and technological colonialism:

DOCTOR INTERNET: Any family history of congenital heart disease?
Physical defects?
Have you or anyone you know been in jail,

A psych ward, or a museum?
WOMAN: Does public housing count?
DOCTOR INTERNET: Depends on the demographic makeup . . .
I see that you're wearing makeup . . .
(Pause.)
WOMAN: What about public toilets?
DOCTOR INTERNET: All depends on the situation.
Was there a glory hole?
(Pause.)
WOMAN: I've only been curious.
But never tried it myself.
Have you?
DOCTOR INTERNET: Let's focus on you, the patient.
WOMAN: Why?
DOCTOR INTERNET: Doesn't obey commands.
Questions the questionnaire.
Easily agitated.
WOMAN: I wasn't—
DOCTOR INTERNET: Delusional . . .
Do you believe in God?
WOMAN: When it's convenient,
Or if I'm told to.
DOCTOR INTERNET: Saint or Sinner?
WOMAN: Do I have to choose?
DOCTOR INTERNET: Conform or deviance?
WOMAN: There's a difference?
DOCTOR INTERNET: Fascinating.
WOMAN: What is?
DOCTOR INTERNET: With all these symptoms
It's a little difficult to make an accurate prognosis.
WOMAN: What does that mean—
Am I going to die?!
DOCTOR INTERNET: Surely. (16–18)

This scene directly and indirectly tackles the inevitable consequences of colonization while addressing social, cultural, and racial policing and sexual regulation, such as the overpathologizing of the Other, in particular the othered-Other and queered-Queer. It speaks to the broader implications of colonial ideologies, such as the incarceration and impoverishment of Indigenous people, and the persisting, generational effects of trauma through social, cultural, spiritual, and economic exploitation of Indigenous bodies and minds (i.e., the scene critiques how Indigenous people have been put on display in museums, psych wards, jails, and public housing). While satire draws on cutting humour, it also reveals some of the real illnesses and perversities of colonialism in North America, and a form of counterpublic performativity, as Muñoz describes, "Counterpublic performances let us imagine models of social relations. Such performance practices do not shy away from the theoretical and practice of cultural critique" (*Disidentifications* 33).

Since creating and presenting *Victorian Secrets*, Magowan and I have gone on to explore other modes of counterperformativity, thus expanding our concepts of decolonization through music, theatre, text, and sonic experimentations. Our current project, entitled *HATE MAIL and Irreconcilable Trolls* (which premiered at Weesageechak Begins to Dance in November 2017) takes up the fragmented and fracturing debate around cultural appropriation and various social, cultural, historical, and contemporary expressions of hate that persist in art, politics, in the public and private sectors, and in the online and offline worlds. While our work continues in the same vein of humour and satire seen in *Victorian Secrets*, this work is somewhat of a departure as it tackles head on various current affairs and heated political issues in Canada while subverting the gross nature of colonialism within art and our political system. Working with public documents (in the public domain), this piece is written for soprano/actor, contrabassoon, and piano and includes electronics. As a creative duo, Magowan and I have been working with musical themes and subjects, and while these may not always be seemingly "queer" on the surface, they are, I would say, radically queered through the lens of political art, composition, and performance.

To return to some of the original points I made earlier pertaining to the question of what is Indigenous queer theatre, there is obviously no clear-cut answer. However, as I have previously argued, much of Indigenous theatre is already queered given the depth of its own marginalization, and consequently its own form of (counter)resistance to dominant hegemony, heteronormativity, and colonialism that prevails within the theatre at large. But within this paradigm exists an even more radical theatre, one that is born of the othered-Other, which becomes a site to instigate deeper resistance. As such, the very existence of the othered-Other—the queered-Queer—is one that ultimately strikes at the hegemonic core of racism and homophobia permeating our theatres and productions. Indeed, the Indigenous queer—the queered-Queer, the othered-Other—may very well be the ultimate radical and productive contrary yet.

QUEER REDO

SARAH GARTON STANLEY

Q2Q: A Symposium on Queer Theatre and Performance in Canada came at me as a fractious, fertile, broken, creative, bitter, unresolvable, and at times beautiful prism of conversation. Bridges were built as others were burning. Generations communicated across the divides with megaphones; and within shared age ranges and formations they whispered with spaghetti tins tied together with string.

I had a really hard time being at the conference. My assessment was that I was not the only one who felt this way. The difficulty was largely related to the fact that, for what felt like the first time in Canadian history, Queer performing artists from across the land were gathering to attempt to take one another seriously. Seriously? Yes. And taking one another seriously, respectfully, for the marginalized, for the often reviled and usually dismissed, is a tough job.

This meeting was timely. In my evolving understanding I see how Queer, LGBTQ, Trans are words that for many years now have been held hostage to the dominant frameworks of white cultural ideals. It makes sense to me that Queer, Trans, and LGBTQ are themselves evolutions from pervert/invert to lesbian/gay, but as a white settler of tremendous inherited privilege I see more each day how that which I previously understood to be *wide* is without a doubt incredibly *narrow*. Any assumptions as to commonalities across queer performing-arts lines are clearly in need of a shakedown, and Q2Q was a key site of this ongoing action.

We gathered in fluorescent-lit rooms at Simon Fraser University, in Vancouver's legendary retrofitted Woodward's Building in the city's Downtown Eastside. The room, itself removed from the neighbourhood's most recent iteration, made it a good metaphor for the complexity of change. The Downtown Eastside was not always a legend for tragedy, and the previous governing definitions for Queer were only the previous governing definitions. Places and ideas age out. They fail. This remains a constant.

In my own experience, failure is a constant partner in the necessary renewal or perpetual redefinition of "Queer" as a word. Something has to fail before space can be created for what is needed to succeed. At Q2Q I was challenged by a participant for placing faith in failure. It was understood by my challenger to be a privilege to valorize failure when survival was at issue.

The challenge was levelled at me from a member of a QTIBPOC alliance that met the day before the conference began. This group—that I envied for their apparent sense of belonging—brought the necessary disruption. Gone, obliterated, never to be seen again, was a shared platform where Queers across generations, socio-economic status, educational background, Queers who were Black, Indigenous, People of Colour or White, could assume that they were coming at that word (Queer) or the world from the same place. And, yes, this assumption needed to be shorn and, yes, it needed to be shorn because it holds white-supremacist values within it. And fuck.

In advance of the conference, Sky Gilbert and I had been working on *The Wrinkle Bar.* Current Buddies in Bad Times Theatre Artistic Director Evalyn Parry had joined us at this very early and unformed stage. Together we were set to share a brief excerpt of the piece at the gathering. In many ways, this piece was about a desire for connection in what was increasingly feeling like a disconnected world. Our piece centres on a rupture in Sky's and my relationship in the aftermath of me succeeding him as the next AD at Buddies.

Within our piece Sky denies that he harboured any negative feelings toward me; he does admit, however, that until I reached out to him he hardly thought about me at all. It is a good piece, with lots of potential for a dramatic mining of connection and disconnection. We did not end up showing any of *The Wrinkle Bar* at Q2Q. Due to disharmonies between the gathered, we chose not to present the piece, but, instead, to build space for conversation. It felt productive.

The Wrinkle Bar begins to unpack the truth about aging in a culture that used to have no aging in view. In Canada, before Trudeau senior famously allowed for the business of the bedroom to be divorced from the business of the nation, the idea of Queers growing old seemed unimaginable to subsequent generations. In the '80s and '90s, in Canada, for men—and, in my world, it crossed over into women's queer cultural considerations—live fast and die young was a mantra. Being prepared for the end was part of the intensity of the moment, of the revolution, and, indeed, harsh reality of the time.

When I was at Buddies in the dying years of the last century, we witnessed the end of HIV/AIDS as a certain death sentence and the beginning of trans culture as an anchoring force in the reshaping of Queer culture. When Sky left Buddies we were not yet online. When I left Buddies we had an info@ email account and a website "under construction." Our phones rang non-stop. The world had a different sound then, but heartbreaks, maligning, malingering, and discontents happened, and so too did salvaging. Salvaging a way forward, night after night, week after week, and year after year. Q2Q caused me to think about what should be salvaged now.

One of the things that stays with me following Q2Q was a Brad Fraser admonishment about our internal struggles within the Q2Q conversation, and his contention that we were doing what the neoliberal forces wanted by dividing ourselves at the bottom, distracting ourselves with oppositional stances down low, so that we can be fucked from above. This is a free remembrance and now similarly a free interpretation of a passing remark he made, but I think it bears consideration. Not as an excuse to lean away from discord, but more to find a way to engage with our vast differences through love and a new language that can help us think, feel, and respond with empathy.

We are living in extremely divisive times. And, likely due to my age and my past, I find myself looking for spots of peace and harmony. But I know that this is not the answer for many. And I know too that I am still here, I am still Queer, and I can take it. I am ready. For whatever needs to happen for us all to be more empowered, for new stories in Queer to be heard. For a new word, if it is needed, to replace that old Queer word, or for new definitions as to how the word can be better employed. A Queer redo.

WORKS CITED

"The 49." *The 49 List*, http://the49list.com/.

Ackroyd, Peter. *Dressing Up: Transvestism and Drag, the History of an Obsession*. Simon and Schuster, 1979.

"Aging With HIV." *HIV.gov*, 15 May 2017, https://www.hiv.gov/hiv-basics/living-well-with-hiv/taking-care-of-yourself/aging-with-hiv.

Ahmed, Sara. *The Cultural Politics of Emotion*. Routledge, 2004.

---. "Evidence." *Feministkilljoys*, 12 Jul. 2016, https://feministkilljoys.com/2016/07/12/evidence/

---. *Living a Feminist Life*. Duke UP, 2017.

---. *On Being Included: Racism and Diversity in Institutional Life*. Duke UP, 2012.

---. *Queer Phenomenology: Orientations, Objects, Others*. Duke UP, 2006.

---. *Wilful Subjects*. Duke UP, 2014.

Ahmed, Shawn. "Who Owns the Pride Movement?" *Globe and Mail*, 27 Jun. 2017, https://www.theglobeandmail.com/opinion/who-owns-the-pride-movement/article35476950/.

Allen, Paula Gunn. "The Savages in the Mirror: Phantoms and Fantasies in America." *Eating Fire, Tasting Blood: Breaking the Great Silence of the American Holocaust*, edited by MariJo Moore, Thunder's Mouth, pp. 16–31.

Althusser, Louis. "Ideology and Ideological State Apparatus (Notes Towards an Investigation). *Lenin and Philosophy and Other Essays*. Monthly Review, 2001.

"Amy Redpath Roddick." *The Montreal Daily Star*, 16 Feb. 1954. *Great Unsolved Mysteries in Canadian History*, http://www.canadianmysteries.ca/sites/redpath/archives/newspaperormagazinearticle/5304en.html.

anitafrika, d'bi.young. "Black Plays Matter: Watah Theatre, Creating Safe Space for Black Artists in These Dangerous Times." *Canadian Theatre Review*, no. 165, 2016, pp. 26-31.

Appleford, Rob. "Daniel David Moses: Ghostwriter with a Vengeance." *Aboriginal Drama and Theatre*, edited by Appleford, Playwrights Canada, 2005, pp. 150–65. Critical Perspectives on Canadian Theatre in English 1.

---. "The Desire to Crunch Bone: Daniel David Moses and the 'True Real Indian.' " *Canadian Theatre Review*, no. 72, Winter 1993, pp. 21–26.

Arboleda-Ríos, Paola. "Astrid Hadad: The Cyborg Goddess. Queer Performance and the Decolonization of the Gendered Self." *Postcolonial Studies*, vol. 17, no. 2, 2014, pp. 189–206.

Atkins, Damien, Paul Dunn, and Andrew Kushnir. *The Gay Heritage Project*. 2013. Manuscript.

Auslander, Philip. *Liveness: Performance in a Mediatized Culture*. Routledge, 2008.

Bailes, Sara Jane. *Performance Theatre and the Poetics of Failure*. Routledge, 2010.

Batson, Charles R., and Denis M. Provencher. "Feeling, Doing, Acting, Seeing, Being Queer in Québec: Michel Marc Bouchard, Rodrigue Jean, and the Queer Québec Colloquium." *Québec Studies*, vol. 60, 2015, pp. 3–22.

Baudrillard, Jean. *The Gulf War Did Not Take Place*. Indiana UP, 1994.

Bellwether, Mira. "Why Not SCUM." *Fucking Trans Women*, http://fuckingtranswomen .tumblr.com.

Berlant, Lauren. "Intimacy: A Special Issue." *Critical Inquiry*, vol. 24, no. 2, 1998, pp. 281–88.

Berlant, Lauren, and Elizabeth Freeman. "Queer Nationality." *Boundary 2*, vol. 19, no. 1, Spring 1992, pp. 149–80.

Bernstein Sycamore, Mattilda. *That's Revolting! Queer Strategies for Resisting Assimilation*. Soft Skull, 2004.

Bersani, Leo. *Homos*. Harvard UP, 1995.

---. "Is the Rectum a Grave?" *AIDS: Cultural Analysis/Cultural Activism*, edited by Douglas Crimp, MIT, 1988, pp. 197–222.

Bettcher, Talia Mae. "Feminist Perspectives on Trans Issues." *The Stanford Encyclopedia of Philosophy*, edited by Edward N. Zalta, Metaphysics Research Lab, Center for the Study of Language and Information (CSLI), Stanford University, 8 Jan. 2014, http://plato.stanford.edu/entries/feminism-trans/.

Bird, Kym. "Leaping into the Breeches: Liberal Feminist Drag in Sarah Anne Curzon's 'The Sweet Girl Graduate.'" *Journal of Australasian Studies*, edited by Joanne Tompkins, Oct. 1996, pp. 168–79.

---. *Redressing the Past: The Politics of Early English-Canadian Women's Drama, 1880–1920*. McGill-Queen's UP, 2004.

Birns, Nicholas. *Theory After Theory: An Intellectual History of Literary Theory From 1950 to the Early 21st Century*. Broadview, 2010.

Black Lives Matter—Toronto. "Rain drop." *Facebook*, 17 Jan. 2017, https://www.facebook.com/blacklivesmatterTO/posts/602991889896305.

---. "Some Tidbits to Mull On." *Facebook*, 28 Jun. 2016, 12:09 p.m., https://m.facebook.com/story.php?story_fbid=516999381828890&id=313499695512194.

Blanchard, Mathieu. "RE: essay draft." Email received by Sean Metzger, 13 Aug. 2017.

Blanchot, Maurice, and Michel Foucault. *Foucault/Blanchot*. Zone, 1987.

Body Politic. Written by Nick Green, directed by Alisa Palmer, Buddies in Bad Times Theatre, Toronto, 24 May 2015.

"Body of Work." *Indigenous Performing Arts Alliance*, http://www.ipaa.ca/about/body-of-work.

Bornstein, Kate. *My New Gender Workbook: A Step-by-Step Guide to Achieving World Peace Through Gender Anarchy and Sex Positivity*. Routledge, 2013.

Bouchard, Michel Marc. *Tom at the Farm*. Translated by Linda Gaboriau, Talonbooks, 2011.

Boulanger, Luc. "Michel Tremblay défie la mort et l'oubli." *La Presse*, 11 Feb. 2012, http://www.lapresse.ca/la-tribune/arts/201204/02/01-4511741-michel-tremblay-defie-la-mort-et-loubli.php.

Bredbeck, Gregory W. "The New Queer Narrative: Intervention and Critique." *Textual Practice*, vol. 9, no. 3, 1995, pp. 477–502.

Brotman, Shari, et al. "Coming Out to Care: Caregivers of Gay and Lesbian Seniors in Canada." *Gerontologist*, vol. 47, no. 4, 2007, pp. 490–503.

Bruno, Giuliana. *Surface: Matters of Aesthetics, Materiality, and Media*. U of Chicago P, 2014.

Burton, Rebecca. "Adding It Up: The Status of Women in Canadian Theatre." *Playwrights Guild of Canada*, Oct. 2006, http://www.playwrightsguild.ca/sites/default/files/AddingItUp.pdf.

Butler, Judith. *Antigone's Claim: Kinship Between Life and Death*. Columbia UP, 2000.

---. *Bodies that Matter: On the Discursive Limits of "Sex."* Routledge, 1993.

---. *Gender Trouble: Feminism and the Subversion of Identity*. Routledge, 1990.

---. "Imitation and Gender Insubordination." *The Lesbian and Gay Studies Reader*, edited by Henry Abelove, Michèle Aina Barale, and David M. Halperin, Routledge, 1993, pp. 307–20.

---. "Performative Acts and Gender Constitution: An Essay in Phenomenology and Feminist Theory." *Theatre Journal*, vol. 40, no. 4, 1988, pp. 519–31.

---. *Precarious Life: The Powers of Mourning and Violence*. Verso, 2006.

Califia, Pat. *Sex Changes: The Politics of Transgenderism*. Cleis, 1997.

Campbell, Alyson, and Dirk Gindt, editors. *Viral Dramaturgies: HIV and AIDS in Performance in the Twenty-First Century*. Palgrave Macmillian, 2018.

Canadian AIDS Society/Société canadienne du SIDA. "HIV and Aging in Canada." *Canadian AIDS Society/Société canadienne du SIDA*, 2013, http://www.cdnaids.ca/2013-updated-hiv-aging-fact-sheets/.

Carpenter, Humphrey. *Secret Gardens*. Houghton Mifflin, 1985.

Carvalho, John. "Fact and Fiction: Writing the Difference Between Suicide and Death." *Contemporary Aesthetics*, 20 Nov. 2006, http://www.contempaesthetics.org/newvolume/pages/article.php?articleID=463.

Case, Sue-Ellen. "Classic Drag: The Greek Creation of Female Parts." *Theatre Journal*, vol. 37, no. 3, 1985, pp. 317–27.

Caserio, Robert L., Lee Edelman, Judith Halberstam, José Esteban Muñoz, and Tim Dean. "The Antisocial Thesis in Queer Theory." *PMLA*, vol. 121, no. 3, May 2006, pp. 819–28.

Castiglia, Christopher, and Christopher Reed. *If Memory Serves: Gay Men, AIDS, and the Promise of the Queer Past*. U of Minnesota P, 2012.

"Catalogue of Works." *Ad Hoc Assembly*, https://adhocassembly.wordpress.com/indivisible-report/catalogue-of-works/.

Césaire, Aimé. *Discourse on Colonialism*. Monthly Review, 2000.

Chauncey, George. *Gay New York*. HarperCollins, 1994.

Chávez, Brittany. "A Living Legacy: What Disidentification Will Continue to Mean for Queer Performance Artists of Color." *QED: A Journal in GLBTQ Worldmaking*, vol. 1, no. 3, 2014, pp. 150–53.

Clum, John M. *Acting Gay: Male Homosexuality in Modern Drama*. Columbia UP, 1992.

---. *Staging Gay Lives: An Anthology of Contemporary Gay Theater*. Westview, 1996.

"Coming Out Saison 2." *Indiegogo*, 23 Jun. 2016, https://www.indiegogo.com/projects/coming-out-saison-3-la-finale#/.

Connell, Raewyn [Robert]. *Masculinities*. U of California P, 1995.

Crisp, Quentin. *An Evening with Quentin Crisp*. Directed by L. Brandon Krall, Media Triangle, 2010.

Cvetkovich, Ann. *An Archive of Feelings: Trauma, Sexuality, and Lesbian Public Cultures*. Duke UP, 2003.

Daley, Andrea. "Lesbian and Gay Health Issues: OUTside of Canada's Health Policy." *Critical Social Policy*, vol. 26, no. 4, 2006, pp. 794–816.

D'Augelli, A., S. Hershberger, and N. Pilkington. "Lesbian, Gay, Bisexual Youth and Their Families: Disclosure of Sexual Orientation and its Consequences." *American Journal of Orthopsychiatry*, vol. 68, no. 3, 1998, pp. 361–71.

Dean, Joanna E. *Religious Experience and The New Woman: The Life of Lily Dougall*. Indiana UP, 2007.

Deleuze, Gilles, and Félix Guattari. *Anti-Oedipus: Capitalism and Schizophrenia*. Viking, 1977.

Delgado, Celeste Fraser, and José Esteban Muñoz, editors. *Everynight Life: Culture and Dance in Latin/o America*. Duke UP, 1997.

Dénommé-Welch, Spy, and Catherine Magowan. *Giiwedin*. 2010. Typescript.

---. *HATE MAIL and Irreconcilable Trolls*. 2017. Typescript.

---. *Victorian Secrets*. 2014. Typescript.

Deveau, Dave. Artist Statement. "The Queer Playwright," *Q2Q Conference*, 22 Jul. 2016, https://q2qconferencedotcom.files.wordpress.com/2016/05/statement-dave-deveau.pdf.

de Vries, Brian, and Catherine F. Croghan. "LGBT Aging: The Contributions of Community-Based Research." *Journal of Homosexuality*, vol. 61, no. 1, 2014, pp. 1–20.

de Vries, Brian, and Gil Herdt. "Aging in the Gay Community." *Gay, Lesbian, Bisexual, and Transgender Aging: Challenges in Research, Practice, and Policy*, edited by Tarryn M. Witten and Evan E. Eyler, Johns Hopkins UP, 2011, pp. 84–129.

Dickinson, Peter. "Brothers' Keepers, or, The Performance of Mourning: Queer Rituals of Remembrance." *Queer Theatre in Canada*, edited by Rosalind Kerr, Playwrights Canada, 2007, pp. 134–59. Critical Perspectives on Canadian Theatre in English 7.

---. *Here is Queer: Nationalisms, Sexualities and the Literatures of Canada*. U of Toronto P, 1999.

Dinshaw, Carolyn. *Getting Medieval: Sexualities and Communities Pre- and Postmodern*. Duke UP, 1999.

Dolan, Jill. *Theatre & Sexuality*. Palgrave Macmillan, 2010.

---. *Utopia in Performance: Finding Hope in the Theater*. U of Michigan P, 2005.

Donnelly, Pat. "Michel Tremblay's *L'Oratorio de Noël*: Remembrance via Alzheimer's." *Montreal Gazette*, 21 Feb. 2012, http://www.montrealgazette.com/health/michel+tremblay+oratorio+no%C3%ABl+remembrance+alzheimer/6163277/story.html.

Driskill, Qwo-Li. "D4Y DBC (Asegi Ayetl): Cherokee Two-Spirit People Reimaging Nation." *Queer Indigenous Studies: Critical Interventions in Theory, Politics and Literature*, edited by Driskill, Chris Finley, Brian Joseph Gilley, and Scott Lauria Morgensen, U of Arizona P, 2011, pp. 94–112.

Driskill, Qwo-Li, Daniel Heath Justice, Deborah Miranda, and Lisa Tatonetti, editors. *Sovereign Erotics: A Collection of Two-Spirit Literature*. U of Arizona P, 2011.

Driskill, Qwo-Li, Chris Finley, Brian Joseph Gilley, and Scott Lauria Morgensen. Introduction. *Queer Indigenous Studies: Critical Interventions in Theory, Politics and Literature*, edited by Driskill, Finley, Gilley, and Morgensen, U of Arizona P, 2011, pp. 1–28.

Driver, Susan, editor. *Queer Youth Cultures*. SUNY, 2008.

Duggan, Lisa. *The Twilight of Equality?: Neoliberalism, Cultural Politics, and the Attack on Democracy*. Beacon, 2004.

Edelman, Lee. *Homographesis: Essays in Gay Literary and Cultural Theory*. Routledge, 1994.

---. *No Future: Queer Theory and the Death Drive*. Duke UP, 2004.

"The Epidemiology of HIV in Gay Men and Other Men who have Sex with Men." *CATIE*, 29 Jul. 2017, http://www.catie.ca/en/fact-sheets/epidemiology/epidemiology-hiv-gay-men-and-other-men-who-have-sex-men.

Escobar, Sam. "I'm Not Male. I'm Not Female. Please Don't Ask Me About My Junk." *Esquire*, 31 Mar. 2016, https://www.esquire.com/lifestyle/sex/news/a43461/what-is-non-binary-gender/.

Etemadi, Izad. "Leila Orders Coffee." *YouTube*, 11 May 2015, https://www.youtube.com/watch?v=Lwayf5FtxMY.

Evans, Alex. "How Homo can Hollywood Be? Remaking Queer Authenticity from *To Wong Foo* to *Brokeback Mountain*." *Journal of Film and Video*, vol. 61, no. 4, Winter 2009, pp. 41–54.

Faderman, Lillian. *Odd Girls and Twilight Lovers: A History of Lesbian Life in Twentieth-Century America*. Penguin, 1991.

---. *Surpassing The Love of Men: Romantic Friendship and Love Between Women from the Renaissance to the Present*. William Morrow, 1981.

Filax, Gloria. *Queer Youth: In the Province of the "Severely Normal."* UBC P, 2006.

Flawless, Lucy (Eric Rich). Personal interview with Cameron Crookston, 2 May 2016.

Foucault, Michel. "Discourse and Truth: the Problematization of Parrhesia." *Foucault, Info*, http://foucault.info//system/files/pdf/DiscourseAndTruth_MichelFoucault_1983_0.pdf.

---. *The History of Sexuality. Vol. 1: The Will to Knowledge*. 1976. Translated by Robert Hurley, Penguin, 1990.

---. *The Order of Things*. Routledge, 2002.

Fraser, Brad. *Five @ Fifty*. Playwrights Canada, 2012.

---. "Releasing the Dead." *Daily Xtra*, 18 Apr. 2013, http://www.dailyxtra.com/toronto/news-and-ideas/opinion/releasing-the-dead-58976.

---. *True Love Lies*. Playwrights Canada, 2010.

Freeman, Elizabeth. "Packing History, Count(er)ing Generations." *New Literary History*, vol. 31, no. 4, Autumn 2000, pp. 727–44.

---. "Queer Belongings: Kinship Theory and Queer Theory." *A Companion to Lesbian, Gay, Bisexual, Transgender, and Queer Studies*, edited by George E. Haggerty and Molly McGarry, Blackwell, 2007, pp. 295–314.

---. *Time Binds: Queer Temporalities, Queer Histories*. Duke UP, 2010.

Frye, Northrop. *Fools of Time: Studies in Shakespearean Tragedy*. U of Toronto P, 1981.

Fuss, Diana. "Inside/Out." *Inside/Out: Lesbian Theories, Gay Theories*, edited by Fuss, Routledge, 1991, pp. 1–12.

Garber, Marjorie. *Vested Interests: Cross-Dressing and Cultural Anxiety*. Routledge, 1992.

Garebian, Keith. "The Indian Medicine Shows: Two One-Act Plays." *Books in Canada*, vol. 27, no. 3, 1998, pp. 35–37.

"The Gay Heritage Project." *Buddies in Bad Times Theatre*, 2015, http://buddiesinbadtimes.com/show/gay-heritage-project/.

The Gay Heritage Project. Written and performed by Paul Dunn, Damien Atkins, and Andrew Kushnir, directed by Ashlie Corcoran, Buddies in Bad Times Theatre, Toronto, 31 Nov. 2013.

"Gender." *The World Health Organization*, http://www.who.int/gender-equity-rights/understanding/gender-definition/en/.

Gilbert, Helen. "Black and White and Re(a)d All Over Again: Indigenous Minstrelsy in Contemporary Canadian and Australian Theatre." *Theatre Journal*, vol. 55, no. 4, 2003, pp. 679–98.

Gilbert, Sky. *Ejaculations from the Charm Factory: A Memoir*. ECW, 2000.

---. *A Few Brittle Leaves*. 2013. Manuscript.

---. "If That's What It Means to Be Gay, I Quit." *The Globe and Mail*, 1 Dec. 2009, http://www.theglobeandmail.com/opinion/if-thats-what-it-means-to-be-gay-i-quit/article4294235/.

Gindt, Dirk. "Queer Embodied Absence: HIV/AIDS and the Creation of Memory in Gordon Armstrong's *Blue Dragons* and Daniel MacIvor's *The Soldier Dreams*." *Journal of Canadian Studies*, vol. 48, no. 2, 2014, pp. 122–45.

---. " 'Your Asshole is Hanging Outside of Your Body?': Excess, AIDS, and Shame in the Theatre of Sky Gilbert." *The Uses of Excess in Visual and Material Culture, 1600–2010*, edited by Julia Skelly, Ashgate, 2014, pp. 249–76.

Goldman, Jessica. "Review of *UNSEX'd*." *Calgary Eyeopener*, CBC Radio, 30 Oct. 2013.

Gómez-Peña, Guillermo. "The New Global Culture: Somewhere between Corporate Multiculturalism and the Mainstream Bizarre (a border perspective)." *The Drama Review*, vol. 45, no. 1, Spring 2001, pp. 7–30.

Gonick, Marnina. *Between Femininities: Ambivalence, Identity, and the Education of Girls*. SUNY, 2003.

Gopinath, Gayatri. *Impossible Desires: Queer Diasporas and South Asian Public Cultures.* Duke UP, 2005.

Grace, André P. "Camp fYrefly: Linking Research to Advocacy in Community Work with Sexual and Gender Minority Youth." *Out Spoken: Perspectives on Queer Identities*, edited by Wes D. Pearce and Jean Hillabold, U of Regina P, 2013, pp. 127–42.

Green, Nick. *Body Politic*. 2015. Manuscript.

Gudgeon, Chris. *The Naked Truth: The Untold Story of Sex in Canada*. Greystone, 2003.

Hadjimatheou, Chloe. "Christine Jorgensen: 60 Years of Sex Change Ops." *BBC Magazine*, 31 Nov. 2012, http://www.bbc.com/news/magazine-20544095.

Halberstam, Judith [Jack]. *In a Queer Time and Place: Transgender Bodies, Subcultural Lives*. New York UP, 2005.

---. *The Queer Art of Failure*. Duke UP, 2011.

---. "Who are 'We' After Orlando?" *Bully Bloggers*, 22 Jun. 2016, https://bullybloggers.wordpress.com/2016/06/22/who-are-we-after-orlando-by-jack-halberstam/.

Halferty, J. Paul. "For the Future, the Past: LGBT2Q Theatre, Performance, and Scholarship in Canada." *Theatre Research in Canada/Recherches théâtrales au Canada*, vol. 35, no. 2, 2014, pp. 255–58.

Halperin, David M. *How to Be Gay*. Belknap of Harvard UP, 2012.

---. "How to Do the History of Male Homosexuality." *GLQ: A Journal of Lesbian and Gay Studies*, vol. 6, no. 1, 2000, 87–123.

Halperin, David M., and Valerie Traub. "Beyond Gay Pride." *Gay Shame*, edited by Halperin and Traub, U of Chicago P, 2009, pp. 3–40.

Hawkes, David. *Ideology*. Routledge, 1996.

Hays, Matthew. "Michel Tremblay, Canada's Greatest Playwright." *The Lesbian and Gay Review Worldwide*, vol. 12, no. 3, 2005, p. 32.

Hayter, Simon. "Winners and Losers: Virtuoso Wordplay Gives Way to Nasty Verbal Sparring in This Tour De Force." *The Globe and Mail*, 28 May 2013, https://www.theglobeandmail.com/arts/theatre-and-performance/theatre-reviews/winners-and-losers-virtuoso-wordplay-gives-way-to-nasty-verbal-sparring-in-this-tour-de-force/article12196260/.

Healy, Brendan. Email received by Richie Wilcox, 12 Apr. 2015.

Hennessy, Rosemary. *Profit and Pleasure: Sexual Identities in Late Capitalism.* Routledge, 2000.

---. "Queer Visibility in Commodity Culture." *Cultural Critique*, no. 29, Winter 1994–1995, pp. 31–76.

Hickling, Alfred. "True Love Lies." *The Guardian*, 4 Feb. 2009, https://www.theguardian.com/stage/2009/feb/04/theatre-stage-culture-review1.

Hildebrand, Lucas. *Inherent Vice: Bootleg Histories of Videotape and Copyright.* Duke UP, 2009.

Hill, Dominique. "A Vulnerable Disclosure: Dangerous Negotiations of Race and Identity in the Classroom." *Journal of Pedagogy*, vol. 5, no. 2, 2014, pp. 161–81.

Hill, Greg A. "Caught . . . (Red-Handed)." *Caught in the Act: Viewer as Performer*, edited by Joseé Drouin-Brisebois, National Gallery of Canada/ABC Art Books Canada, 2008, p. 163.

Hill, Kelly. "A Statistical Profile of Artists and Cultural Workers in Canada. Based on the 2011 National Household Survey and the Labour Force Survey." *Statistical Insights on the Arts*, vol. 12, no. 2, Oct. 2014. *Hill Strategies Research*, 7 Oct. 2014, http://www.hillstrategies.com/content/statistical-profile-artists-and-cultural-workers-canada.

Hobbes, Michael. "Together Alone: The Epidemic of Gay Loneliness." *Huffington Post*, 2 Mar. 2017, http://highline.huffingtonpost.com/articles/en/gay-loneliness/.

Hocquenghem, Guy. *Homosexual Desire.* Duke UP, 1993.

Horkheimer, Max, and Theodor W. Adorno. *Dialectic of Enlightenment: Philosophical Fragments.* Stanford UP, 2002.

"How." *Selfconscious*, http://selfconscious.ca/category/who-what-why/us/.

Huffer, Lynne. *Are the Lips a Grave?: A Queer Feminist on the Ethics of Sex.* Columbia UP, 2013.

Hughes, Holly, and David Román, editors. *O Solo Homo: The New Queer Performance.* Grove, 1998.

Hunt, Sarah, and Cindy Holmes. "Everyday Decolonization: Living a Decolonizing Queer Politics." *Journal of Lesbian Studies*, vol. 19, no. 2, 2015, pp. 154–72.

Hurley, Erin. *National Performance: Representing Quebec from Expo 67 to Céline Dion.* U of Toronto P, 2011.

Hyte, Farra N. (Chantelle Helena Carr). Personal interview with Cameron Crookston, 13 May 2016.

Jarman-Ivens, Freya. *Queer Voices: Technologies, Vocalities, and the Musical Flaw*. Palgrave MacMillan, 2011.

"John Easton Mills (1846-1847)." "Democracy in Montreal," *Montréal*, http://www2.ville.montreal.qc.ca/archives/democratie/democratie_en/expo/maires/easton-mills/index.shtm.

Jones, David C. *Out on Stage in Lotusland: A Cabaret Retrospective*. *Q2Q Conference*, 20 Jul. 2016, https://q2qconference.com/schedule/.

Joseph, Miranda. *Against the Romance of Community*. U of Minnesota P, 2002.

Justice, Daniel Heath, Mark Rifkin, and Bethany Schneider. Introduction. *GLQ: A Journal of Lesbian and Gay Studies*, vol. 16, nos. 1–2, 2010, pp. 5–39.

Kaufman, Donald L. "The Indian as Media-Hand-Me-Down." *American Indian Theater in Performance*, edited by Hanay Geiogamah and Jaye T. Darby, UCLA American Indian Studies Center, 1999, pp. 114–22.

Kerr, Rosalind, editor. *Queer Theatre in Canada*. Playwrights Canada, 2007. Critical Perspectives on Canadian Theatre in English 7.

King, Moynan, editor. *Canadian Theatre Review: Queer Performance: Women and Trans Artists*, vol. 149, 2012.

---. "Queer Performance in the Post-Millennial Scramble." York University, 2015. Ph.D. dissertation proposal.

---, editor. *Queer/Play: An Anthology of Queer Women's Performance and Plays*. Playwrights Canada, 2017.

---. "Revenge as Radical Feminist Tactic." *nomorepotlucks*, vol. 28, Jul./Aug. 2013, http://nomorepotlucks.org/site/revenge-as-radical-feminist-tactic-in-the-scum-manifesto-moynan-king/2013.

King, Moynan, and Ellen-Ray Hennessy. "The Genius of Sky Gilbert." *Compulsive Acts: Essays, Interviews, Reflections on the Works of Sky Gilbert*, edited by David Bateman, Guernica Editions, 2014, pp. 243–49.

Knausgaard, Karl Ove. *A Man in Love: My Struggle: 2*. Random House, 2013.

Knowles, Ric. General Editor's Preface. *Performing Indigeneity*, edited by Yvette Nolan and Knowles, Playwrights Canada, 2016, pp. v–vii. New Essays on Canadian Theatre 6.

---. Introduction to *The Indian Medicine Shows*. *Staging Coyote's Dream: An Anthology of First Nations Drama in English, Volume II*, edited by Monique Mojica and Knowles, Playwrights Canada, 2008, pp. 45–46.

---. "Look. Look Again. Daniel David Moses' Decolonizing Optics." *Crucible of Cultures: Anglophone Drama at the Dawn of a New Millennium*, edited by Marc Maufort and Franca Bellarsi, P.I.E. Pater Lang, 2002, pp. 187–98.

Kristeva, Julia. *Hatred and Forgiveness*. Columbia UP, 2012.

Kushnir, Andrew. Personal interview with Stephen Low, 29 Nov. 2013.

"Lady Amy Redpath Roddick, Poetess, Philanthropist, Dies." Roddick Papers, Rare Books and Special Collections, McGill University, MS 818 c. 3 file 3.9.

LaRiviere, Serafin. "Secrecy, Violence & Sex." *Daily Xtra*, 23 Sep. 2009, http://www.dailyxtra.com/toronto/arts-and-entertainment/secrecy-violence-and-sex-7123.

Latchford, Frances. "Unidentified Remains: The Impolitics of Non-identity." *Atlantis*, vol. 36, no. 2, 2014, pp. 20–35. http://journals.msvu.ca/index.php/atlantis/article/view/1817/pdf_4.

Leslie, Deborah, and John Paul Catungal. "Social Justice and the Creative City: Class, Gender and Racial Inequalities." *Geography Compass*, vol. 6, no. 3, 2012, 111–22.

Levin, Laura, and Marlis Schweitzer. "Performance Studies in Canada: Mapping Genealogies and Geographies of Performance Culture." Introduction. *Performance Studies in Canada*, edited by Levin and Schweitzer, McGill-Queen's UP, 2017, pp. 3–39.

Licata, Salvatore J. "The Homosexual Rights Movement in the United States: A Traditionally Overlooked Area of American History." *The Gay Past: A Collection of Historical Essays*, edited by Licata and Robert W. Peterson, Routledge, 1986, pp. 161–90.

Liss, David, and Shirley J. Madill. *The Triumph of Mischief: Kent Monkman*. Art Gallery of Greater Victoria; Art Gallery of Hamilton; Glenbow Museum, Calgary; Museum of Contemporary Art, Toronto; St. Mary's University Art Gallery, Halifax, 2008.

Lo, Jacqueline, and Helen Gilbert. "Toward a Topography of Cross-Cultural Theatre Praxis." *TDR*, vol. 46, no. 3, 2002, pp. 31–53.

Love, Heather. *Feeling Backward: Loss and the Politics of Queer History*. Harvard UP, 2007.

---. "Spoiled Identity: Stephen Gordon's Loneliness and the Difficulties of Queer History." *The Transgender Studies Reader*, edited by Susan Stryker and Stephen Whittle, Routledge, 2006, pp. 521–36.

Luscombe, Tim. *PIG*. Draft 4A, 2013. Manuscript.

Ly, Minh. *Ga Ting (Family)*. Scirocco, 2016.

MacArthur, Michelle. "Achieving Equity in Theatre: A Report With Best Practice Recommendations." *Equity in Theatre*, April 2015, https://equityintheatre.com/sites/default/files/FINAL%20EIT%20Report_4%2022%2015.pdf.

Mamet, David. *True and False: Heresy and Common Sense for the Actor.* Vintage, 1999.

Martin, Luther H., Huck Gutman, and Patrick H. Hutton, editors. *Technologies of the Self: A Seminar with Michel Foucault*. U of Massachusetts P, 1988.

Martinez, Shantel. " 'For Our Words Usually Land on Deaf Ears Until We Scream': Writing as a Liberatory Practice." *Qualitative Inquiry*, vol. 20, no. 1, 2013, pp. 3–14.

Mays, Vickie M., Linda M. Chatters, Susan D. Cochran, and Joanna Mackness. "African American Families in Diversity: Gay Men and Lesbians as Participants in Family Networks." *Journal of Comparative Family Studies*, vol. 29, no. 1, Spring 1998, pp. 73–87.

McInnes, David, and Christyn Davies. "Articulating Sissy Boy Queerness within and against Discourses of Tolerance and Pride." *Queer Youth Cultures*, edited by Susan Driver, SUNY, 2008, pp. 105–21.

McMaster, Gerald. "The Geography of Hope." *Triumph of Mischief: Kent Monkman*, by David Liss and Shirley J. Madill, Art Gallery of Greater Victoria, et al., 2008, pp. 95–101.

McRuer, Robert. "Composing Bodies; or, De-Composition: Queer Theory, Disability Studies, and Alternative Corporealities." *JAC: A Quarterly Journal for the Interdisciplinary Study of Rhetoric, Culture, Literacy, and Politics*, vol. 24, no. 1, 2004, pp. 47–78.

---. "*As Good As It Gets*: Queer Theory and Critical Disability." *GLQ: A Journal of Lesbian and Gay Studies*, vol. 9, nos. 1–2, 2003, pp. 79–105.

Menon, Madhavi. *Indifference to Difference: On Queer Universalism.* U of Minnesota P, 2015.

Metzger, Sean. *The Chinese Atlantic: Seascapes and the Theatricality of Globalization.* Indiana UP, forthcoming.

---. "*Le Rugissement du Lion*: Mapping and Memory in Montreal's Chinese/Canadian Street Theatre." *Asian Canadian Theatre*, edited by Nina Lee Aquino and Ric Knowles, Playwrights Canada, 2011, pp. 86–97. New Essays in Canadian Theatre 1.

Metzger, Sean, Francisco-J. Hernández Adrián, and Michaeline Crichlow. "Introduction: Islands, Images, Imaginaries." *Third Text*, vol. 28, nos. 4–5, 2014, pp. 333–43.

Miller, Arthur. "Death of a Salesman: A Modern Tragedy." *Modern Theories of Drama: A Selection of Writing on Drama and Theatre, 1840–1990*, edited by George W. Brandt, Oxford UP, 1998, pp. 106–14.

Miller, Tim, and David Román. "Preaching to the Converted." *Theatre Journal*, vol. 47, no. 2, May 1995, pp. 169–88.

Mitchell, Allyson. *Art Institutions and the Feminist Dialectic*, 2008, http://feministdialectic.ca/en/video.php?id=1.

---. "Deep Lez Statement." http://www.allysonmitchell.com/action/deeplez.cfm.

Morales, Aurora Levins. *Remedios: Stories of Earth and Iron from the History of Puertorriqueñas*. Beacon, 1998.

Morganroth Gullette, Margaret. "Politics, Pathology, Suicide, and Social Fates: Tony Kushner's *The Intelligent Homosexual's Guide to Capitalism and Socialism with a Key to the Scriptures*." *Modern Drama*, vol. 59, no. 2, 2016, pp. 231–48.

Morgensen, Scott Lauria. *Spaces Between Us: Queer Settler Colonialism and Indigenous Decolonization*. U of Minnesota P, 2011.

Moses, Daniel David. *The Indian Medicine Shows*. *Staging Coyote's Dream: An Anthology of First Nations Drama in English, Volume II*, edited by Monique Mojica and Ric Knowles, Playwrights Canada, 2008, pp. 43–110.

Moses, Naomi. " 'Who is Pure Enough to Shelter It?': A Celebration of Forbidden Love in Amy Redpath Roddick's *The Romance of a Princess*." British Women's Drama, York University, Dec. 2009. Course paper.

Moss, Jane. "Dramatizing Sexual Difference: Gay and Lesbian Theater in Québec." *American Review of Canadian Studies*, vol. 22, no. 4, 1992, pp. 489–98.

Muñoz, José Esteban. *Cruising Utopia: The Then and There of Queer Futurity*. New York UP, 2009.

---. *Disidentifications: Queers of Color and the Performance of Politics*. U Minnesota P, 1999.

---. "Feeling Brown: Ethnicity and Affect in Ricardo Bracho's The Sweetest Hangover (and Other STDs)." *Theatre Journal*, vol. 52, no. 1, 2000, pp. 67–79.

Muraco, Anna. "Intentional Families: Fictive Kin Ties Between Cross-Gender, Different Sexual Orientation Friends." *Journal of Marriage and Family*, vol. 68, no. 5, 2006, pp. 1313–25.

Namaste, Viviane K. *C'était du spectacle!: L'histoire des artistes transexuelles à Montréal, 1955–1985*. McGill-Queen's UP, 2005.

Nehamas, Alexander. *The Art of Living*. U of California P, 1998.

Nestruck, J Kelly. "Matthew Jocelyn Ducks Real Discussion on Canadian Stage Diversity Failure." *Globe and Mail*, 29 Jan. 2016, https://www.theglobeandmail.com/arts/theatre-and-performance/matthew-jocelyn-ducks-real-discussion-on-canadian-stage-diversity-failure/article28457878/.

Noir, Elle (Chris Cochrane). Personal interview with Cameron Crookston, 1 Jun. 2016.

O'Hara, Jean, editor. *Two-Spirit Acts: Queer Indigenous Performances*. Playwrights Canada, 2013.

Oswald, Ramona Faith. "Resilience Within the Family Networks of Lesbians and Gay Men: Intentionality and Redefinition." *Journal of Marriage and Family*, vol. 64, no. 2, May 2002, pp. 374–83.

"Our History." *Buddies in Bad Times Theatre*, 20 Jun. 2017, http://buddiesinbadtimes.com/about/history/.

Patton, Cindy. *Inventing AIDS*. Routledge, 1990.

Pearl, Monica B. *AIDS Literature and Gay Identity: The Literature of Loss*. Routledge, 2013.

Pecic, Zoran. *Queer Narratives of the Caribbean Diaspora*. Palgrave, 2013.

Pérez, Hiram. *A Taste for Brown Bodies: Gay Modernity and Cosmopolitan Desire*. NYU, 2015.

Phelan, Peggy. *Unmarked: The Politics of Performance*. Routledge, 1993.

PIG. By Tim Luscombe, directed by Brendan Healy, performed by Bruce Dow, Paul Dunn, and Blair Williams, Buddies in Bad Times Theatre, Toronto, 13 Sep. 2013.

"pig play." *The Urban Dictionary*, second definition, 16 Dec. 2011, http://www.urbandictionary.com/define.php?term=pig play.

Playwrights Guild of Canada. "PGC's Annual Theatre Survey for 2013/14–Breakdown by Budget Size." n.d.

Playwrights Guild of Canada. "PGC's Annual Theatre Survey for 2015/16." n.d.

Poon, Colleen S., and Elizabeth M. Saewyc. "Out Yonder: Sexual-Minority Adolescents in Rural Communities in British Columbia." *American Journal of Public Health*, vol. 99, no. 1, 2009, pp. 118–24.

Poutanen, Mary Anne. Personal interview with Kym Bird, Jul. 2008.

---. "Redpath Sugar Museum, Toronto." *Amy Redpath Diary*, http://www.redpathsugars.com/museum_index.html.

Probyn, Elspeth. *Love in a Cold Climate: Queer Belongings in Québec*. GRECC, 1994.

---. *Outside Belongings*. Routledge, 1996.

Pruden, Harlan. "Position Paper." Acts of Faith round table, Q2Q: A Symposium on Queer Theatre and Performance in Canada, Vancouver, 21 Jul. 2016.

Redpath, Linda. Personal interview with Kym Bird, 27 Jul. 2007.

"Redpath Mansion Mystery." *Great Unsolved Mysteries in Canadian History*, http://www.canadianmysteries.ca/sites/redpath/home/indexen.html.

Richardson, Lindsay. "Montreal group gets $25,000 to fight bullying in the LGBTQ community." *Montreal Gazette*, 20 Jun. 2016, http://Montrealgazette.com/news/local-news/countering-bullying-in-the-gay-community.

Ridley, Hilda M. "A Daughter of Montreal." *Canadiana*, Spring 1950. Roddick Papers, Rare Books and Special Collections, McGill University.

Rifkin, Mark. *When Did the Indian Become Straight? Kinship, the History of Sexuality, and Native Sovereignty*. Oxford UP, 2011.

Rocheleau, Alan-Michel, and Luke Sandford. "Gay Theater in Québec: The Search for an Identity." *Yale French Studies*, vol. 90, 1996, pp. 115–36.

Roddick, Amy Redpath. "A Chance Meeting." *The Iroquois Enjoy A Perfect Day, A Change Meeting And Other Poems*, John Dougall & Son, 1939, pp. 19–36.

---. "Diaries." Roddick Papers, Rare Books and Special Collections, McGill University.

---. "Her Face." *The Birth of Montreal: A Chronicle Play*, John Dougall & Son, 1921, p. 152.

---. "In A Train." *The Flag and Other Poems*, John Dougall & Son, 1918, p. 25.

---. "Last Will and Testament." Jan. 1925. Roddick Papers, Rare Books and Special Collections, McGill University.

---. "The Parson's Daughter." *The Armistice And Other Poems*, John Dougall & Son, 1919, p. 44.

---. *The Romance of a Princess*. John Dougall & Son, 1922.

---. "Sappho in Exile." *From Montreal Elsewhere*, John Dougall & Son, 1929, p. 80.

---. "Where Willows Intertwine." *The Armistice And Other Poems*, John Dougall & Son, 1919, p. 25.

Rogers, Amanda. "Emotional Geographies of Method Acting in Asian American Theater." *Annals of the Association of American Geographers*, vol. 102, no. 2, 2012, pp. 423–42.

Román, David. "Dance Liberation." *Theatre Journal*, vol. 55, no. 3, Oct. 2003, pp. 377–94.

---. "Not-About-AIDS." *GLQ: A Journal of Lesbian and Gay Studies*, vol. 6, no. 1, 2000, pp. 1–28.

---. *Performance in America: Contemporary U.S. Culture and the Performing Arts*. Duke UP, 2005.

Ronell, Avital. "Deviant Payback: The Aims of Valerie Solanas." *The SCUM Manifesto* by Valerie Solanas, Verso, 2004, pp. 1–31.

Sandahl, Carrie. "Why Disability Identity Matters: From Dramaturgy to Casting in John Belluso's *Pyretown*." *Text and Performance Quarterly*, vol. 28, nos. 1–2, 2008, pp. 225–41.

Schneider, Rebecca. *The Explicit Body in Performance*. Routledge, 1997.

---. *Performing Remains: Art and War in Times of Theatrical Reenactment*. Routledge, 2011.

Scott, Shelley. *Nightwood Theatre: A Woman's Work is Always Done*. Athabasca UP, 2010.

Sedgwick, Eve Kosofsky. *Epistemology of the Closet*. U of California P, 1990.

---. *Tendencies*. Duke UP, 1993.

Senelick, Laurence. *The Changing Room: Sex, Drag and Theatre*. Routledge, 2000.

Sethi, Meera. "The Mainstreaming of Dissent: Women Artists of Colour and Canadian Arts Institutions." *Resources for Feminist Research*, vol. 29, nos. 3–4, 2002, pp. 1–15.

Shakespeare, William. *King Lear: Total Study Edition*. Coles, 1999.

Shewey, Don. *Out Front: Contemporary Gay and Lesbian Plays*. Grove, 1988.

Shields, David. *Reality Hunger*. Knopf, 2010.

Sinfield, Alan. *Out on Stage: Lesbian and Gay Theatre in the Twentieth Century*. Yale UP, 1999.

Sing Turner, Valerie. "The Danger of a Single Story." *Canadian Theatre Review*, no. 165, 2016, pp. 20–25.

Sly, Katie. Artist Statement. "Queer Theatre and Performance to Come," *Q2Q Conference*, 24 Jul. 2016,. https://q2qconferencedotcom.files.wordpress.com/2016/05/statement-katiesly.pdf.

Small Axe. By Andrew Kushnir, directed by Alan Dilworth, performed by Sarah Afful, Michael Blake, Lisa Codrington, Andrew Kushnir, Chy Ryan Spain, and Marcel Stewart, produced by Project Humanity, the Theatre Centre, Toronto, 17 Jan. 2015.

Smith, Andrea. "Not an Indian Tradition: The Sexual Colonization of Native Peoples." *Hypatia*, vol. 18, no. 2, 2003, pp. 70–85.

---. "Queer Theory and Native Studies: The Heteronormativity of Settler Colonialism." *GLQ: A Journal of Lesbian and Gay Studies*, vol. 16, nos. 1–2, 2010, pp. 42–68.

Solanas, Valerie. *The SCUM Manifesto*. Verso, 2004.

Sophocles. *Antigone*. Translated by Paul Woodruff, Hacket, 2001.

Stacey, Judith. "The Families of Man: Gay Male Intimacy and Kinship in a Global Metropolis." *Signs*, vol. 30, no. 3, Spring 2005, 1911–35.

Stanley, Sarah Garton. "Failure Points." *Canadian Theatre Review*, vol. 150, 2012, pp. 100–02.

---. "Failure Theatre: An Artist's Statement." Queen's U, 2013. M.A. dissertation.

St. Bernard, Donna-Michelle. "Counter: Offensive." "The Queer 'Real,' " *Q2Q Conference*, 22 Jul. 2016, https://q2qconferencedotcom.files.wordpress.com/2016/05/counter-offensive-by-dm-for-q2q.pdf.

Strommen, E.F. " 'You're a what?' Family Member Reaction to the Disclosure of Homosexuality." *Journal of Homosexuality*, vol. 18, nos. 1–2, 1989, pp. 37–58.

Stryker, Susan. *Transgender History*. Seal Press, 2008.

Tagore, Proma. *Shapes of Silence: Writing by Women of Colour and the Politics of Testimony*. McGill-Queen's UP, 2009.

Tannahill, Jordan. *Age of Minority: 3 Solo Plays*. Playwrights Canada, 2013.

---. Email received by Jay Whitehead, 15 Jun. 2015.

---. "The New Intimacy: *rihannaboi95* and Web Theatre." *Canadian Theatre Review*, no. 159, Jul. 2014, pp. 9–12.

---. *rihannaboi95*. *Age of Minority: 3 Solo Plays*. Playwrights Canada, 2013, pp. 31–58.

---. *Theatre of the Unimpressed: In Search of Vital Drama*. Coach House, 2015.

Tension, Dmanda (Ashick, Ryan). Personal interview with Cameron Crookston, 7 May 2016.

Theatre Outré. "About." *Facebook*, 20 Jun. 2017, https://www.facebook.com/pg/TheatreOutre/about/?ref=page_internal.

"Theatre Outré In Lethbridge Says Homophobic Emails, Petition Forced Them To Close Their Doors." *The Huffington Post Alberta*, 30 Jan. 2014, http://www.huffingtonpost.ca/2014/01/29/theatre-outre-lethbridge_n_4689596.html.

Thomas, Colin. "Jordan Tannahill Writes Plays For And About Queer Youth." Colin Thomas, 13 Nov. 2014, http://colinthomas.ca/2014/11/13/jordan-tannahill-writes-plays-queer-youth.

---. "Playwright Minh Ly Uses Family Portrait in *Ga Ting* to Reflect Realities of Being Gay and Asian." *The Georgia Straight*, 2 Mar. 2016, https://www.straight.com/arts/648596/playwright-minh-ly-uses-family-portrait-ga-ting-reflect-realities-being-asian-and-gay.

Thorkelson, Erika. "Complex Play *Ga Ting* Struggles, Despite Moments of Genuine Intensity." *Vancouver Sun*, 9 Mar. 2016, http://www.vancouversun.com/Theatre+review+Complex+play+Ting+struggles+despite+moments+genuine+intensity/11773973/story.html.

Torres, Justin. "In Praise of Latin Night at the Queer Club." *Washington Post*, 13 June. 2016, https://www.washingtonpost.com/opinions/in-praise-of-latin-night-at-the-queer-club/2016/06/13/e841867e-317b-11e6-95c0-2a6873031302_story.html?utm_term=.605af5761c47.

Tremblay, Michel. *Messe solennelle pour une pleine lune d'été*. Leméac, 1996.

---. *L'Oratorio de Noël*. Leméac, 2012.

Trump, Donald. "After consultation with my Generals and military experts." *Twitter*, 26 Jul. 2017, 5:55 a.m., https://twitter.com/realdonaldtrump/status/890193981585444864?lang=en.

Turcotte, Louise. "Queer Theory: Transgression and/or Regression." *Canadian Women's Studies*, vol. 16, no. 2, 1996, pp. 118–21.

Turner, Victor. *From Ritual to Theatre: The Human Seriousness of Play*. PAJ, 1982.

UNAIDS. "HIV and Aging." *UNAIDS*, 2013, http://www.unaids.org/sites/default/files/media_asset/20131101_JC2563_hiv-and-aging_en_0.pdf.

Vacante, Jeffery. "Evolving Racial Identity and the Consolidation of Men's Authority in Early Twentieth-Century Quebec." *Canadian Historical Review*, vol. 88, no. 3, 2007, pp. 416–38.

---. "Quebec Manhood in Historical Perspective," *Canadian Men and Masculinities: Historical and Contemporary Perspectives*, edited by Christopher J. Greig and Wayne J. Martino, Canadian Scholars', 2012, pp. 23–41.

---. "Writing the History of Sexuality and 'National' History in Quebec." *Journal of Canadian Studies*, vol. 39, no. 2, 2005, pp. 31–56.

Van Alphen, Ernst. "Affective Operation of Art and Literature." *RES: Anthropology and Aesthetics*, no. 53/54, Spring/Autumn, 2008, pp. 20–30.

Velez, Ali. "Dozens of Broadway Stars Recorded a Powerful Song for Orlando." *BuzzFeed*, 20 Jun. 2016, https://www.buzzfeed.com/alivelez/broadway-for-orlando-love-sweet-love?utm_term=.tl3AjE8YkE#.kc2VBrJ3pr.

"Vigile à Montréal, après la Tuerie d'Orlando," *La Presse*, 12 Jun. 2016, http://www.lapresse.ca/photos/201606/12/12-16885-vigile-a-montreal-apres-la-tuerie-dorlando.php#1210968.

Vizenor, Gerald. *Manifest Manners: Narratives on Postindian Survivance*. U of Nebraska P, 1999.

Walcott, Rinaldo. *Black Like Who?: Writing Black Canada*. Insomniac, 2003.

Walker, Johnnie. "Peaking at 60?" *Daily Xtra*, 23 Apr. 2013, http://www.dailyxtra.com/toronto/arts-and-entertainment/peaking-at-60-58898.

Wallace, Robert, editor. *Making Out: Plays by Gay Men*. Coach House, 1992.

---. *Producing Marginality: Theatre and Criticism in Canada*. Fifth House, 1990.

Warner, Michael. *Publics and Counterpublics*. Zone, 2005.

Warner, Sara. *Acts of Gaiety: LGBT Performance and the Politics of Pleasure*. U of Michigan P, 2012.

Watmough, David, editor. *Canadian Theatre Review: Homosexuality and the Theatre*, vol. 12, 1976.

Weiss, Peter Eliot. *Remembering Shanghai. Plague of the Gorgeous and Other Tales*, Scirocco Drama, 1996, pp. 97–123.

Weston, Kath. *Families We Choose: Lesbians, Gays, Kinship*. Columbia UP, 1991.

Whitney, Elizabeth. "The Dangerous Real: Queer Solo Performance in/as Active Disruption." *Comparative American Studies in International Journal*, vol. 14, no. 3–4, 2017, pp. 246–60.

Wilcox, Richie, editor. *Daniel MacIvor*. Playwrights Canada, 2015. New Essays on Canadian Theatre 5.

Wilde, Oscar. *The Importance of Being Earnest*. *Plays*, Penguin, 1985, 247–314.

---. "The Soul of Man Under Socialism." *De Profundis and Other Writings*, Penguin, 1977.

Wilson, Ann, editor. *Canadian Theatre Review: Sexuality, Gender and Theatre*, vol. 59, 1989.

Witten, Tarryn M. "The Aging of Sexual and Gender Minority Persons: An Overview." *Gay, Lesbian, Bisexual, and Transgender Aging: Challenges in Research, Practice, and Policy*, edited by Witten and Evan E. Eyler, Johns Hopkins UP, 2011, pp. 1–58.

Wood, James. *The Nearest Thing to Life*. Brandeis UP, 2015.

Wyllie, Andrew. *Sex on Stage: Gender and Sexuality in Post-War British Theatre*. Intellect, 2009.

Yellow Bird, Michael. "Cowboys and Indians: Toys of Genocide, Icons of American Colonialism." *Wicazo Sa Review*, vol. 19, no. 2, 2004, pp. 33–48.

Zeidler, Christina. Personal interview with Moynan King, 28 Oct. 2012.

NOTES ON CONTRIBUTORS

T. Berto's first play, *BASH*, won the Toronto Fringe Best New Play Prize in 2000. Since then he has had plays mounted in Ontario, British Columbia, Alberta, and New York. His play *ROW* has (in various forms) been presented at Buddies in Bad Times, the Roundhouse in Vancouver, and in 2014 at the SummerWorks Performance Festival. *ROW* recently won an Arch and Bruce Brown Foundation Award for playwriting. He has had five short plays at the Loud & Queer festival in Edmonton. In 2009, *A SINGULARITY OF BEING* won the macIDeas Toronto Best New Play Prize and Best of the Fringe. He lives in Guelph.

Kym Bird is Director of the Graduate Program in Interdisciplinary Studies at York University, where she is also an Associate Professor of drama in the Humanities Department, Faculty of Liberal Arts and Professional Studies. An award-winning teacher and scholar, her field of research is early Canadian women dramatists, about which she has written several articles. Her book, *Redressing the Past: The Politics of Early English-Canadian Women's Drama, 1880–1920* (McGill-Queen's 2004), won the 2004 Association of Canadian Theatre Research Ann Saddlemyer Prize. Her present project is an anthology of early Canadian women's plays, contextualized in discourses of the public and private, the domestic world, and the world of work, as well as those of reform, race, nationalism, and empire.

Eury Colin Chang is a Ph.D. candidate in the Department of Theatre and Film at UBC. His dissertation, *A History of Asian Canadian Theatre, 1971–2017*, documents the dramatic contributions of Canadians of Asian descent since the formation of the Multiculturalism Act. Prior to his academic career, Chang worked as the editor of *The Dance Central* from 2004–2012 and for the quarterly magazine *Ricepaper (Asian Canadian Arts & Culture)* from 2008–2012. His research has been published in *Theatre Research in Canada* and *Contemporary Directions in Asian American Dance*.

Cameron Crookston is a Ph.D. candidate at the University of Toronto in the Centre for Drama, Theatre and Performance Studies, in collaboration with the Mark S. Bonham Centre for Sexual Diversity Studies. His research examines drag performance in North America as a form of queer cultural memory. In the past he has presented papers and participated in roundtable discussions at the Popular Cultural Association of Canada's national conference, Performance Studies International, and the Canadian Association for Theatre Research.

Ryan Cunningham (Nehiyaw-Cree) is an actor, director, producer, curator, and founding CEO of Cunning Concepts & Creations, a production and management company that produces and tours performing arts productions around the world. He is originally from amiskwacîwâskahikan (Edmonton, Alberta), where in 2009 he co-founded Alberta Aboriginal Performing Arts and served as Artistic Director from 2009–2014. He is also the former artistic director of Native Earth Performing Arts (2014–2017), Canada's longest-running Indigenous theatre company. As an actor, Ryan has worked professionally in TV, theatre, and film across Canada for over two decades and can be seen in all five seasons of the award-winning APTN television series *BLACKSTONE*. Currently he is performing in his second season at the Shaw Festival and is a board member of two national arts service organizations: IPAA (Indigenous Performing Arts Alliance) and the CanDance Network.

Spy Dénommé-Welch is a composer and writer of Anishinaabe identity. He co-created the Dora Mavor Moore Award–nominated opera *Giiwedin*, and is now completing his second full opera, as well as a new chamber work that will be presented in the summer of 2018. He has written and co-composed *Victorian Secrets* (2014) and *HATE MAIL and Irreconcilable Trolls* (2017). He is a member of the Playwrights Guild of Canada, the Canadian Music Centre, and a faculty member at Brock University.

Peter Dickinson is a professor at Simon Fraser University, with a joint appointment in the School for the Contemporary Arts and the Department of English. He is also Director of SFU's Institute for Performance Studies. A performance studies scholar, Peter's articles on theatre, dance, film, and performance art have appeared in *Canadian Theatre Review*, *Dance Research Journal*, *Modern Drama*, *Screen*, *TDR: The Drama Review*, *Text and Performance Quarterly*, *Theatre Journal*, *Theatre Research in Canada*, *Theatre Survey*, and numerous other journals and edited collections. He is also the author, editor, or co-editor of eight books and special journal issues, including *World Stages, Local Audiences: Essays on Performance, Place and Politics* (Manchester University Press, 2010); *Women and Comedy: History, Theory, Practice* (Fairleigh Dickinson University Press, 2014); and *Mega-Event Cities: Art/Audiences/Aftermaths* (*PUBLIC* 53, Spring 2016). Peter's produced plays include *The Objecthood of Chairs* (2010), *Positive ID* (2012), and *Long Division* (2016/2017).

Born, raised, and based on the unceded traditional lands of the Coast Salish peoples (Vancouver), Filipino Canadian author **C.E. Gatchalian** writes drama, poetry, fiction, and non-fiction. His plays, which include *Falling In Time*, *Broken*, *Motifs & Repetitions*, and *People Like Vince*, have appeared on stages nationally and internationally, as well as on radio and television. A two-time finalist for the Lambda Literary Awards, he was the 2013 recipient of the Dayne Ogilvie Prize, awarded annually by the Writers' Trust of Canada to an LGBT author of merit. Formerly Artistic Producer of **the frank theatre company**, he is the recipient of two Jessie Richardson Theatre Awards for his work as a theatre artist and producer. His non-fiction book, *Double Melancholy*, is due out from Arsenal Pulp Press in Spring 2019. Please visit his website, cegatchalian.com.

Sky Gilbert is a poet, novelist, playwright, filmmaker, theatre director, and drag queen extraordinaire. He was the co-founder and artistic director of Toronto's Buddies in Bad Times Theatre—one of the world's largest gay and lesbian theatres—from 1979 to 1997. He has had more than forty plays produced and written seven critically acclaimed novels and three award-winning poetry collections. He has received three Dora Mavor Moore Awards, as well as the Pauline McGibbon Award and the Silver Ticket Award. There is a street in Toronto named after him: Sky Gilbert Lane. His latest novel, *Sad Old Faggot* (ECW Press), was critically acclaimed.

Dirk Gindt has a Ph.D. in Theatre Studies and is an associate professor in the Department of Culture and Aesthetics at Stockholm University. He is the co-editor of *Viral Dramaturgies: HIV and AIDS in Performance in the Twenty First Century* (Palgrave Macmillan, 2018) and the author of the monograph *Tennessee Williams in Sweden and France 1945–1965* (Bloomsbury Methuen Drama, 2019), which unpacks the sexual anxieties and racial fantasies that the American playwright's works provoked in post-war Europe. Gindt's current research project, "Lest We Forget," critically analyzes the impact of HIV and AIDS on queer theatre and performance in Sweden and Canada.

Moynan King is a performer, director, curator, writer, and scholar. Recent acting credits include roles in CBC's *Baroness von Sketch Show* and John Greyson's *Last Car*. She is the author of six plays, the creator of performance installations, including *The Beauty Salon* and *Mothering*, and was the co-creator and director of *trace*. Moynan was co-founder and director of the Hysteria Festival (2003–2009), co-director of the Rhubarb! Festival (2003–2005), and has curated many cabarets. She is the editor of the *CTR* issue *Queer Performance: Women and Trans Artists*, and the book *Queer/Play: An Anthology of Queer Women's Performance and Plays*.

Stephen Low received his Ph.D. from Cornell University in April 2016, where he also received his Masters in Theater Studies in 2014. He received his first Masters from the University of Texas at Austin in the Performance as Public

Practice program. His scholarly interests include twentieth-century theatre and performance, musicals, queer theory, sex and sexuality, gender, critical race studies, and gay culture. His dissertation, "Toward an Aesthetic of Gay Culture," identifies an aesthetic of theatricality as the constitutive feature of contemporary gay culture. His scholarship has been published in *Modern Drama* and *Theatre Research in Canada.*

Sean Metzger is an associate professor in the UCLA School of Theater, Film, and Television and the president of Performance Studies international. He is the author of *Chinese Looks: Fashion, Performance, Race* (Indiana University Press, 2014) and a forthcoming book called *The Chinese Atlantic: Seascapes and the Theatricality of Globalization*. His co-edited volumes include *Embodying Asian/American Sexualities* (Lexington, 2009); *Futures of Chinese Cinema: Technologies and Temporalities in Chinese Screen Cultures* (Intellect, 2009); and *Awkward Stages: Plays about Growing Up Gay* (Cambria, 2015). He has also co-edited special issues of *Cultural Dynamics* (2009) and *Third Text* (2014).

Jean O'Hara is a professor in Theater and Gender Studies at Marlboro College. The primary focus of her work is theatre that addresses socio-political issues. Jean has worked in partnership with Klamath Theatre Project, Native Earth Performing Arts, the Centre for Indigenous Theatre, and Spiderwoman Theater. She is a Theatre of the Oppressed practitioner who has worked nationally and internationally. Jean has been directing and teaching for the past eighteen years and is the editor of *Two-Spirit Acts: Queer Indigenous Performances.* Currently, she is working with the Mopan Maya community to help archive their traditional stories in their native language.

Kathleen Oliver's first play, *Swollen Tongues*, won the 1997 National Playwriting Competition and has been produced across Canada, in London, and (in a French translation) in Paris. Her other plays include *Carol's Christmas* and *The Family Way*, which were both produced in Vancouver. Kathleen teaches English at Langara College in Vancouver and is a regular contributor to *The Georgia Straight*, where she has been writing about theatre for nearly twenty years. She lives in Vancouver with her partner and son.

Evalyn Parry is the current artistic director of Buddies in Bad Times Theatre in Toronto. An award-winning, interdisciplinary performance creator, she is a director, writer/performer, songwriter, and collaborator whose work is inspired by intersections of social justice, history, and auto/biography. As creator/performer recent shows include *SPIN* (which has toured extensively around the continent), *Kiinalik: These Sharp Tools* (Buddies), *Gertrude and Alice* (Independent Aunties/Buddies); directing credits include *The Youth/Elders Project* (Buddies), and the Dora Mavor Moore Award–winning *Obaaberima* by Tawiah M'Carthy (Buddies). She is the recipient of the KM Hunter Award for Theatre, the Ken McDougall Award for Directing, and the Colleen Peterson Songwriting Award.

Cordula Quint is a director and Associate Professor of Drama at Mount Allison University, where she teaches dramatic theory, literary and theatre studies, and studio praxis (acting and directing). Forthcoming is her book *Robert Wilson's Hamletmachine: Mise en Scène of Postmodern Groundlessness*. She is currently working on another monograph about contemporary theatre directors Robert Lepage, Ariane Mnouchkine, and Robert Wilson. Her articles have appeared in various journals and anthologies, including *Canadian Theatre Review*, *Theatre Journal*, *WHERE THE BOYS ARE: Cinemas of Masculinity and Youth*, *Popping Culture*, *Global Challenges and Regional Responses*, *Space and the Postmodern Stage*, and the *New England Theatre Journal*.

Dalbir Singh is a Ph.D. candidate in Performance Studies at the University of Toronto. He taught courses there as well as at the University of Waterloo and the University of Guelph. At Waterloo, he taught the first theatre course exclusively focused on racial identity and Canadian theatre. He has edited five collections of plays and critical essays on topics including Tamil culture and identity, post-colonial theatre, South Asian Canadian drama, and queer Canadian theatre. As a result, he has published the work of such notable writers as Donna-Michelle St. Bernard, Ravi Jain, Guillermo Verdecchia, Anusree Roy, and Yvette Nolan.

Originally from Montréal, **Sarah Garton Stanley** now lives and studies in Kingston and works in Ottawa and beyond. She is Associate Artistic Director, English Theatre, at the National Arts Centre, where she curates the Collaborations and the Cycle(s). She is also Creative Catalyst at SpiderWebShow. Sarah is a former artistic director of Buddies in Bad Times Theatre. Throughout her career she has directed, created, and dramaturged from coast to coast and internationally. Sarah is currently a Ph.D. student in Cultural Studies at Queen's University.

Jay Whitehead is a faculty member in the Department of Theatre and Dramatic Arts at the University of Lethbridge, where he primarily teaches classes in acting and performance. He received his M.F.A. in acting from York University and completed the Meisner Certificate Training Program from the True Acting Institute with Larry Silverberg. Whitehead is the artistic director and founder of Theatre Outré in Lethbridge, Alberta, and his creative work as an actor, director, and writer has been seen Calgary, Lethbridge, Halifax, Toronto, Saint John, Vancouver, and Dublin. Recent publications include articles in *alt.theatre* and *Canadian Theatre Review*.

Richie Wilcox is a multitalented director/singer/actor whose work has been seen across Canada and toured internationally. He is an artistic associate for Theatre Outré, where he has directed *UNSEX'd*, *Castrati: An Electro Drag Opera*, *Late Company*, and more. Wilcox is an artistic co-producer of Halifax's live art company Heist, where he most recently directed *Girls! Girls! Girls!* the award-winning *The Princess Show*, *Nation*, and his original show *New Waterford Boy*. He recently became one of three co-festival directors of Queer Acts.

Laine Zisman Newman received her Ph.D. from the University of Toronto's Centre for Drama, Theatre and Performance Studies and the collaborative programs in Sexual Diversity Studies and Women and Gender Studies. Her primary research focuses on the influence of space on queer women's performance practices. In addition to her research, Zisman Newman is founder and chair of Toronto's Queer Theory working group at the Jackman Humanities Institute and co-founder of Equity in Theatre, a national organization that works to improve equity in the professional Canadian performance industry. She is currently an instructor at the Mark S. Bonham Centre for Sexual Diversity Studies at the University of Toronto.

INDEX

D

T

U

V

W

X

Y

Z

First edition: May 2018
Printed and bound in Canada by Imprimerie Gauvin, Gatineau

Cover photos of Berend McKenzie, d'bi.young anitafrika, and Isolde N. Barron provided courtesy of Katrina Tadros
Cover design by Leon Aureus

PLAYWRIGHTS CANADA PRESS

202-269 Richmond Street West
Toronto, ON
M5V 1X1

416.703.0013
info@playwrightscanada.com
www.playwrightscanada.com
@playcanpress

MIX
Paper from responsible sources
FSC® C100212